Big ideas in education

What every teacher should know

Dr Russell Grigg

Crown House Publishing Limited
www.crownhouse.co.uk

First published by
Crown House Publishing
Crown Buildings,
Bancyfelin,
Carmarthen,
Wales, SA33 5ND, UK
www.crownhouse.co.uk
and
Crown House Publishing Company LLC
PO BOX 2223, Williston, VT 05495, USA
www.crownhousepublishing.com

p. 64 tables from *Skills for Life* brochure, are reproduced with permission. © 2006, OCR.
p. 94 extract from Costa, A. and Kallick, B. (2014) *Dispositions: Reframing Teaching and Learning* is reproduced with kind permission. © 2014, Corwin Press.
p. 102 model text from Costa, A. and Kallick, B. (2008) *Learning and Leading with Habits of Mind: 16 Characteristics of Success* is reproduced with kind permission. © 2008, ASCD.
p. 246 extract from Merideth, E. M. (2007) *Leadership Strategies for Teachers* is reproduced with kind permission. ©2007, Corwin Press.
pp. 256–257 extract from Grigg, R. (1998) *History of Trinity College Carmarthen* is reproduced with kind permission.

Cover image: © auryndrikson – fotolia.com

British Library Cataloguing-in-Publication Data

A catalogue entry for this book is available from the British Library.

Print ISBN: 978-178583027-3
Mobi ISBN: 978-178583045-7
ePub ISBN: 978-178583046-4
ePDF ISBN: 978-178583047-1
LCCN 2016937209

Printed and bound in the UK by Bell & Bain Ltd, Thornliebank, Glasgow

To Tom and Mia, for their travelling 'Jack Army' support wherever we go.

Contents

Acknowledgements

I am very grateful to Emma Tuck and colleagues at Crown House Publishing for their meticulous attention to detail during the editorial process. Without their helpful and supportive comments, this book would not have been possible. I have also benefited considerably from discussions and banter with Professor David Egan and the companionship of the team at the Wales Centre for Equity in Education. Finally, I owe a special thanks to my partner, Helen, for her creativity, generosity and acts of kindness.

Introduction

Imagine a competition to vote for the greatest idea in the history of education. Which idea would win your vote? The concept of schooling itself opens up lots of possibilities, from the introduction of certain types of schools (grammar, private, comprehensive, faith, etc.) to ideas about learning virtually 'in the cloud' without the need for physical school spaces. Perhaps your idea would be something to do with the role of education in promoting equity, such as the beginning of free elementary education in 1890 or, more recently, grants to support learners from low-income families. What about an idea relating to children's physical well-being, such as the provision of school meals pioneered in Bradford in the 1880s? Or, on the same theme, the introduction of breakfast clubs in the 1990s? How about something to do with school equipment or resources? Historic examples might include the blackboard, the first 'primer' reading books, school uniforms or even the humble school bell. Their significance may be difficult to appreciate in a modern digital age when children learn via interactive whiteboards, use e-books and other multimedia resources and when schools have sophisticated timekeeping systems, but these were, once upon a time, significant breakthroughs. The bell, for example, alerted children to when school was to start and this was particularly useful in rural areas. There are also ideas relating to school design, from the first playgrounds and school gardens to open-air schools and state-of-the-art eco-schools.

Perhaps you would vote for a particular curriculum idea or initiative, such as the principle of a national curriculum, particular assessment practices or the introduction of a baccalaureate-style qualification for post-16-year-olds. Or, at the other end of the age range, you might decide that a play-based approach to learning, which characterises early years provision, is the greatest idea in education. Then there are a host of subject-specific ideas and approaches, such as learning through investigations in science or the move from religious instruction to religious education. In Wales, the inclusion of Welsh as a compulsory subject in the curriculum might win many votes, while the same might be the case with the introduction of modern foreign languages into English primary schools.

Some ideas draw on a more philosophical and moral basis than others. As such, they often provoke controversy. The increasing emphasis on children's rights during the twentieth century led to the widely (though not universally) supported idea that corporal punishment should end in state schools, which happened in 1987. Surely few would seriously question the efficacy of this. Yet it was not until 2003 that legislation was extended to private schools in all parts of the United Kingdom. Moreover, in 2005, headmasters of private Christian schools unsuccessfully challenged the ban on corporal punishment, claiming that it was a breach of their freedom of religion under Article 9 of the European Convention on Human Rights. Ideas then can be controversial. Take the philosophical view that children should be treated as independent and autonomous individuals which lies at the heart of human rights. This is alien to many belief systems, such as Confucianism, where the collective need of the family and society take precedence over individual needs. *— Like comunism,*

Religious and Phil idea (from China (SS) - 479bc)

Suggestions should not be limited to schools. What about the spread of higher education beyond Oxford and Cambridge (established in the thirteenth century) to 'new universities' throughout cities in the United Kingdom? Or a specific idea, such as the opening up of universities to women (which began in London in 1878), the start of the Open University or moves towards a masters level teaching profession? Perhaps you think that teaching, as a profession, is in itself the most significant idea. There is also a bank of ideas associated with education management and leadership, such as performance-related pay or dedicated time for teachers to plan, prepare and assess.

In sum, there are plenty of contenders for our imaginary competition. The popularity of some ideas has waned (e.g. learning styles) while others have stood the test of time, even though their relevance to modern life is seriously questioned (e.g. the three-term school year). If such a competition were to be run, it would need clarification on what we mean by an idea and how to assess its significance.

Definitions and characteristics

The word 'idea' has lots of meanings and applications. It can refer to:

» **Particular thoughts** – e.g. 'This idea of paying teachers by performance really interests me.'

» **Specified plans, aims or objectives** – e.g. 'The governors' idea is to cut back on waste within school.'

» **Mental representations of something** – e.g. 'She has a good idea of the classroom layout.'

» **The belief that something is the case** – e.g. 'The parents have the idea that their child has been poorly treated by the school which has not met his needs.'

» **Comparative thoughts** – e.g. 'His idea of a good school is not the same as mine.'

» **Vague notions or inklings** – e.g. 'The head teacher has no idea what she is letting herself in for.'

» **A philosophical model** – e.g. 'Plato's view of the world was one of ideals or forms, the highest of which was the form of good which empowers humans to understand the spiritual, immaterial world.'

One of the most entertaining definitions is 'a flight of fancy, result of thought, product of reflection, proposal for action, a candidate for euthanasia in any institution because of the terror it induces in the staff, especially senior ones' (Burgess, 2002: 71).

The significance of an idea can be judged in terms of its impact in education, although measuring this is challenging. At the University of California, Berkeley, students have the opportunity to suggest their own big ideas in business to be assessed by expert panels of judges. The proposals are evaluated in terms of creativity, how well they address a pressing social issue, value for money, research and market viability.[1]

Big ideas have been defined as 'highly selected concepts, principles, rules [and] strategies that facilitate the most efficient and broadest acquisition of knowledge' (Kame'enui et al., 2002: 9). Usually, big ideas share several characteristics – Table 1.1 focuses on how these apply to education.

---

1 See http://bigideas.berkeley.edu/toolkit-judging/.

Characteristic	Meaning
Important	Big ideas have broad educational significance. They may open up new ways of looking at issues and help educators to make sense of seemingly isolated facts.
Distinctive	Big ideas have unique selling points or propositions. They stand out for their originality.
Empowering	Big ideas are transformative, or potentially so, in that they can change people's attitudes, behaviours or beliefs and contribute to improvements in teaching and learning. For teachers, the critical feature is that they have 'pedagogical power' (Gunter et al., 2007: 49).
Adaptable	Big ideas can be adapted to different contexts – for example, educators can apply the idea irrespective of who or where they teach.
Simple	Big ideas are clearly expressed, concise and straightforward to understand.

Table 1.1. Characteristics of big ideas in education.

At first glance it may not seem that all the ideas in this book are important, distinctive, empowering, adaptable or simple to understand. Arguing, for example, that education goes beyond the school gates may not seem particularly important. But economists forecast that by 2033 one in four people will be over 65 (Whitehead, 2009). This ageing population will place an unsustainable burden on taxpayers unless people work longer and update their knowledge and skills. This is why the government has called on the over sixties to consider further education. As David Willetts, former minister of state for universities and science, put it: 'There is evidence that the idea that you first study and then stop isn't what the world is like any more' (cited by Ross, 2013). So, the idea of lifelong learning challenges the conventional thinking that limits education to schooling and the young. Education is extended to include all ages who participate in a range of learning environments, including preschool groups, community projects, online courses, weekend retreats, summer schools, apprenticeship schemes, placements and foreign exchanges.

Some big ideas, although widely endorsed, are not always consistently understood or implemented in schools. Take the example of assessment data being used to improve (rather than prove) learning. This idea of assessment for learning was introduced in the late 1980s, but the authors, Paul Black and Dylan Wiliam, have since complained that most schools are doing it wrong (see Stewart, 2012). The bottom line is that although big ideas are well conceived, in practice they can be misunderstood, ignored or only partially implemented.

Ideas become big when they offer a particular insight. The original Greek meaning of 'idea' was 'to see' (from *idein*), and the notion of 'getting it' (simplicity) remains a powerful characteristic of big ideas. When teaching history, for example, learners improve their chronological awareness when they understand that there is often a time gap between when something is invented and when it is adopted by the general public. This is a big idea. It means that when they are studying the Victorians, they come to realise that the sixty-four years of Queen Victoria's reign (1837– 1901) was an age of inventions, but many of these did not filter through to ordinary folk for some time. Historically, on average, technologies such as the steamship, telegraph and electricity were adopted forty-seven years after they are invented, with the United States and the United Kingdom leading the way in adoption rates for much of the past two centuries. This matters because the longer the lag in technology adoption for any given nation, the lower the per capita income (Comin and Hobijn, 2008).

Steven Johnson (2011) points out that very few ideas begin with individuals experiencing 'eureka' moments of sudden discovery. Rather, they take time to develop and people build on what others have suggested – what he describes as 'liquid networks'. In education, ideas filter through to classrooms and lecture halls, sometimes over many years. These are often adapted from other fields such as sport (e.g. coaching techniques), business (e.g. target setting), technology (e.g. tablets) and industry (e.g. vocational training).

Choice and structure

The aim of this book is to provide readers with a concise and reliable introduction to a dozen ideas which are at the core of educational practice. It is not exhaustive in its coverage. The dozen ideas chosen are general rather than subject-specific in nature. The first two, education and childhood, invite the reader to look at teaching in wider society. This should enhance our understanding that children and young people's experiences in school are shaped by many factors beyond the classroom. The next three ideas concern elements of learning which teachers promote – knowledge, skills and dispositions, followed by four ideas about aspects of teaching – ethics, instruction, curriculum and feedback. These raise questions about why, how and what to teach. Finally, there are three ideas that are essentially about improving the quality of education through reflective practice, research and professional leadership.

Some big ideas in education have not been included even though there are strong arguments to do so – specifically about the teaching of literacy and numeracy, or more generally about parental engagement, tackling educational disadvantage or promoting behaviour for learning. However, the twelve included cover a broad range of topics and taken together should equip teachers with a good understanding of current thinking in a diverse, fluid and dynamic field.

Each of the big ideas is discussed within the framework of four questions: what is the big idea, who is behind it, why is it important and what can you do? To begin with, the meaning of each idea is explained. This includes a general discussion of the context today and, where appropriate, how it is presented and interpreted in different ways. Then the origin and development of the idea is discussed, including the contributions of key individuals, before considering why it should matter to teachers and examples of practical strategies to use. Some ideas reflect the influence of psychology and other social sciences on our growing understanding of how children learn and develop – for example, recognising the importance of cultivating positive dispositions. Others are rooted in a more philosophical discussion – for instance, what education is for and the kind of knowledge and skills children and young people need to become educated citizens in the twenty-first century.

So why bother reading this book? In short, it offers readers a synthesis of ideas presented in a largely objective manner, free from ideological positioning. Having been involved in education for more than twenty-five years, as a historian, teacher, teacher educator, leader, inspector, consultant and researcher, one of the conclusions I have reached is that there is far too much polarisation in education – what Robin Alexander (2010: 21) calls a 'discourse of dichotomy'. Talking about education purely in terms of 'child-centred versus teacher-centred', 'traditional versus progressive', 'formal versus informal' or 'teaching versus learning' sets the profession back – it is both divisive and not particularly representative. In my experience, most teachers are not so fixed in their thinking or practices that they can be labelled one thing or another. Good teaching is more nuanced, inclusive and contextual than this, drawing on a range of approaches and strategies – for example, in planning, the deployment of resources and classroom skills. We need to adopt a more balanced view in discussions about education: technologies can be both a help and a hindrance; there are times when teachers should instruct and at other times guide; children need to acquire both knowledge and skills. We then need to focus on the important things. So, while it is necessary to understand the arguments about how the curriculum is organised (e.g. subjects, themes, areas of experience), what really matters is what learners take from school and how we can ensure that the quality of teaching is consistently good.

There is another reason why this book may be of interest. The recent spate of publications (e.g. Adey et al., 2012; Christodoulou, 2014), which set out to debunk myths in education, suggests that many teachers are uncertain about some of the core ideas that shape what they do. Didau (2015) goes further and claims that teachers are simply wrong about lots of ideas – for example, the value of group work or that they should talk a lot less in class. Believing in half-truths and myths is not an occupational hazard confined to teaching. Over several years, Ben Goldacre (2009) has been exposing dodgy medical data and questionable 'scientific' practices, while organisations such as the Child Poverty Action Group, the Joseph Rowntree Foundation and others remind us of the myths about those experiencing poverty, such as 'they' are on the fiddle or 'they' don't want to work (Baptist Union of Great Britain, the Methodist Church, the Church of Scotland and the United Reformed Church, 2013). Too often in education we make assumptions – for instance, lessons should last between forty-five and sixty minutes; young children should be guided rather than instructed; research is undertaken by academics in university; and, fundamentally, schools are places where children are taught. Throughout the book, these kinds of assumptions are questioned and the reader is invited to reflect on and beyond their own experiences.

When I was training to be a teacher in the 1980s, I followed a four-year BA Ed programme that included modules on the history, philosophy, sociology and psychology of education. We were introduced to the Greek trinity of Socrates, Plato and Aristotle, and the likes of John Locke, Basil Bernstein, John Holt and Paulo Freire. At the time, much of this seemed far too abstract and irrelevant to those of us eager to get into school. They are certainly perceived as luxuries in the world of teacher education today. Many of those entering the profession do so via shorter school-based courses where there is an understandable emphasis on acquiring the technical and practical skills that teachers need. University colleagues are under pressure to 'fit in' what they can and, inevitably, there is limited (if any) time to spend on some of those who have been dead for centuries. Throughout this book I have resurrected some of these names to illustrate their relevance to the issues that teachers face today. It was the twelfth-century philosopher Bernard of Chartres who is credited as first using the oft-quoted expression, 'If I have seen further, it is by standing on the shoulders of giants', but we also need to look around at what is happening in the world today. So this book includes brief reference to past and present figures and organisations relevant to each idea.

We have a responsibility as teachers to be well informed about our practices and the evidence that underpins what we do and what could be done better. This book is a modest attempt to provide a base camp for the reader to explore further.

Chapter 1

Education

Education goes beyond the school gates
and is a lifelong experience

What is the big idea?

Think about something that you are very good at doing or passionate about. Perhaps it's playing golf or some other sport, gardening, singing or playing a musical instrument, showing compassion to others, running a business, supporting a charitable cause or organising things. While a teacher at school may have provided the initial inspiration, more than likely you developed these skills and passions outside school. This could have been due to the influence of family and friends, members of clubs and societies or perhaps something that caught your eye on a television programme or on the Internet triggered your interests. The point is that learning – the acquisition of new knowledge and skills – is a continual process from the moment of birth. Scientists tell us that prenatal babies can recognise specific rhythms and patterns of stories they hear. In one study, doctors gave day-old infants dummies that were connected to tape recorders. Depending on the babies' sucking patterns, the dummies either turned on a tape of their mother's voice or that of an unfamiliar woman's voice. Within ten to twenty minutes, babies were able to adjust their sucking rate to turn on their own mother's voice (Flynn McCarthy, 2014). — *Pre-natal babies able to learn in the womb*

If learning begins in the womb, when does it end? According to a report by an insurance company, life in Britain really begins at 60. The

life insurance?

researchers revisited the premise of an American psychologist, Walter B. Pitkin, who suggested in 1932 that 'Life begins at 40'. Pitkin thought that with the advent of the machine age, workers would be set free from back-breaking labour and enjoy more prosperous times when their thirties were over. The new research, based on the views of 2,000 adults, points out that the concept of what it means to be old changes as we age. For those under the age of 35, the word 'old' applies to those aged 61 and over. For those over 70, being 'old' doesn't begin until they reach the age of 77 – only four years short of Britain's average life expectancy (Doughty, 2015). Between 2006 and 2013, Internet use by the over-65s more than tripled, while 25 per cent of over-55s own a smartphone (Tame, 2015). Although something of a cliché, a generation of 'silver surfers' presents a growing market for business and learning, illustrated by the Barclays Digital Eagles scheme, which provides advice on technology for the older generation. In higher education, there are a growing number of mature students over 50 studying for degrees to improve their qualifications or pursue their love of a particular subject. In 2012, Bertie Gladwin became Britain's oldest recorded graduate at the age of 90, having left school at 14 to work as a greengrocer's delivery boy. A former MI6 agent, he gained a master's degree in intelligence history from Buckingham University (Garner, 2012).

Education, training, schools and learning

Most dictionaries and commentaries describe education as a process of learning aimed at equipping people with knowledge and skills to enable them to become well-adjusted members of society. There is less agreement over what exactly such knowledge and skills should be and what education is for (see Chapter 3). Do schools exist to equip children with literacy, numeracy and other basic skills needed to become an active citizen? What about other aspects of learning, such as spiritual and moral values, social and emotional skills, artistic appreciation or a sense of heritage? Are schools about building open-mindedness, risk taking, creative and critical thinking skills? Most commentators conclude that schools exist to pass on cultural heritage and to prepare young people for life. When asked what is the point of education, former Education Secretary Michael Gove replied:

Handwritten margin note: Age is all relitive. This will be true for pupils also

*To introduce people to the best that's been thought and written.
Our children may never enjoy the prodigious wealth of Roman
Abramavich's children, but they're just as capable of enjoying
Dostoyevsky or Wagner or appreciating the Gherkin or the Shard –
but only if the education they've had has given them an understanding
of everything from metaphor to scientific principles. (cited by
Horowitz, 2014)*

Gove highlights a particular classical view of what it means to be well
educated. The ancient Greeks believed that it involved cultivating the
intellect through a study of great literature. Later, medieval universities
added the arts and sciences to what became known as a liberal education
– liberal in the sense of liberating the learner from preconceptions, dogma
and parochial attitudes. By the nineteenth century, the value of education
in its own right – the joy of reading poetry, exploring nature, looking at
paintings or debating the meaning of life – was increasingly undermined
by a more instrumental view of education as a means to an end, namely
preparation for work. *Training* in specific skills rather than a broader
education assumed importance.

The notion of training rather than educating remains prevalent today
for example, in the emphasis on teacher training rather than teacher
education – reflecting a focus on development of technical skills in an
instrumental, competence-led model rather than broadening the mind of
young teachers through teacher enquiry, reflective practice and personal
development (see Chapter 10). Sir Ken Robinson (2015: xii), using
his customary wit, recalls debating as a student the difference between
education and training: 'The differences were clear enough when we
talked about sex education. Most parents would be happy to know their
teenagers had sex education; they'd probably be less happy if they'd had
sex training.'

The longstanding link between education and schools is understandable – one would hope that in every case the latter promotes the
former. Yet around a quarter of secondary schools require improvement
compared to one in seven primary schools (Ofsted, 2014a). But this is
not the full story. Thomas (2013: 106) reckons that around 40 per cent of
children leave school disengaged, uninspired and bored. Another estimate
suggests that a third of 14- to 16-year-olds are not taking part fully in

lessons, have given up or resist (Stamou et al., 2014). While the main business of schools is to educate pupils, not everything that happens in school is educational – schools perform other functions such as childcare, certification, selecting for further training and preparing youngsters for occupational roles.

It is common for the terms education and schooling to be used interchangeably as if they are the same thing – they are not. There have been many quips about this. The American writer Mark Twain pointed out that he never let his schooling interfere with his education, while Albert Einstein, perhaps the greatest intellectual of all time, suggested that 'Education is what remains when we have forgotten everything that has been learned at school' (cited by Thomas, 2013: 2).

Education is more than the act of teaching or learning. Education is the process whereby one generation initiates the next into the ways of the world, acquiring the knowledge they need to make sense of it (Furedi, 2009). Formal education implies a sense of order and direction, where learners are supported to know and achieve things that they might not gain on their own. Much education takes place informally through spontaneous conversations with family, friends and neighbours, self-taught projects and the myriad of folk teachers who offer their expertise through online videos on channels such as YouTube.

Advances in cognitive and social psychology, educational practice and neuroscience are helping us to better understand the process of learning. We know that there are certain conditions which facilitate effective learning. These include frequent opportunities for learners to collaborate and talk purposefully about their learning, practise particular skills and receive constructive, timely and specific advice on how to improve (see Chapter 9). Motivation is also important. Learners are more likely to begin and keep at a task they actually want to do. Motivation increases the amount of time learners spend on a task (Larson, 2000). When learners are extrinsically motivated by the prospect of good grades, public recognition or other rewards, they tend to perform tasks as a means to an end. On the other hand, learners who are intrinsically motivated engage in tasks because they get pleasure from doing so, recognise the importance of the learning or perhaps believe it is the morally right thing to do. Sometimes learners are motivated by both intrinsic and external factors but, on balance, those who are intrinsically motivated achieve deeper levels of learning. Sotto (1994) boldly claims that for many children around the world, the experience of going to school inhibits their motivation to learn: they are bored, made to look foolish, asked to study things that are unreal and reach a point when they know that they are not going to do well no matter how hard they try. More recent commentators acknowledge that school learning is often dull and uninspiring (e.g. Paton, 2009), but most children enjoy the overall school experience. According to the Children's Society's *Good Childhood Report* (2015), on average students gave their schools seven out of ten. This was based on a sample of 8,000 children aged between 10 and 17.

Discussing definitions may seem all rather abstract and academic. But understanding these terms strikes at the heart of what teachers do and how they see themselves. Teachers who feel that their primary role is to nurture children's natural inclinations are likely to teach in a very different way to those who value a body of knowledge that they think must be passed on to the next generation. This reflects a difference in the very etymology of the word education, which can be traced back to three Latin terms:

1. *Ducere* – to lead.
2. *Educere* – to bring out.
3. *Educare* – to mould or nourish.

The first and second terms were associated with leading troops into battle, with drill having a strong military resonance, whereas *educare* carried the notion of nurturing and tending, as in gardening.

Issues and challenges

These different meanings hint at a longstanding debate about what education should aim to do and the role of teachers therein. Should teachers lead through formal instruction or develop pupils' latent abilities by guiding, coaching and facilitating? What is their role in the Google Age, where learners can instantly verify what they are told? There is no universally agreed answer to these kinds of questions. In some cultures, particularly in Asian countries where Confucian beliefs emphasise obedience and listening, teachers are held in high esteem and valued for imparting knowledge. A successful education is often equated with hard work, self-discipline, remembering lots of things and passing tests. Despite the success of Asian schools, their systems are frequently criticised for relying on rote learning: one study found that for each of their twice-a-semester exams, South Korean students have to remember between 60 to 100 pages of facts in order to do well (Jones, 2013). Generally, in Western countries, there is more scope for independent thinking, dialogue between teachers and pupils, self-assessment and informal teaching methods and classroom organisation.

Learning based on repitition and memorization

One of the goals of education is surely to promote independent or self-directed learning. This is based very much on learners taking personal responsibility for setting their own learning goals and reflects models that value lifelong learning. Most studies suggest that children learn best when they are given opportunities to use their full range of senses, ask questions, talk, work alongside knowledgeable others and apply their knowledge in practical real-life contexts (Watkins, 2003; Husbands and Pearce, 2012).

One of the aims of this book is to support trainee and experienced teachers in reaching an informed view in a world where the profession is too readily vilified in the press. When there are problems in society, the tendency is to blame schools – they seem to be responsible in some way for everything from teenage pregnancy (Merrick, 2014) to the 'mental health epidemic' among young people (Tait, 2015). Schools and teachers are not miracle workers. In the 1970s, the sociologist Basil Bernstein controversially declared that 'education cannot compensate for society' (Bernstein, 1970). He wrote this at a time when neo-Marxists on the far left and eugenicists on the far right both claimed that schooling could do nothing to 'transform' society or address its inequalities and divisions. This fatalism did little to help the comprehensive school ideal or, more generally, lift aspirations in the teaching profession and working-class communities. Michael Apple (2013), an American professor, discusses the question of whether education can truly change society. Born in a very poor family, he attended schools in tough areas to qualify as a teacher and then progressed to graduate work at Columbia University. Education opened up possibilities for Apple but without challenging the structures that create poverty in the first place. Sir Michael Wilshaw, Her Majesty's Chief Inspector, put it as follows: 'It is sometimes said that "schools cannot do it alone", but this is not quite true: exceptional schools can

Events are predetermined and therefore unevitable

make up for grave disadvantages faced by young people. In the process, they often become surrogate parents' (Ofsted, 2013a: 5). — *Debatable*

There is no doubt that excellent schools and teachers can make a huge difference in children and young people's lives. We know, for example, that the significant improvements in many London schools since 2000 have paid off in terms of educational outcomes for pupils from disadvantaged backgrounds. The success is largely attributed to effective leadership at all levels. This is manifested in many ways, from the recruitment and retention of quality teachers to high levels of data literacy among leaders (Baars et al., 2014). But there is a danger that the work of schools has become so demanding that growing numbers of teachers are suffering from low morale, excessive stress and burnout (Precey, 2015). The relentless focus on measurable outcomes and the rhetoric around targets, results and league tables can detract from the joy of educating children and young people.

Perhaps the greatest challenge for policy-makers and leaders is ensuring that more children have access to high quality teaching. We know that those fortunate enough to be taught by a very effective teacher can make 40 per cent more learning gains in a single year when compared to those taught by a poorly performing teacher. Those pupils from disadvantaged backgrounds feel the greatest impact: over a school year, these pupils gain 1.5 years' worth of learning with very effective teachers, compared with 0.5 years with poorly performing teachers (Sutton Trust, 2011). In other words, this difference amounts to a whole year's learning. Imagine the impact of being taught by a string of very effective teachers.

The topics of education and schooling usually attract heated debate, partly because we all feel qualified to offer an informed opinion, as ex-pupils, students or parents. These experiences do not, however, necessarily put us in a position to make a fair and accurate assessment of the educational system as a whole. Our views are often selective and subjective, whereas an academic study of education can afford a more balanced and rounded interpretation. Put simply, we need to know what the most reliable evidence says about the topics discussed in this book. This is not straightforward, for various reasons. First, the experts themselves differ over the value of particular research studies and how these should be interpreted. They may have ideological views on how children should be educated. Second, substantial longitudinal studies in education are

[handwritten margin notes: Because all go through some level of schooling everyone feels they can contribute an opinion]

expensive to fund and do not provide the quick answers that politicians and educators often demand. Third, a lot of research has not always been made available in concise, readable formats for busy teachers. Fourth, despite the development of action or practitioner-led models of research (see Chapter 11), the priority for teachers is to teach. Research is not necessarily something that is valued ahead of, say, personal experience.

L should more enphsis be put on research in ITE?.

Why are some schools more successful than others?

Over the years, the literature on school effectiveness and improvement has shown that the key differences between good and not so good schools revolve around the quality of leadership, teaching and the learning environment. Specifically, good leaders have strong values and high expectations, are continually looking to improve further, operate a high degree of internal consistency, invest in their staff and put students first (Hopkins, 2013). They create a climate in which pupils want to learn, and their achievements do not happen by chance. In a classic study of the 15,000 hours that children typically spend in school (Rutter et al., 1979), researchers found the ethos or tone was critical to its success. In schools that had a good ethos, teachers held high expectations of learners' academic achievement and behaviour, valued student participation and offered a stimulating curriculum including extracurricular activities. One of the most significant findings was that problem behaviours decreased the longer students attended these successful schools. Yet, the researchers noted that schools within close proximity of each other, with almost exactly the same pupil intake in terms of social background and intellectual ability, engendered widely different experiences and results.

Today, reducing the variation in the quality of education between schools remains a major challenge. Put simply, children's education should not depend on their postcode. Yet children living in local authorities such as Camden and North Tyneside have a 98 per cent chance of attending a good or outstanding primary school, whereas in Doncaster and Medway it is less than 60 per cent (Ofsted, 2014a: 38–39). The picture is equally mixed in secondary schools. Ofsted also reports that in areas of London like Haringey, Islington and Lambeth, despite high levels of social disadvantage, there is nothing but good and outstanding secondary schools. In places such as St Helens, Oldham and Hartlepool, the chances of attending a good school are less than 40 per cent. But there are no single reasons for such variation and comparing schools is not an exact science.

How do you judge the quality of a school and the teaching therein? There is substantial literature on what makes for great teaching and learning (Husbands and Pearce, 2012; Ko and Sammons, 2013; Coe et al., 2014; Siraj and Taggart, 2014; Grigg, 2015). Some studies provide forensic levels of detail through observing excellent teachers at work. So, for example, we know the kinds of effective language that teachers use, such as when a Year 5 teacher boosts the self-esteem of a shy boy by saying in front of the whole class: 'Very good boy spending his time reading whilst he's waiting' (Siraj and Taggart, 2014: 29).

Classroom observations remain the most direct means of assessing the quality of teaching. The views of learners and parents are often perceptive, while external sources such as inspection reports provide a useful overview. Over the last few decades, many schools have become sophisticated in their use of data to track the performance of learners (as individuals, groups and as a cohort). Data is a good thing to be embraced. It enables leaders and teachers to know where there are strengths and areas of underperformance – for example, between groups of learners, subjects or in comparison to average national standards. The acid test of a school's worth is the extent to which it provides good 'value added' on measurable child outcomes (Siraj and Taggart, 2014).

Despite the growth in the use of attainment data for comparative purposes, statistics are best treated as a source for raising questions rather than providing definitive conclusions. Using programs such as Student Information Management System (SIMS), computer analysis of learners' reading or mathematical test results can help schools to evaluate what learners know. This takes on added significance when considered over a period of say three or four years to establish more meaningful trends. But raw data does not, for example, tell school leaders how much help children are getting at home. Moreover, test results are snapshots that do not necessarily provide an accurate view of learners' abilities over time. They also do not reveal the extent to which pupils enjoy learning and school life. This is why establishing a regular dialogue with learners is so important.

Most explanations as to why schools in similar socio-economic contexts vary in their provision arrive at common-sense conclusions:

factors such as the quality of leadership and teaching and the learning environment are most significant. Ofsted reiterate what Rutter and his research team observed thirty-five years ago, namely that 'the right school culture is critical for improvement' (Ofsted, 2014a: 5).

Whether the length of the school day matters is more debatable. Countries whose pupils perform well on international tests – Canada, Finland and Norway – have a shorter school day than students in the UK (from around 8.30 a.m. to 2.30 p.m.). One study in North Tyneside found that starting the school day an hour later significantly improved grades in basic subjects (Savill, 2010). There is also biological evidence that changes in teenagers' body clocks means that their sleep cycle begins an average two hours later than an adult's, making adolescents predisposed to sleep between midnight and 9 a.m. (Everett, 2016). Many parents would concur that their teenage children are not very alert first thing in the morning. Yet, studies have also shown that additional instruction time can have a positive impact on learning outcomes particularly for weaker students (Lavy, 2015; Cattaneo et al., 2016). In 2016, the government announced plans to add an extra hour to the school day in secondary schools. But no matter how long children spend in school, how the time is used is most significant in terms of explaining why some schools are more successful than others.

Who is behind it?

The ancient Greek philosopher Plato (c.428–347 BC) was perhaps the first Western thinker to raise questions about the role of education and school (*skhole*) in society. He dreamed of an ideal state in *The Republic* and mapped out a lifelong learning process for its rulers: from learning to read, write and do sums by the age of 6, studying philosophy and politics by the age of 30 and beginning to rule at the age of 50. Plato formed an open-air Academy (from which we get the word 'academic') in which fellow intellectuals debated subjects such as philosophy, mathematics and astronomy. He believed that schools should not force young people to study slavishly because 'nothing that is learned under compulsion stays with the mind' (cited by Thomas, 2013: 4). Rather, children should discover knowledge for themselves through play and enquiry.

Aristotle (384–322 BC), one of Plato's leading students, also believed in the lifelong nature of learning. He described learning in seven-year cycles. The first phase of early childhood was based on learning through play, toys and physical exercise. Formal schooling began at the age of 7 and lasted until the age of 21. However, learning did not stop then – Aristotle wanted it to extend to the 'Whole of Life' with a focus on self-improvement (Giardiello, 2013). His Lyceum is regarded as the first Open University with its focus on philosophy, history and scientific study. Since these very early days, questions have been asked about the purpose of schooling. Aristotle acknowledged: 'For in modern times there are opposing views about the tasks to be set, for there is no generally accepted assumptions about what the young should learn' (cited by Thomas, 2013: 17). What these ancient philosophers did was to begin a longstanding debate over how children should be viewed, the nature of learning and what society should value most in its educational system.

Over the years, four views of the role of schools have emerged. In reality, there are blurred lines between these views and many educators are not constrained by one philosophy or another. First, there is a classical humanist view that sees schools and educators as the gatekeepers to our heritage. Their primary role is to pass on the best of our cultural knowledge to young people. The emphasis is on valuing formal knowledge arranged in subjects or academic disciplines. What matters is that learners acquire such knowledge through traditional didactic methods and assessments, usually in the form of examinations. The public and grammar schools epitomise this ideology.

A second more instrumental or utilitarian view stresses the need for formal education to prepare young people for life beyond school. Advocates are quick to talk about employability and the needs of business. They want to see schools bridge the gap between classroom learning and the real world. One of the major challenges for policy-makers, leaders and practitioners is getting to grips with the kind of knowledge and skills that will be needed in the future (see Chapter 4). The continual revisions to the national curriculum, since it was first introduced in England and Wales in 1988, illustrate not only political tensions but also shifts in educational thinking as curriculum designers try to keep up with social, cultural and technological changes in society – for instance, in the move from teaching information and communication technology (ICT), which was originally part of the technology programme of study alongside textiles and food, towards a discrete focus on computer science and programming skills.

A third child-centred view values freedom, discovery, nature and individuality. It originated in the Enlightenment and Romanticism of the late seventeenth and eighteenth centuries when the likes of the philosophers John Locke (1632–1704) and Jean-Jacques Rousseau (1712–1778) saw children not as mini-adults but as free-thinking individuals. Rousseau believed that the child should not be kept in 'a stuffy room' but taken out 'into a meadow every day' (Rousseau, 1979 [1762]: Book II) where he would learn from encounters with nature. These progressive educators see schools as places to guide learners in their growth as independent, critical and creative thinkers.

A fourth view questions the existence of schools in their current form. The radical notion that traditional schooling could be a barrier to children's learning was at the centre of the de-schooling movement in the 1960s and 1970s. The leading proponent, Ivan Illich (1926–2002), a former Catholic priest, suggested that schools suppressed children's individuality and creativity. He wanted to replace schools with skill exchanges and 'learning webs' built on an apprenticeship-style education in which youngsters followed their interests – from car mechanics to philosophy. His idea was that education should be available to the individual whenever he or she wanted it – that is, self-directed rather than institutionalised learning. He famously suggested that if you asked someone where they learned what they knew, almost everyone would say outside school – while viewing TV, from friends or peers, on the street, reading and so forth.

While the de-schooling movement was subjected to severe criticism for its idealised vision, the spirit of children learning at their own pace and time without the institutional constraints of schools has been adopted by the home schooling movement. The American educator John Holt (1923–1985) was vociferous in his criticism of conventional formal education, notably in *How Children Fail* (1964), *Instead of Education: Ways to Help People do Things Better* (1976) and *Teach Your Own: The John Holt Manual on Homeschooling* (1981). For Holt, what mattered was not something called 'a better education' but 'a life worth living, and work worth doing' (Holt, 2004 [1976]: xii). Today, based on local authority data, it is estimated that at least 36,000 children are educated

[handwritten margin note: At the forefront of the "home education" and "un-schooling" movement. Linked to youth centred ideas of 60s & 70s.]

at home because parents object to schools for various philosophical, political, cultural or religious reasons or due to their children's special needs (Jeffreys, 2015).

Formal schooling has attracted criticism from many quarters during its history. In the nineteenth century, some politicians and farmers complained about the possible threat to the social order from educating the labouring classes and the consequent loss of the workforce from the fields. In the twentieth century, there were moves to set up alternative schools by the likes of A. S. Neill (1883–1973) and Rudolf Steiner (1861–1925). Sociologists such as Basil Bernstein (1924–2000) and Pierre Bourdieu (1930–2002) argued that working-class children often struggle at school because the system is culturally biased against them (Bernstein, 1970; Bourdieu, 1991). Schools embrace middle-class values, speech (Standard English) and behaviours, which disadvantage working-class children because they have to learn behaviours that middle-class children take for granted, such as how to sit still for a story or speak assertively. The middle classes possess what is known as 'cultural capital', or knowledge and experience in life that enables them to advance through the school system at a much faster rate than their working-class peers. More recently, Stephen Ball (2008) and other writers have kept this debate alive, pointing out that despite all the rhetoric and 'good' policies to produce fairer educational outcomes, the class divide is as stark as it was in the nineteenth century.

In the twenty-first century, the notion of parental choice has led to the establishment of free schools, while the rise of technologies has brought into question the role of the traditional school and teacher. Concepts such as 'virtual schools' and 'flipped learning' have struck a chord with those who want to redefine the relationship between schools and education. Students who attend virtual schools learn via the Internet rather than 'going to school' – one estimate suggests more than 1.5 million children in the United States learn in this way (Hanover, 2011). In England, virtual schools tend to focus on supporting children looked after by the local authority and may have only a few enrolled at any one time. However, the Wey Education Schools Trust is planning to open the first online school where children as young as 9 log in to a web-based classroom at 9.15 a.m. before receiving up to four hours of direct tuition each day (Paton, 2014b).

Flipped learning involves using class time for discussion to master content, while children are introduced to new material through online videos watched at home. An American professor, Eric Mazur (1997), pioneered the idea through what he called peer instruction in which he coached students in class (rather than lectured to them), while they used technologies to gain basic information as homework. Salman Khan is most often associated with flipped learning. In 2004, he began to record videos for the younger cousin he was tutoring because she felt that recorded lessons would let her skip sections she had mastered and replay those that she was finding difficult. Today, the Khan Academy's massive open online courses (MOOCs) include more than 100,000 interactive activities on a wide range of subjects under the strapline 'free, for everyone, forever'. More recently, Khan has opened a small-scale laboratory ('school of the future') where mixed-aged children are given scope to be creative, take calculated risks and learn from their mistakes. Through self-paced learning, his vision is to offer a free first-class education globally over the next fifteen or so years.

So, education and learning are not dependent on schools or teachers. Sugata Mitra, professor of educational technology at Newcastle University, famously illustrated this with his hole-in-the-wall experiment in a New Delhi slum in 1999. He installed a computer in a wall, connected it to the Internet and observed how passing children responded. Their natural curiosity led them to explore, even though they had no previous computer experience and the browser was in English – a foreign language they did not speak. Within hours they were playing games, recording their own music and teaching themselves.[1] Mitra has conducted further research in Gateshead where groups of children worked together, independent of the teacher, using computers to solve a problem. He describes a follow-up discussion between the teacher and a Year 4 child:

---

[1] In Mitra's (2010) TED talk, 'The Child-Driven Education', he points out that in a follow-up experiment in Hyderabad, he gave a speech-to-text computer program to a group of children who spoke English with a strong Telugu accent. When they first used it the computer could not understand their speech, so Mitra left it with them to see whether they could overcome the problem. When he returned two months later, he found they had developed a more neutral British accent to enable them to talk to the computer. A short while later, Mitra wanted to know whether 12-year-old Tamil children could teach themselves biotechnology in English on their own. One child told him, 'Apart from the fact that improper replication of the DNA molecule causes genetic disease, we've understood nothing else.'

Child: Aren't we going to do any work?
Teacher: What were you doing so far?
Child: Learning.
Teacher: And what is 'work'?
Child: When you tell us things and we have to write them down.
(Mitra and Crawley, 2014: 82)

When tested several months later, the children demonstrated high levels of knowledge, the depth of which surprised the teacher.

Mitra's goal is to create Self-Organised Learning Environments (SOLEs) in which learners teach themselves and each other using technologies with minimal adult supervision. In summarising his research between 1999 and 2013, Mitra concludes that children can achieve educational objectives by themselves and understand content years ahead of their time through the use of technologies (Mitra and Crawley, 2014). In simple terms, Mitra is at one end of an opinion line that wants schools to give learners more time using technologies and to investigate 'big' motivating questions, rather than spend their time listening to teachers who seek to transfer core knowledge. Mitra's latest research involves the setting up of 'Granny Clouds' in which volunteers from the older generation teach children online (Cadwalladr, 2015).

Such developments are examples of the innovative use of technologies to bring together different generations within the learning process. For a number of years, there have been well-articulated arguments for schools to move ahead and integrate into lessons the very tools that students are using to learn in their own time, such as social networking and mobile devices (Schrum and Levin, 2009). Despite this, how well are schools embracing technologies and encouraging learners to use them as part of their everyday learning in the classroom? To what extent are teachers confident and skilled enough to 'let go' and empower learners to use technologies to support their learning across the curriculum? Unfortunately, it seems that not enough schools are moving learners from being 'consumers' to 'producers' of knowledge, using technologies such as e-books, podcasts and blogs to enhance this process.

It is one thing to acknowledge that education has become a lifelong process in which individuals continue to learn in a variety of contexts beyond school, but it is quite another for this belief to be reflected in practice. One way of doing this is to rethink the whole concept of schools – less as places of formal instruction where teachers 'deliver' a pre-set curriculum and more as centres for lifelong learning, not constrained by set times and routines. In the United States, this is manifested in the '21st Century Community Learning Centers' (CCLC) programme in which schools stay open longer, offering a range of enrichment activities including classes and workshops on basic and vocational skills, recreational interests in the arts and sport and preparation for employment. In the UK, there is a long tradition of 'community learning' and schools opening up facilities to local people. In England, the extended schools programme was launched in 2005 and was designed to improve levels of educational achievement for disadvantaged children by enabling them to learn in non-school hours, with breakfast and homework clubs, classes for parents and families, and art, sport, drama and computer classes (DCSF, 2005). According to the Education Endowment Foundation, a leading education research centre, extending school time can improve behaviour, relationships and raise attainment, particularly for learners from low-income households.[2] However, it is worth reflecting carefully on whether the quality of learning and teaching can be improved during school hours *before* committing additional resources to extending hours.

Why is it important, and what can you do?

In 2001, then Prime Minister Tony Blair famously declared that his top priority was 'education, education, education'. A Conservative Party retort was that it had similar priorities – although not necessarily in the same order. No one disagrees about whether education matters, but most politicians have plenty to say about how best to put their commitments into practice. The all-round benefits of receiving a good education are pretty clear. These include the increased likelihood of a better job and higher income as well as health benefits. On average, among fifteen Organisation for Economic Co-operation and Development (OECD) countries with available data, a 30-year-old college-educated man can expect to live eight years longer

---

2 See https://educationendowmentfoundation.org.uk/evidence/teaching-learning-toolkit/extending-school-time/ .

than a 30-year-old man who has not completed his secondary education (OECD, 2013a). Better-educated individuals live healthier lives than those with less education and their children are also more likely to flourish. It also appears that for every additional year spent in formal education, individuals benefit from larger and more diverse networks (social capital) and the opportunities these bring (Halpern, 2005).

Of course, obtaining a degree is no longer a guarantee of securing well-paid employment and enjoying a comfortable standard of living. Twenty or so years ago, jobs that were done by school leavers are now seen to need a degree – for instance, in nursing and policing. The expansion of educational opportunities since the Second World War has, in some respects, left the UK with an over-educated workforce. In a thought-provoking critique of government investment into education, Professor Alison Wolf (2002) asked the question, 'Does education matter?' She argued that while we produce more graduates than ever before, this has not resulted in a better-educated workforce or a more prosperous economy.

More recent research by Professor Eric Hanushek has shown that developing the cognitive skills of the population – for example, reflecting critically on written information, drawing conclusions based on evidence and making connections – has a decisive influence on long-term economic growth, both at an individual level and for society at large (Hanushek and Woessmann, 2010; OECD, 2010). Each year the OECD publishes a report called *Universal Basic Skills: What Countries Stand to Gain*. The report for 2015, written by Hanushek and Woessmann, shows clearly that the quality of schooling is a good predictor of the wealth a country will produce in the long run. It is estimated that a high-income country such as the United States would gain US$27 trillion in additional income if it ensured that all of its 15-year-olds left school with decent basic skills, over the working life of these students (OECD, 2015: 10).

Good schooling matters then. But the question remains, how is it that schools with similar student intakes, resources and exposure to ideas produce such different outcomes in terms of ethos and expectations on the one hand, and learning and achievement on the other (Hopkins, 2007)? Surely, in our age of phenomenal human achievement in areas such as technology, communication and medicine, it is possible for all schools to become good schools. One response is to say that this is rather naive and that there will always be variation in quality, depicted statistically in normal distribution along the 'bell curve'. Another response is to point out that defining good schools in data terms alone is not straightforward – attainment data may appear to be strong but the school may be coasting. So, the focus on raising standards in schools described by Ofsted as 'requiring improvement' or 'inadequate' is not the complete answer. High expectations of learners and staff are critical in all contexts, and schools already considered 'good' should not be complacent but aspire to become excellent. Or, put another way, all teachers need to ask themselves, 'Am I doing everything I can to remove barriers to learning so that learners can achieve their potential?' Schools should be adopting what Martha Nussbaum, a professor of law and ethics, calls a 'capabilities approach' to learning: 'What is each person able to do and be?' (Nussbaum, 2011: 18).

Schools do not operate in a vacuum but, instead, as part of a broader educational system (e.g. government directives, trade union activity, local authority policies) that shapes its direction and performance. An international report by McKinsey & Company, a leading management consultancy firm, entitled *How the World's Most Improved School Systems Keep Getting Better* (Mourshed, 2010), found that significant improvements can be achieved within six years. Irrespective of context or where school systems are on their improvement journey, the report highlights six key factors to securing improvement: building the instructional skills of teachers and the management skills of principals; assessment practices; improving data systems; facilitating improvement through the introduction of policy documents and education laws; revising standards and curriculum; and ensuring an appropriate reward and remuneration structure for teachers and principals.

The ultimate goal is to move learners – whether children or adults – from shallow to deep and profound modes of learning (see Table 1.2). Shallow learning, the most common in schools, is characterised by recalling and repeating information. Learners respond to external stimuli, such as tests, rewards or praise. Deep learning involves understanding and reflection, turning information gathered from different sources into meaningful knowledge that can be applied in a range of contexts. Learners are self-motivated. Profound learning occurs when learners question established truths, redefine problems and create alternatives, adding to our stock of knowledge. The modes are well illustrated when learning a language. A novice learner visiting France might know enough

French phrases for everyday exchanges, such as asking for directions (shallow), but struggle to engage in any extended conversations, initiate discussions or read newspapers (deep). Those who have mastered French go beyond the technical skills of communication to appreciate and possibly contribute to the wider cultural context – for example, by writing a short story in French or participating in a television debate over a contemporary issue (profound).

Shallow	Deep	Profound
Replication	Understanding	Meaning
Application	Transfer	Creativity
Information	Knowledge	Wisdom
Experience	Reflection	Intuition — _not boring_
Extrinsic	Intrinsic _naturally essential_	Moral
Acceptance	Interpretation	Challenge
Dependence	Independence	Interdependence

Table 1.2. The characteristics of shallow, deep and profound learning.
Source: West-Burnham (2003: 55).

In order to develop deep learning, Biggs and Collis (1982) proposed the SOLO (Structure of Observed Learning Outcomes) taxonomy, which describes increasing complexity in a student's understanding of a subject through five stages: _In terms of history_

1. **Pre-structural** – where learners acquire bits of unconnected information. _– Dates, people, facts_
2. **Unistructural** – simple and obvious connections. _– led an army_ _How one person_
3. **Multistructural** – numerous connections are made, but the 'meta' connections are missed, as is the big picture. _— What caused a rev (a few factors)_
4. **Relational** – learners are now able to appreciate the significance of the parts making up the whole. _Significance of one factor over another in causing rev._
5. **Extended abstract** – learners make connections within and beyond subjects, generalising and transferring principles.

Show what this meant for a country for example, what impact this had for russian society.

These are not straightforward terms. Hattie (2013: 29) explains the taxonomy as 'one idea, many ideas, relate ideas and extend ideas'; the first two relate to surface knowing and the latter two to deep knowing. The SOLO taxonomy depends on a firm knowledge base (the first two stages) before any real thinking can take place. The key point is that both surface *and* deep learning are necessary; there is little point in learners being able to make connections in isolation. Leaders are only able to promote deep and profound learning if they establish strong relationships in school. The ultimate test of leadership is whether such learning occurs.

Learning is not the same as performance. Herein lies one of the major challenges in our school system. Too many children and young people are judged solely by their success, or otherwise, in tests or competitions. These achievements do not always reflect depth of learning. Learning occurs when individuals retain knowledge in their long-term memory and are able to apply this. The problem is that it is difficult to know when learning has actually happened; like thinking, we can't physically see it and so we have to infer when it occurs. So, the fact that a child has scored ten out of ten in a spelling test might suggest that the words have been learned. They have clearly been recalled accurately at the moment of the test. But to move from rote learning to deeper learning, the learner needs to use and understand the words accurately when writing in a range of contexts.

The good news is that there is plenty of evidence to show what effective teachers do. Here are some well-established practices to build on:

» Seek out what motivates learners – each week invite different children to talk to the class about their passions for five minutes. Make it a memorable occasion using a lectern or special chair, mood music or display table, or use websites such as Pinterest.

» Use varied and stimulating resources – show the children a thought-provoking image each day (e.g. during registration). Try sites such as www.livescience.com/50717-amazing-images.html.

» Ask a range of thought-provoking 'What if?' questions such as, 'What if you couldn't read?' Then share real-life accounts to illustrate the points – for example, the story of the teacher, John Corcoran, who worked his way through high school and college without reading.

» Invite into school retired people who can discuss with pupils new skills they are learning – what are their challenges and joys?
» Initiate a community project that brings people together.

While such practices can enhance children's progress in school, there are also factors beyond the classroom that shape children's education. Over the last decade or so, the notion of community or extended schools has gained support, based on the principle of building closer dialogue between schools, families and the wider community. They seek to provide for a range of services or activities outside of the normal school day to help meet the needs of children as well as their parents, families and local community – for instance, the provision of clubs, activities and evening classes. There is a danger of schools imposing professional views of what is 'needed' on the communities they serve, however, working closely with parents and the community should be a central aim for all schools.

There is abundant evidence to show that parental involvement in children's education from an early age has a major impact on their achievement well into adulthood (DCSF, 2008c). In schools that are most successful in working alongside parents, the following are evident:

» There are open and clear channels of communication (e.g. text messaging alerts, emails, website, newsletters, 'positive news' phone calls, outdoor notices, face-to-face meetings).
» There are good family learning opportunities (e.g. after-school clubs, parent–child homework sessions, fathers' storytelling weeks).
» There are regular opportunities for parents to contribute to school decisions beyond those who serve on the governing body (e.g. through surveys).
» The school is actively involved in community projects, drawing on the contribution of parents.

Conclusion

In November 2015, the House of Commons Education Committee announced an inquiry into the purpose and quality of education in England. The chair, Neil Carmichael, explained that the committee wanted to know, 'What is the purpose of our educational system?' He provided some helpful prompts for bemused or confused educators: is it to prepare young people for the world of work, to be ready for adulthood, to provide them with broad academic knowledge based on shared culture and values? He added that the answers would help the committee to weigh up whether the curriculum, qualifications, assessment and accountability systems are fit for purpose. The timing of this inquiry is rather odd, given that a new national curriculum was introduced in 2013. A generous view is to point out that this committee is cross-party and its remit is to hold the government to account. It will be interesting to note how many individual teachers take time to respond to the call for evidence.

These questions and others about purpose and quality have occupied educationalists for a very long time: what does it mean to be truly educated, and what is the role of schools therein? Most commentators would agree that being well educated goes beyond what is learned in school and paper qualifications. It involves personal, social and emotional development as well as academic success. It should involve learner engagement as well as achievement. High quality teaching, a rich and stimulating curriculum and strong home–school links can inspire the habits of lifelong learning which learners need to flourish in an uncertain, complex world. Unfortunately, the emphasis on measurable outcomes can sometimes obscure the fact that learning is a continual and complex process, in which mistakes occur that sometimes engender fear of failure and a lack of confidence. Ironically, those schools that see education as an enriching process, beyond being an exam factory, do not underperform in terms of academic results. Rather, student engagement becomes a precursor to high and sustained performance.

But how do we engage learners? There is no catch-all solution – certainly building relationships with students, their peers and parents is key to understanding their interests, motives, likes and dislikes. Learning in the context of real-world scenarios can make a difference (see Chapter 4). Another key factor to consider is where learning occurs, so there are calls for leaders and teachers to literally think outside the (classroom) box. A report by the Innovation Unit points out that some schools are rethinking how they use their available space (which is turned into 'learning zones') so that students and their parents organise their own learning – forming groups, commissioning local experts to cover specific subjects or help out with projects, or working independently (Hampson et al., 2012). In one school, the experimental zone is equipped with webcams, which allow students to monitor their experiments over the weekend. These developments are not dependent on a major investment of resources, but a change of perspective so that learning without limits integrates school and real-world learning.

Summary

» The terms education, training, schooling and learning are often used interchangeably, but they are not the same.
» Education has a much broader and deeper meaning than training in specific skills. Learning begins in the womb and continues into old age. It is not only for the young.
» Children's progress in learning in school is very much dependent on the quality of teaching. This can vary considerably within and between schools.
» The effectiveness of teaching is usually measured in terms of its impact on children's educational outcomes.
» The most effective teachers know their material and how to communicate in a clear and engaging manner.
» While teachers can make a significant difference to children's learning, parental engagement is also important.
» The relationship between education and schooling needs to be redefined to better equip learners for the modern age. This can be achieved, for example, through better integration of technologies in learning and stronger partnerships with parents and the wider community.

Points for reflection and action

» Can you ever imagine a time when schools are no longer needed?
» Take a look at the Cramlington Learning Village website (www. cramlingtonlv.co.uk) to see how the school uses classroom spaces in a very flexible way.

» According to a recent report by the Office for National Statistics, Scotland is the best educated country in Europe, based on the numbers (45 per cent) receiving tertiary and higher education (Johnston, 2014). Do you think too many people are going to university, and is this cheapening the value of degrees? Are qualifications the best measure of an education?

» How can the generations be brought together to share learning? Consider the lessons to be learned from the Intergenerational Centre in Seattle where a nursery is set within a care home for elderly residents (http://washington.providence.org/senior-care/mount-st-vincent/services/child-care). Try to watch a documentary called Present Perfect, based on the centre (www.presentperfectfilm.com).

Chapter 2

Childhood

Children need time and space to explore, enjoy learning and develop as children rather than miniature adults

What is the big idea?

Admittedly, the second big idea in this book is broad ranging in scope and might be better presented as three inter-related points: (1) children learn most effectively by exploring their worlds and building on what they naturally do, (2) learning should be enjoyable and (3) children should not be hurried into adulthood. The role of families, schools and wider society is to ensure that children have the care, support, guidance and resources to flourish during childhood. This chapter provides an overview of the huge body of material related to each of these three inter-related points.

1. Children learn through exploration

Point of disagreement

The first point appears incontrovertible: by nature, children are curious individuals who seek to explore their environment. Babies crawl around, touch and put things in their mouths – this is how they learn. To aid infant physical and cognitive development, we now take for granted the need to stimulate infants through physical contact, baby talk ('motherese') and playing games like peek-a-boo. As consumers, parents and teachers, we buy into the all-pervasive marketing of all kinds of toys, educational materials and furniture designed to draw children out to explore a little more. Yet these assumptions are very different from those held in the

Not true

pre-modern Western world where it was generally agreed that children should be seen and not heard. It is also still the case in some traditional societies, such as the Maya, that the overall objective of childcare is to keep the baby quiet and never stimulated (Lancy, 2008).

But what about when children enter school? There is considerable support for teaching approaches that encourage children's natural tendency to explore, particularly in the early years. Playing and exploring is one of the defining characteristics of the early years foundation stage (EYFS), where effective practice is seen to invite young children to investigate and experience things, to 'have a go' (DfE, 2012). Teachers might create regular opportunities for children to raise questions and use these as a basis for planning a unit of work building on their interests. Their classroom and outdoor environments typically invite children to make independent decisions about learning – for example, what resources they might need, whether they work alone or with others and how they will record what they are learning. The emphasis is on active learning strategies, where learners review what they already know, make connections and develop a spirit of continually questioning what is before them.

For older pupils, enquiry-based learning and similar approaches are used in many schools around the world. They draw on a social constructivist view of learning which stresses the importance of allowing learners to explore their world and for teachers to refrain from the temptation to provide the 'right' answer or over-direct lessons. One of the key features is the opportunity for pupils to ask as well as answer questions and to take a lead in their learning. For older pupils, this might take the form of following a particular enquiry or investigation in an independent learning project in science, geography or history. Learners work through logical steps in trying to solve a problem, including gathering, analysing and presenting data, drawing conclusions and evaluating their work. For younger ones, this might take a more simplified 'plan, do and review' approach – for example, linked to how they might improve their school grounds. In one school I have visited, pupils took photographs of places around the school that made them feel comfortable and gave them a sense of belonging and other places where they felt excluded. The images were then turned into a collage to reflect pupils' feelings of inclusion and as a basis for discussion with the senior leadership team.

2. Children's learning should be enjoyable

The second point, namely that children's learning should be enjoyable, has support from neuroscience. Brain scans reveal that when students are more comfortable and enjoy learning, information flows freely, connections are stronger and memory improves (Kohn, 2004). On the other hand, learning is impeded when boredom, confusion or anxiety levels are high (Willis, 2007). Research led by Paul Howard-Jones suggests that learning through games improves when the reward for success is uncertain. In one project, Year 8 students spin a 'wheel of fortune' to determine how many points they receive for answering quiz questions correctly. Emerging findings show that not being sure of a reward increases dopamine levels in the brain and motivates learners (*The Telegraph*, 2014). Enjoyment, however, is not the same as fun. Enjoyment conveys a sense of satisfaction and this often comes through perseverance, the achievement of a goal and recognition that learning is, at times, damn hard work. Enjoyment can be expressed in terms of the memorable and significant moments experienced by learners in what the psychologist Mihaly Csikszentmihalyi (2002) calls a state of 'flow' – when learners are completely immersed in what they are doing.

3. Children have a right to a childhood

The third point relating to the rights for children to have a childhood (as distinct from adulthood) has become a major political issue over the past twenty-five years or so with the growth of the human rights movement. Childhood is a controversial subject, so much so that it is difficult to reach a consensus over even the most straightforward of questions – for example, when does childhood begin and end? For some fundamentalist Christians, human life begins at the moment of conception. In some traditional societies, such as the Bororo tribe in Brazil, a child is not recognised as an individual until the baby is 'hardened' and ready to be named, usually six or so months after birth. The naming ceremony is a marker at which point the child is 'socially born' into the community (Lancy, 2008: 15). Prior to this, the death of a child is seen as an unremarkable event. If unwanted, the infant may even be abandoned or smothered alive. Legally speaking, in many countries childhood comes to an end when children reach the age of majority (18 in most countries). The difficulty, however, is that children of the same age may be regarded as competent and responsible in one area of life but immature and dependent in another. In England, Wales and Northern Ireland young people can register to vote at 16 but cannot exercise that right until 18 (in Scotland it is 14 and 16 years respectively), whereas they can join the army at 16. In fact, more than one in ten recruits to the British Army are just 16 (Owen, 2014).

More broadly, the question of childhood happiness has been closely examined (Holder, 2012). In a major report, the Children's Society concluded that children's overall well-being is being eroded by excessive individualism in a highly competitive, consumer age (Layard et al., 2009). It argues that by attaching so much importance to individual success, this has led to many family break-ups, an overly competitive education system, relationship problems and an acceptance of income inequality. More recently, an international survey reports that many things trouble children in England, including family life, their appearance, relationships with teachers in school and performance in school. English children were ranked thirteenth out of sixteen countries in life satisfaction, well behind countries such as Romania, Poland and Columbia (see Gayle, 2016).

In many countries, the status of children has improved due to the efforts of the United Nations Children's Fund (UNICEF) and human rights' organisations, but there is still a long way to go before child poverty and misery are rare. The UN Convention on the Rights of the Child came into force on 2 September 1990, based very much on a Western model that sees childhood as a time of play, innocence and learning (Wells, 2009). Critics have argued that the philosophy behind it is alien to some cultures because of its emphasis on the individual child as separate from the family. It has proven impossible to establish universal agreement on what is good for children and what moral and legal responsibilities states have towards them. What we do know is that austerity policies across Europe are hitting the poorest children hardest and affecting their rights to decent health and their overall well-being (Hoffman, 2015).

This is why academics call childhood a social construct – an acknowledgement that what it means to be a child and what society expects from children varies across time, place and society, according to prevailing cultural and social values. While there are biological markers in children's development – smiling, crawling, walking, talking and so on – even within the same community adults respond to children in different ways. On a recent visit to an Amish village in Pennsylvania, the tour guide explained that whereas young adults might be allowed to use mobile phones for emergency purposes in one village, this depended on what the local bishop decreed – ten miles down the road young people were censored for using mobile phones.

There is an industry of experts (from 'child whisperers' to religious leaders) who offer advice on everything from child obesity to smacking, from when children should start school to when they should become criminally responsible for their actions. Unfortunately, all too often, views about children and childhood tend to be expressed as polar opposites: children are either precious innocents in need of protection from all kinds of dangers or 'tiny tearaways' wreaking havoc in the community. Those in the concerned camp worry about the influence of predatory adults, excessive materialism, unhealthy food, school bullying and all-pervasive digital technologies. It is a wonder that they, let alone their children, sleep safely at night.

Some have gone as far as to suggest that children are losing their right to childhood. In 2006, 110 leading child professionals wrote to *The Telegraph* protesting about the 'death of childhood', which they attributed to a variety of reasons from over-competitive schooling to junk food (Fenton, 2006). In particular, there are widespread concerns that children are being targeted as consumers, hurried too quickly into buying into a vast array of clothing, services and goods. There are also genuine fears that children are expected to participate in sexualised behaviour before they are ready to do so – one government commissioned report describes the 'wallpaper' of modern children's lives comprising sexualised images on the Internet, music videos, magazines, newspapers and television (Bailey, 2011). The same report revealed that nine out of ten parents agreed that 'these days children are under pressure to grow up too quickly'.

More generally, there are concerns that the well-being of children in the UK is poor in comparison to other continental countries (UNICEF, 2013; Children's Society, 2015). According to a survey by the Children's Society, only around one in four children (in Years 6 and 8) like going to school, while two-fifths (38%) said that other children had hit them in the past month. Outside of school, the charity reports that only one in five children spend time learning with their family every day (Children's Society, 2015: 37). In the realm of children's play, there are regular reports that children are not enjoying the simple outdoor pleasures of previous generations, such as climbing trees, splashing in puddles or playing conkers. According to the National Trust, on average children today spend about an hour a day outside compared to three hours in their grandparents' generation (Sing, 2014).

It matters whether children are rushed into growing up because this can have a detrimental impact on their health and well-being. They may develop a range of stress-related conditions, such as nervousness, hyperactivity, eating and sleeping disorders, as well as more common headaches and stomach problems. YoungMinds, the leading charity committed to improving children and young people's emotional and mental well-being, estimates that one in ten children and young people aged from 5 to 16 suffer from a diagnosable mental health disorder – that is around three children in every class.[1] Psychotherapist Graham Music has also observed a rise in children's selfish behaviour over three decades of clinical practice. In his book, *The Good Life: Wellbeing and the New Science of Altruism, Selfishness and Immorality* (Music, 2014a), he argues that materialism has produced a toy-crazy generation, where consumer goods are valued over people and narcissistic adults have never learned the intrinsic rewards of social belonging and interdependence. Busy parents feel obliged to give their children what they want, which means that the children do not learn the value of delayed gratification. Research shows that the likelihood of mental health problems increases among those who care more about having the latest status symbols (e.g. mobile phone) or how they look, rather than those who place greater value on being with people they care about or doing things they feel passionate about. When childhood is eroded, there are increased risks of social and behavioural problems, irregular school attendance and later, teen pregnancy, smoking and drug and alcohol abuse. Even if children and young people do not develop these problems, they can miss out on simple pleasures if they are hurried out of childhood.

At the other extreme, children are depicted as nuisances, menaces or little devils, and it is the adults (and other well-behaved children) who

---

1 See http://www.youngminds.org.uk/training_services/policy/mental_health_statistics.

need protection. In 2010 the Prime Minister David Cameron expressed his concern at the 17,000 cases of teachers being attacked by students in a typical year, based on the number of fixed-term exclusions (see Judd, 2010). Strictly speaking, these 'attacks' were against adults (including non-teaching staff) and some suspensions were for shoving or pushing. Nonetheless, reportedly, each year millions of pounds are paid out to teachers in compensation for classroom assaults by 'thugs' (Mulholland, 2012). Two fatal stabbings of teachers by pupils – one in 2014 and another in 2015 – left the nation appalled (Austin, 2015). But these are rare events, hence the shock factor.

In reality, the picture of modern childhood is more complicated than surveys or sensational media sound bites suggest. Much of the material on negative childhood experiences is too sweeping, as if the effects of living in the modern age damage *all* children. So, for example, while commercialism clearly influences children this is not always in a negative sense. An independent assessment of the impact of the commercial world on children's well-being concluded that it offers children exciting opportunities in terms of entertainment, learning, creativity and cultural experiences (DCSF, 2009a). What schools and parents need to do is to teach children how to think critically about their environment through media and consumer literacy projects – and there are many resources to support this (e.g. www.ofcom.org.uk). This is far more productive than seeking to return to a mythical golden age of childhood when family life appeared to be more harmonious than it is today.

In fact, the vast majority of children enjoy a far better quality of life than their predecessors, say 100 years ago. Given regular reports about issues such as child obesity levels, mental health problems and antisocial behaviour, it is easy to overlook the good things about children's lives today. Life expectancy has increased, children are largely free from debilitating illnesses, many attend preschool, are brought up in better housing and have free access to libraries and other cultural services. Moreover, among educators, there is a broad consensus that childhood should be a time and space when children grow and develop in a climate free from fear, ridicule and commercial exploitation.

Who is behind it?

It was not until the seventeenth century, at least according to the French historian Philippe Ariès (1914–1984), that the idea of childhood being seen as a distinct phase from adulthood began to emerge. Before then, he argued that paintings, gravestones and furniture showed that children were represented as mini-adults. According to Ariès, childhood was a relatively modern invention, although we now know that he overstated the case. Historians who have studied a broader range of sources have shown that while children may have dressed similarly to their parents, they still enjoyed the kind of experiences that most children in modern times take for granted. They played games, sang, skipped, argued, fought, asked questions and explored their worlds in their own ways. There is no evidence to suggest that, in general, medieval parents loved their children any less than modern parents. They simply lived in a world with different values and beliefs.

That said, during the sixteenth and seventeenth centuries, it is possible to identify the beginnings of modern-day thinking about education and childhood. The Czech-born John Amos Comenius (1592–1670) argued that education should be a universal right for children and that well-trained teachers should run the schools. Girls, he argued, should be included because they are 'endowed with equal sharpness of mind and capacity for knowledge' (cited by Flanagan, 2006: 77), although he qualified this by saying that their education should be limited to those things appropriate for women. Nonetheless, Comenius' scheme for universal education (from birth to 24) applied to all, irrespective of gender, faith, economic standing or culture. The philosophers John Locke and Jean-Jacques Rousseau both believed in the intrinsic value of childhood but, unlike Comenius, they were only interested in the education of the gentry. For Rousseau, schools should follow their children's inclinations rather than compel them to do things. Forcing children to read books, for example, was 'the plague of childhood' (cited by Flanagan, 2006: 105). It was better for children to have the desire to read first and then to use simple messages concerning them as a stimulus.

During the first half of the twentieth century, official reports endorsed the view that schools should build on children's natural tendencies to explore, ask questions and observe. The Plowden Report (1967) on primary education, for example, advocated individual discovery learning, schools providing first-hand experiences and children participating in creative projects. This is what it had to say in terms of our big idea about childhood: 'A school is not merely a teaching shop. It is a community in which children learn to live first and foremost as children and not future adults' (Plowden, 1967: para. 505).

In the modern age, social commentators from different backgrounds have argued that childhood is not what it once was and has lost its innocence. For one thing, children are spending less time outdoors than previous generations – one writer has gone so far as to suggest that children are suffering a kind of 'nature deficit disorder' (Louv, 2005). More generally, concerns about childhood have been expressed over several decades across the Western world. The American Neil Postman (1982) bemoaned the 'disappearance' of childhood, while David Elkind first wrote about the damaging effects of 'the hurried child' in 1981. In his updated edition, he refers to the combined pressures of the Internet, classroom culture, school violence, movies and television, which have blurred the boundaries of what is age appropriate (Elkind, 2006).

Childhood has been compressed so that children are not children for long. In the Western world, there is considerable pressure on children to 'be mature' and 'grow up'. In the UK, the popular writer Sue Palmer (2006) suggests that childhood has become 'toxic', suffering under the pressures of commercialisation and 'sexualisation' (this new word describes the grooming of girls – never boys – into premature sexual behaviour). One journalist argues that the government is at fault because it does not do enough to regulate the market that sells, for example, thongs to little girls because it's not perceived to be a middle-class problem. While the middle class dresses 'its children in pretty polka-dot dresses, the useless underclass will dress its little girls as tarts' (Moore, 2011). Is it poverty that makes children grow up 'too soon'? In one study, researchers found children from low-income families wore branded trainers to hide their poverty, reasoning that they could not be poor if they owned expensive shoes (Elliott and Leonard, 2004). They tried to transfer Nike's popularity to themselves by wearing 'cool' trainers. They also preferred to play with other children who had prestige branded products than those who did not.

While the idea that children are not small adults seems obvious, some parents seem to think that they are. Television programmes, such as the

US reality show *Toddlers & Tiaras*, feature 3- and 4-year-olds dressing like their mothers in bling in the competitive world of child beauty pageants. Meanwhile, children aged between 8 and 12 ('tweenagers') are particularly susceptible to media influence. The American historian Joan Brumberg (1997) calls young girls' obsession with dieting, personal grooming and shopping 'the body project'. She looked at the diaries of young girls to see how the idea of self-improvement has changed over the years. Her conclusion is that whereas nineteenth-century young women were interested in how to improve their internal character (e.g. to think before speaking, to show self-restraint, to show interest in others, to work harder at school), the modern-day girl is interested in her external appearance (e.g. the new haircut, good makeup, new clothes and accessories). Added to this should be the rise of the 'selfie' – sharing self-taken photographs online – with one survey suggesting that nine out of ten American teenagers post photos of themselves online (BBC, 2013).

It is sometimes easy to overlook the basic point that children *are* children, but the big idea here is that they need time and space to explore, question, grow and develop without the pressures associated with adulthood. In some schools, this finds support through the play-based curriculum in the early years and enquiry-based approaches to learning among older children. But, generally, assessment and national curriculum pressures among teachers has constrained opportunities for teachers to build on children's natural curiosity.

One of the consequences of a standards-driven and attainment-focused culture in schools has been concern that this has increased stress among children and young people. The National Union of Teachers reports that there are 'anxious, stressed and disaffected pupils at all levels of education and in all types of schools'. Nine out of ten teachers surveyed attributed this to tests, exams and the fear of failure (Adams, 2015). The Labour government recognised that enjoyment in learning was important and made it central to its policies in the 2000s. The landmark Green Paper *Every Child Matters* (DfES, 2003) identified enjoyment as one of five key outcomes for education, placing it on the same level of importance as being healthy and safe. In *21st Century Schools: A World-Class Education for Every Child*, the Department for Children, Schools and Families made it clear that one of its key objectives was to ensure children 'enjoy their learning' (DCSF, 2008a: para. 3.4). There are schools that create a climate conducive to learning with an emphasis on high academic standards without sacrificing breadth or balance in the curriculum. While they retain a focus on literacy and numeracy, they do not do so at the expense of squeezing out the arts and humanities (see Chapter 8).

Why is it important, and what can you do?

For schools, one of the main implications of these debates about childhood is to give appropriate attention to values-based education, where there is a focus on building strong relationships and emotional resilience. As Williamson and Payton (2009: 39) point out: 'A curriculum dedicated to supporting a "good childhood" should address such problems as "teaching to the test" and children's fear of failure, and it should take greater account of children's socio-economic backgrounds'. Children in the same school, let alone country, can come from very diverse backgrounds. It is therefore essential to get to know children as *individuals*, understanding their needs, interests and motivations. Whatever children's backgrounds, they share common needs and rights – including the need to belong and be loved, to play and express their views. They also have in common the fact that they are growing, changing and learning. But children differ in how their development is manifested, their rate of learning and the circumstances in which they find themselves. Moreover, the biological state of being a child can be very different to the social and cultural experience of childhood.

A few years ago, the concept of personalised learning was the dominant motif in education policy-making. The Department for Children, Schools and Families produced a range of supporting resources as part of its vision for *21st Century Schools*, now half-forgotten in the National Archives. Personalised learning rested on the notion of high expectations for every child and the mantra of 'participation, fulfilment and success' (DCSF, 2009d: 7). What does this mean in practice? It demands 100 per cent participation from pupils and sets high and realistic challenges. It does not 'spoon feed'; it is challenging and demanding. It expects pupils to be able to articulate their ideas, understanding and thinking by actively promoting pupil talk. Lesson organisation is fit for purpose –

for example, it may involve direct whole-class teaching or, alternatively, may have significant elements of enquiry-based individual or group work (DCSF, 2009d: 10).

Personalised learning is not the same as individualised learning where pupils work independently on their own work. Rather, it seeks to 'open doors' for all pupils so they can access the curriculum and work towards the same challenging goals. Professor Dylan Wiliam (2015) cites an example from a mathematics lesson. A traditional British approach to finding the area of a trapezium is to model an example to the class and then give all the pupils the opportunity to practise twenty on their own. Wiliam points out that a Japanese teacher gives the class one method of finding the area of a trapezium and then the class, working as individuals, pairs or groups, suggest as many different ways of finding the area of a trapezium as they can. They then present and compare their findings at the front of the class. Wiliam concludes that, although it is a whole-class activity, it is personalised because each pupil accesses the task in different ways – some demonstrate sophisticated thinking using ratio, while others use the more straightforward method of dissection.

Personalised learning seeks to move education away from a model based on the mass market to take greater account of the cultural background, learning preferences and abilities of individuals. Professor Stephen Heppell (2006: 1) uses the metaphor of moving from 'factory education to free-range' and cites examples of how technologies such as podcasts and iPods promote the kind of creative and social skills central to personalised learning. The concept has since lost its way, lacking political support from the coalition and then Conservative governments and criticised for its woolliness. However, the spirit of personalised learning is still reflected in schools where there is an emphasis on giving pupils individual attention through tutorials, intensive coaching for groups of pupils who are struggling, partnership 'contracts' between home and school, and strong learner voice.

Personalised learning begins with knowing children as individuals, where each has at least one adult in the school who they can confide in and have confidence that they will be listened to – form tutors in secondary schools, for example, have a key role to play here. Coates (2015) took great pride in her 'assertive mentoring' programme where every student in Years 11 and 13 met with a mentor once a month to discuss predicted grades based on current performance, where they were falling short of expectations and how the school could support them. Research into what pupils think about school shows that they value opportunities to talk to adults about their experiences and opinions. As one child put it: 'Miss talks with us, not at us'; unfortunately, this is not the experience shared by all children: 'Ours don't do nuffink' (Carline, 2008: 53, 55).

John Hattie's much-cited research shows that when children become teachers themselves, it can have a very powerful impact on the quality of their learning (Hattie, 2009). How often do children *teach* in your school? In the novel *A Kestrel for a Knave* (Hines, 1968), popularised in the film *Kes,* Billy Casper is a 15-year-old brought up on a tough estate, dismissed by his mother as 'a hopeless case', abandoned by his father, abused by his half-brother and bullied at school. His salvation comes in the form of a young kestrel, which Billy takes from a nest on a farm, trains and nurtures. He helps himself to a second-hand book on the subject from a shop because he can't get a library card. Billy begins to develop a love for falconry and receives rare praise at school from his English teacher after delivering an impromptu impassioned talk on his relationship with the bird. Billy Casper's rare 'feel-good' moment in school happens when Mr Farthing (Colin Welland), the English teacher, takes a genuine interest in his hobby.

Central to personalised learning is giving pupils individual and collective responsibilities. Many teachers are quite innovative in the way they allocate individual roles in curriculum projects and everyday school life – pupils may act as health and safety officers, noticeboard or website consultants, form captains, classroom environment engineers, school ground architects, registrars or homework coordinators. There has been plenty of research on the value of putting children's decision making at the heart of school life (Ruddock and Flutter, 2003). Most schools in the UK operate school or student councils but these vary considerably in how often they meet and the impact they have (Bennett, 2012). Unfortunately, they can be tokenistic – as when children are asked for their views on school uniform or decorating the toilets but little else – and even manipulative – when teachers and leaders only hear what they want to hear, ignoring criticism. In schools where the pupil voice is taken seriously, however, learners are regularly invited to express their views on the core matters of teaching and learning through fundamental questions such as, 'Why are we learning this?', 'What are we doing well?' and 'What can we do to improve?'

But learner voice is not without its challenges. Children who do well at school and comply with its rules are more likely to be heard than those children who struggle, yet the voices of the latter are equally important (Williamson and Payton, 2009). There is also the broader question of how children's views are influenced by more vociferous peers and the fickle nature of children's decision making. If children's voices are to be heard then they need to understand the consequences of their decisions and the fact that schools (as with all organisations) have limited resources and cannot satisfy everyone at all times.

Conclusion

In many respects most children today are far better off than they have ever been – for example, in terms of access to education, physical health, opportunities to see the world, recreation, housing and material well-being. Life in the twenty-first century opens up many exciting possibilities largely facilitated through digital technology and extended educational opportunities. But clearly children and young people are growing up in a world that also brings many pressures. For some children, this means a lack of basic needs such as a regular breakfast before going to school or a lack of sleep. For others, it means taking on adult responsibilities such as caring for incapacitated relatives. Then there are the children who are immersed in virtual worlds. There are many organisations that are actively promoting and protecting children's rights, from the National Society for the Prevention of Cruelty to Children (NSPCC), founded in 1889, to the Save Childhood Movement, which began in 2013. These organisations, many of them run on a voluntary basis, would not exist unless there was a need to do so. The key message is that children and young people today are living very different lives to when their parents and teachers were children, or even ten years ago. The challenge for teachers, parents and other educators is to provide the necessary support and guidance so that children can make the most of their lives.

Summary

» Childhood is socially and culturally defined, which means that the experience and length of childhood differs according to prevailing values and customs in time, place and society.

» Every generation has raised concerns about children and childhood but the rise of digital technologies present significant opportunities and challenges for the young generation of today.

» Many organisations have long campaigned to protect children's rights.

» Children in the UK have certain rights enshrined in the United Nations Convention on the Rights of the Child (UNCRC), including the right to be educated and listened to.

» Teachers should build on children's natural curiosity by encouraging them to question, explore and discover. This can be achieved through approaches such as enquiry-based learning.

» Personalised learning means understanding and providing for children's needs and setting high expectations for all. It includes genuinely listening to what they have to say and enabling them to participate in the school's decision-making processes.

Points for reflection and action

» According to a recent survey of 5,000 10- to 15-year-olds by the Institute for Social and Economic Research, the three things that matter most to children are having close friends, playing sport and having a stable family (Urquhart, 2012). What are the implications of this for schools and society at large?

» Do you think childhood has become over-protected and too 'bubble wrapped'? See whether you revise your view after watching the TED Talk entitled '5 Dangerous Things You Should Let Your Kids Do' by Gever Tulley (founder of the Tinkering School), available at: https://www.ted.com/talks/gever_tulley_on_5_dangerous_things_for_kids?language=en.

» It has been suggested that boring lessons is a major reason why children are absent from school – one survey in 2009 found that eight out of ten teenagers were fed up with school (Paton, 2009). In your own experience as a child, how boring did you find school? As a teacher (be honest), how exciting do you make your lessons? How do you know?

» How often do you find out what children think about school? Jot down what you think they might say if asked the following questions and then compare your answers to what they actually say:

- Do they enjoy school?
- Which parts do they like/dislike most? Why?
- What are schools for?
- Where and when do they think they learn best?
- Which bits of learning do they find easy or a hard slog? Why?
- When do they find learning exciting?
- What do good learners do?

Chapter 3

Knowledge

Knowledge is the foundation for learning

What is the big idea?

Knowledge, in all its forms, is of premium value – to past, present and future generations. In 1952, the editors of *History Today* asked a teasing question: 'When did it become impossible to know everything?' (Snowman, 2001). They concluded that the great Renaissance humanists, who had access to the collective wisdom of the age, were the last educated men to know the broad outline of European learning. Over the last 400 or so years, knowledge has grown rapidly and specialists have emerged in all fields. According to Snowman, this has meant that there are now few individuals on earth who have the necessary theoretical and practical knowledge, even to make the simplest tool, if society crumbled. In *The Knowledge*, Lewis Dartnell (2015) speculates over what key knowledge we would need to rebuild a post-apocalyptic society. He points out that the distributed nature of knowledge would it make very difficult for any survivors to reboot civilisation, even if they had access to the latest science and technology manuals.

The third big idea in this book is that knowledge is the basis of learning. The process of learning involves making connections between new information and prior knowledge. The most important goals in education – developing literate and numerate pupils, equipping them to become creative and critical thinkers, cultivating values such as tolerance and respect for others – all rest on knowledge. Yet we have a strange view of knowledge. On the one hand we love the *Trivial Pursuit*-style collection of facts – consider the British obsession with lists, pub quizzes and long-running programmes such as *Mastermind*. Yet we also look down on those who appear to be very knowledgeable, often dismissing them as know-it-alls, swots or geeks. But success in all walks of life depends on a strong knowledge base.

The term 'knowledge' can mean many things. Perhaps the greatest thinker in the modern age, Albert Einstein (1954: 80), put it best: 'Knowledge exists in two forms – lifeless, stored in books, and alive, in the consciousness of men. The second form of existence is after all the essential one; the first, indispensable as it may be, occupies only an inferior position.'

Knowledge is often seen in terms of facts and figures (what academics call *declarative* knowledge) – the capital of France, the longest river in the UK, the first Tudor monarch, the elements of the water cycle. But it means more than this. It includes knowing what to do (*procedural* knowledge) – knowing how to ride a bicycle, bake a cake, mend a burst water pipe, what to do in an emergency. It also includes knowing the best course of action to take when solving problems (*strategic* knowledge) – who to select as goalkeeper, who to invite to a wedding, whether to travel by train or car. *Conceptual* knowledge enables learners to classify and organise their learning through general concepts such as change, similarity, difference, cause and effect, as well as specific concepts such as evaporation (science), books (English) and subtraction (mathematics). The ancient Greeks suggested that the starting point for learning was another form of knowledge called self or *metacognitive* knowledge – an individual's knowledge about personal strengths and weaknesses and the ability to control one's thinking. Flavell (1976: 232), who popularised the term metacognition, offered the following explanation: 'I am engaging in Metacognition if I notice that I am having more trouble learning A than B; if it strikes me that I should double check C before accepting it as fact.' Metacognitive knowledge, then, describes what individuals know about their thinking, the possible approaches they could use to solve problems and the demands particular tasks bring.

We may think of knowledge as set in stone. Clearly, there is knowledge that is reliable and beyond dispute but there is also a lot that is contentious. Even in fields such as science and medicine, there are different views on the causes of disease, appropriate treatments, ethical practices and the precise nature of particles, just as historians differ over dating and interpreting evidence. Knowledge cannot be separated from values and beliefs. Decisions are made in schools over which knowledge is important enough to feature in the curriculum and specific lessons and which is edited out. Once knowledge has been filtered through the syllabus, teachers' mouths, textbooks and websites, learners can be left with the belief that it is true and absolute. It can be a sobering experience when children discover mistakes in textbooks or find out that what teachers say is incorrect. This is why it is important not to present oneself as the font of knowledge and to embrace technologies as a means of confirming the provisional nature of knowledge.

One simple way of codifying knowledge is set out in Figure 3.1.

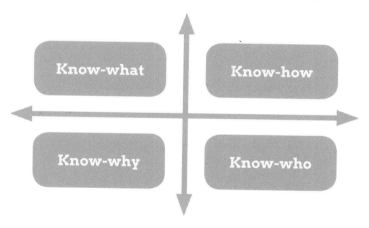

Figure 3.1. Simple knowledge codification.

Know-what refers to factual knowledge. In fields such as law and medicine, this kind of knowledge is particularly valuable and potentially life-saving. For teachers, it is commonly agreed that strong subject knowledge should underpin their practice. In countries such as South Korea, Finland, Hong Kong and Singapore, there is a focus on recruiting top graduates into the teaching profession. A Middle Eastern policy-maker working in a country that struggles to recruit top graduates into teaching observed: 'One cannot give what one does not have' (McKinsey & Company, 2007: 17).

Know-why means knowledge derived from studying the scientific principles and laws of nature. This kind of knowledge is often generated in specialised organisations such as research laboratories and universities. For teachers, exploring why things happen in their context is a key part of any classroom-based research. It typically involves selecting a teaching issue to investigate, trying out some promising change in teaching, monitoring the impact and reflecting on the findings (see Chapter 11). More generally, keeping teachers informed about the reasoning behind school policies and practices, or why particular decisions are made by school leaders or education policy-makers, reflects on the quality of care and communication within an organisation.

Know-how refers to knowledge of how to do something (skills). This knowledge is typically limited to a particular setting, industry or profession. Teachers should know how to maintain discipline in a classroom, engage the interest of learners and plan lessons to meet their different needs.

Finally, know-who relates to information about relationships – who knows what and who knows how to do what. For heads and other senior leaders, this kind of knowledge is important to ensure the smooth running of the school. It typically involves partnerships with parents, other schools, the local authority, businesses, specialist services and agencies. Professional networks and learning communities have a key role to play in supporting teachers, particularly those teaching in small rural schools.

One of the major differences between expert and beginning teachers is what they do with their knowledge – in other words, expert teachers' know-how (procedural knowledge) is far more sophisticated than for novice teachers. However, like experts in other fields, outstanding teachers often struggle to explain this knowledge to others. The knowledge is tacit rather than explicit. What goes on in a classroom is not only the *intentional* pedagogy or what is written in the lesson plan. As one teacher put it: 'When I show other teachers and colleagues how I dance in a classroom, they can see the steps but it's not the same as the dance itself, which can only really exist there when I'm in the classroom with the students' (cited by Shim and Roth, 2008: 11).

Even when lessons are video-recorded and the teaching discussed and reflected on, it is not possible to capture everything – for example, the way a teacher reads a group discussion and knows when (and when not) to step in, the subtle use of body language or the reason behind a change of direction. As Polanyi (1967: 4) puts it in his seminal work on the subject of tacit knowledge: 'We can know more than we can tell.'

Who is behind it?

The study of knowledge (epistemology) can be traced back to the ancient Greeks. Plato famously set up the first Academy, where students searched for true knowledge and virtue. He also imagined an ideal state in *The Republic* in which a knowledgeable class of guardians advised philosopher kings. But while the guardians needed to know their subject, they also needed to know the limits of their knowledge. Plato was a pupil of another intellectual giant, Socrates (469–399 BC). He stressed the importance of self-knowledge, knowing one's own prejudices and motives and developing a rational mind. Without such self-knowledge, Socrates argued, men would act only in their own interests. For Socrates, knowledge was not something that was transmitted but gained through questioning, investigation and reflection. He was critical of paid teachers of philosophy (called Sophists) for being too obsessed with acquiring the 'know-how' of getting on in life. Debates around the kind of knowledge that is seen to be significant, and how best to acquire it, remain very much alive.

In modern times, one of the key thinkers who highlighted the primary importance of knowledge was the American psychologist Benjamin Bloom (1913–1999). He defined knowledge as 'the recall of specifics and universals, the recall of methods and processes, or the recall of a pattern, structure, or setting' (Bloom et al. 1956: 201). Bloom led a group of educators who explored the design of curricula and assessment. They were first interested in the question of classifying the development of knowledge and intellectual skills, followed by mapping out affective or emotional development. What mattered to Bloom and his colleagues was not so much *comparing* the achievement of students but how individuals could be helped to achieve a particular educational goal. Bloom had 'a nose for the significant' (Eisner, 2000: 6).

Bloom's contribution can be seen today in the renewed interest in mastery learning, where subject content is broken down into units with clear objectives that are pursued until they are achieved. Bloom's hierarchy of educational objectives put knowledge (of facts, propositions, principles, etc.) at the base of a pyramid, working through comprehension and application (of knowledge and understanding to problems) to the higher order skills of analysis, synthesis and evaluation (see Figure 3.2). For Bloom, learners need to first recall knowledge, whether specific facts or complete theories, before they can proceed to the next cognitive level. Bloom's work has been critiqued and revised but continues to exert significant influence, particularly in curriculum and assessment (Guskey, 2001).

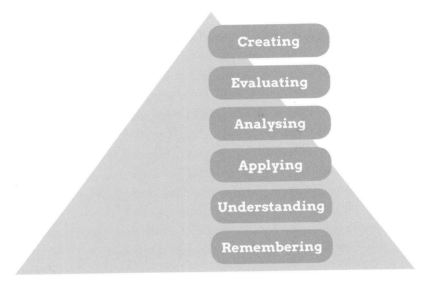

Figure 3.2. Bloom's revised taxonomy
(after Anderson and Krathwohl, 2001).

The literature on effective teaching shows that one of the things that distinguishes experts from novices is their ability to transfer knowledge in meaningful ways to learners. It is not simply that they know more 'stuff' because this does not automatically enable a person to teach this well. As Hattie and Yates (2014b) point out, the reverse is often true because the more someone knows about a subject, the more difficult it is to see the subject from another person's view. An 'expert blind spot' emerges where knowledge becomes an obstacle to teaching. This is why the ability to transfer knowledge in an accessible manner, what Shulman (1987) calls 'pedagogical content knowledge', is essential for teachers. They do so by making use of a full range of techniques such as metaphors, visual sources, models and examples from real life.

Another important figure in epistemology is E. D. Hirsch (b. 1928), a former English literature professor in the United States. In the 1980s, he introduced the notion of 'cultural literacy' to describe the kinds of facts, ideas and works of literature that he thought people needed to know to become active members of their society. He believed that there was a 'knowledge deficit' in US society based on his experiences of mostly black college students who struggled to read with understanding simple passages about the American Civil War. It was not that they lacked reading ability. Rather, they struggled because they did not have the factual knowledge to enable them to grasp the context of what they were reading. Hirsch concluded that there were 'cultural have-nots' who grew up in homes without knowledge of art, heritage, literature and so forth, an idea that is now commonly accepted. The answer, for Hirsch, is for schools to try to compensate by providing a knowledge-rich curriculum (Hirsch, 2007).

Former Education Secretary Michael Gove was influenced by the likes of Hirsch when he introduced the revised national curriculum in 2013 with its focus on 'core knowledge'. Gove believes that knowledge precedes higher order thinking skills and so should have primacy in the curriculum. He believes there is a core or essential body of knowledge that children need to learn. He has support from writers such as Michael Young (2007), Robert Peal (2014) and Daisy Christodoulou (2014), all of whom have called for knowledge to be brought back to the fore and to feature prominently in the curriculum. Peal argues that it is not a question of knowledge *and* skills but rather knowledge *then* skills; it is simply not possible for young people to engage in critical debate without first knowing the subject they are talking about. Thinking, so the argument runs, does not happen in a vacuum. It must have context, purpose and content. Young is of the view that schools should promote the kind of knowledge that young people may not acquire at home or in the community.

This is a convincing argument. Some teachers hold the view that they 'teach children not subjects', but this is an overly simplistic notion that fails to take account of the fact that children can enjoy and be intellectually stimulated by the acquisition of knowledge. As Ledda (2010) controversially points out:

> If one wants educated children, it is knowledge, not the child that should lie at the heart of educational process. Education means teaching children things they have no inclination whatsoever to learn.

That's why nothing motivates children to study more than seeing teachers who have great respect for knowledge.

However, there is a danger in a knowledge-centred approach to teaching which squeezes out opportunities for pupils to be creative and curious. Moreover, the fundamental question of which knowledge takes priority remains highly contentious. There are also philosophical questions over whether there is a discrete, fixed incontestable body of knowledge 'out there' for learners to consume. The historian Richard Johnson (1976) rediscovered the phrase 'really useful knowledge', which was first used by radical workers attending nineteenth-century evening classes who rejected the official programme in favour of political and economic studies.

While there are debates over the value and nature of what is worth knowing, the challenge for the learner is simply stated: to remember whatever they are taught. The psychologist George Miller (1920– 2012) pioneered the idea of 'cognitive overload', which describes the limited capacity of the short-term working memory to hold a handful of words or numbers at any one time. Miller's famous paper, 'The Magical Number Seven, Plus or Minus Two' (1956), highlighted that, on average, people can only recall seven randomised numbers, six letters and four or five words. He went on to describe the importance of techniques such as paraphrasing, chunking (breaking items up into smaller units), summarising, highlighting and note taking to improve recall. The modern-day consensus holds that information is first absorbed through the sensory memory (lasting less than a second) from which we quickly form perceptions. Then the information is processed or encoded through the short-term memory, lasting on average between twenty to thirty seconds. It is easier to encode visual items than abstract ideas, so we can easily picture the concept of a 'dog' but struggle with cynology (the study of dogs). Finally, information passes into the long-term memory that is virtually unlimited in capacity and relatively permanent. To retrieve information, it needs to pass through both sensory and short-term memories and be effectively encoded in the long-term memory. Encoding can be facilitated through the use of visual and auditory cues – for example, when learners associate information with physical characteristics such as size, shape, colour and sound – and when the material becomes personally relevant.

Why is it important, and what can you do?

Today we have access to more information than any other previous generation in the history of humankind. The figures are staggering: scientists have calculated that the amount of information stored on computers around the world is around 295 exabytes (a number with twenty zeros in it). This is the equivalent of 315 times the number of grains of sand in the world! Around 1.9 zettabytes of information is communicated through broadcast technology such as television each year. This is rather like every person in the world reading 174 newspapers every day (Hilbert and López, 2011). But as Rheingold (2010) put it so bluntly, a lot of this 'infowhelm' is 'Information Crap'.

It is simply not possible for pupils to think at higher cognitive levels without drawing on prior knowledge. Even in the Google Age, pupils cannot know what they do not know. They cannot search the Internet without knowing what to look for. They cannot decide whether the information they find is useful or relevant unless they can measure its worth against reliable reference points. Studies show that students with a high level of 'background' knowledge are able to understand and analyse complex texts much better than their peers without that knowledge, who tend to come from poorer, less privileged backgrounds (Willingham, 2010). In response to this, the Core Knowledge Education Foundation in the United States (www.coreknowledge.org) and Core Knowledge UK (www.coreknowledge.org.uk) are examples of support for schools to developing knowledge-rich programmes of study.

Research suggests that most pupils already know something about what the teacher is going to teach them – the New Zealand researcher, Graham Nuthall (2007), suggests that this is, on average, about 50 per cent of the topic. But prior knowledge differs significantly from one pupil to the next. And it is because of this, as well as variations in the way pupils engage with classroom activities, that pupils take away different things from each lesson. In other words, pupils achieve different learning outcomes even from engaging in the same lesson activity. Learning, then, is a highly individualised experience.

Those pupils who do well at school, as judged by their success in examinations, do so largely because they have good memories. They are able to recall large bits of information and recycle these in assessed

Strategy	Description
KWHL grids	KWHL stands for: what learners already *know*, what they *want* to know, *how* they will find out and what they have *learned* during the unit of work. These can be displayed on the wall or written in children's books and added to as the unit of work unfolds.
Mnemonics	Patterns of letters, ideas or associations to help remember things – for example: • Compass points (North, East, South, West – e.g. Never Eat Shredded Wheat, Naughty Elephants Squirting Water). • Planets (Mercury, Venus, Earth, Mars, Jupiter, Saturn, Uranus, Neptune, Pluto – e.g. My Very Educated Mother Just Served Us Nine Pizzas). • Spelling (because – e.g. Big Elephants Can Add Up Sums Easily). • Conjunctions (For, And, Nor, But, Or, Yet, So – e.g. FAN BOYS).
Chunking	The process of rearranging bits of information into larger blocks is called chunking. For example, to recall a telephone number with the sequence 0792808942, it would be easier to group the digits as 0792-808-942. Meaning plays a role in chunking – it is easier to recall TV FBI CIA JFK than TBFBICIAJFK (Bower, 1972).
Summaries	Summaries restate key ideas in a concise manner, either through words, orally, art, drama or music. They can be presented individually, in pairs or small groups. Research shows clearly that summaries are very effective teaching strategies (Marzano et al., 2001).
Graphic organisers	These are communication tools that use visual symbols to represent abstract or implicit information, to organise ideas or to express relationships between ideas. Examples of particular approaches include David Hyerle's (2008) Thinking Maps and Tony Buzan's (2003) Mind Maps.

Table 3.1. Strategies to improve information recall.

conditions. How much learners remember depends on many factors, including the type of material, degree of motivation, recall methods and amount of time available. The importance of developing children's working memories is generally neglected in schools. However, there are many practical things teachers can do to improve pupils' recollection of information (see Table 3.1).

Martha Burns, a leading neuroscientist, explains why some students retain information better than others. When people are highly stimulated the brain releases a chemical called dopamine; drugs and gambling trigger the release of dopamine very effectively but this can lead to serious consequences. There are less harmful ways of achieving a mental high and, according to Burns, dopamine is released whenever someone learns something new and exciting. She likens dopamine to the 'save button' in the brain – its presence enables learning to stick (cited by Gallo, 2014). For teachers, the advice is to find new ways of delivering information and to ensure there is a novelty factor in all lessons so that dopamine levels increase. This is not as tough as it may appear: an unusual picture, soundtrack, artefact, newspaper headline, puzzle, moral dilemma, statistic, animal, photo album, item of clothing, natural object (from a beach, woodland or river), mystery, question, joke, riddle or toy can all spice up a lesson.

Teachers can do various things in order to develop the four kinds of knowledge identified in Figure 3.1. Know-what and know-why is generally acquired through reading books, articles, newspapers, blogs and attending professional development events, such as in-service training, university courses and education conferences. Trade unions and subject associations provide information for their members on the kind of professional development available. There are also commercial organisations and consultants offering their services. Developing the two other forms of knowledge, know-how and know-who, requires practical experience. Teachers can increase their knowledge of how to do things well through an apprenticeship model where they observe expert colleagues, through team teaching, coaching and participation in research projects. In recent years, the Japanese lesson study approach to teacher enquiry has become popular (DCSF, 2009b) and there is some US research evidence that lesson study contributes to higher standards in students' mathematical knowledge (Gersten et al., 2014). The technique involves three teachers working collaboratively to tackle specific barriers to learning. The focus is on three 'case study' pupils rather than the whole class, in order for the teachers to acquire in-depth knowledge of the effects of their teaching on pupils' learning (see Chapter 11). Teachers' awareness of who knows what in education can be developed through joining professional networks. Increasingly, this is mediated through social media, where idea-sharing tools like RSS feeds, digital discussion forums and blogs have added a new dimension to professional learning networks.

Conclusion

Invariably, whenever knowledge is discussed in education it provokes debate. Take a simple example: the government is considering introducing online tests to check whether 11-year-olds know their times tables up to 12 x 12. Fair enough. Christine Blower, the leader of the National Union of Teachers, is not so sure. Although not against children learning their tables, she argues that they should be taught how to look up the answers on their mobile phones (Fenton, 2015). Professor Sugata Mitra goes further by questioning why we bother teaching spelling, times tables and other curriculum lists when the real challenge is to get children to engage in interesting questions and problems (Mitra, 2013). Many (including myself) would disagree with these views, arguing for instance that it's quite useful at the checkout to be able to work out in your head whether you have been overcharged and not need to rely on your phone. However, this is not the point here. What is important is for teachers to recognise that what counts as worthwhile knowledge is contestable and that the things we take for granted should be questioned if we are to develop a commitment to informed enquiry.

This chapter is not arguing for a knowledge-centred curriculum because this can result in neglecting learners' interests and restricting opportunities for creativity and spontaneous and independent learning. Both knowledge and skills are necessary in a well-rounded education. By knowledge, as this chapter has shown, we are not only referring to factual content. Perhaps it is more helpful to think in terms of 'ways of knowing' because this makes less of a distinction between knowledge and skills. While we want children and young people to think independently, they must have something of substance to think about. Those who argue that children can simply look up information on the Internet miss the point. Background knowledge is integral to, rather than separate from, higher order thinking processes. Michael Young (2007) has argued that the reason parents send their children to school is for them to access 'powerful knowledge' that they cannot gain at home or in their everyday lives. This is specialist knowledge that provides reliable explanations about how life works or new ways of thinking about the world. While teachers should draw on pupils' prior knowledge, this is often of a particular type and limited to local experience. One of the core purposes of schooling is to introduce learners to generalised principles derived from a broader and deeper knowledge base.

Summary

» The study of knowledge (epistemology) can be traced back to the ancient Greeks. The various forms of knowledge can be classified in different ways – for example, declarative (facts and figures), procedural (knowing what to do), strategic (knowing how to solve problems), metacognitive (self-knowledge) and conceptual (knowing ideas).

» The place of knowledge in the school curriculum is often debated and knowledge is widely seen as contestable.

» Professor Eric D. Hirsch is one of the key figures behind the development of core knowledge in the curriculum.

» Excellent teachers have very secure knowledge and can transfer this in an accessible and engaging manner.

» Higher order thinking does not happen in a vacuum. It requires something to think about – knowledge.

» There are various strategies to support the effective recall of information including mnemonics, reviewing and relearning.

Points for reflection and action

» Some schools in the UK, such as the Cuckoo Hall Academies Trust in north London (www.chat-edu.org.uk), have introduced a 'core knowledge' curriculum. What does the term imply to you?

» Find out more about Core Knowledge UK (www.coreknowledge.org.uk), introduced by the education charity Civitas, and their approach to the curriculum. How does the programme compare to your experiences?

» Research the impact of KIPP (Knowledge Is Power Program) charter schools in the United States.

» Reflect on how well you use the strategies and tools noted in Table 3.1 to improve how well learners retain knowledge. For example, can you summarise the teaching points in your last lesson in a sentence?

Chapter 4

Skills

Learners need to develop a broad range of skills
in real-life, relevant contexts

What is the big idea?

Skills are abilities to do something well. They vary considerably in nature from writing a letter to kicking a football. Educators sometimes put them forward as a corrective to a knowledge-centred curriculum – the clichéd argument runs that as so much knowledge soon becomes obsolete, it is better to focus on developing the kinds of skills learners will need for future life and employment. Martin Johnson, writing on behalf of the Association of Teachers and Lecturers (ATL) Union, claims:

— Skills vs knowledge.

We need to do things differently, and to do better, if we are to prepare young people for a world in which what is known to be true changes by the hour; a world in which access to information is at the touch of a keyboard, where rote learning of facts must give way to nurturing through education of essential transferable skills that enable the next generation to navigate the information age. That is why we advocate a skills-based curriculum. (Johnson, 2007: 9)

Historically, there has been something of a consensus around the kinds of skills schools should teach, although often described in different terms. Priority has been given to the three R's of reading, writing and arithmetic, personal and social development, a range of vocational skills and, in more *goes against our idea of traditional education.*

recent times, digital competence. One of the common threads through time has been the recognition that school leavers need to be equipped with skills so they can fit into society and are work ready. *Skills for Life* describes the 'basic' and 'key skills' needed for everyday life (OCR, 2006), as set out in Table 4.1. In England, 'functional skills' are the ability to

Basic Skill	Examples of situations when these skills are used
Literacy – the ability to read, write and speak in English	• Completing a form • Phoning for a doctor's appointment
Numeracy – the ability to add, subtract, multiply and divide	• Understanding an electricity bill • Checking your change in a shop
Information and communication technology (ICT) skills – the ability to use ICT systems	• Using websites to find information • Sending a text message

Key Skill	Examples of situations when these skills are used
Application of number	Working out how much wallpaper you need to decorate a room
Communication	Having a discussion with colleagues at work
Information and communication technology	Designing a poster for an event
Working with others	Working with neighbours to organise a Neighbourhood Watch scheme
Improving own learning and performance	Deciding which course to attend to help get into University
Problem solving	Making sure mail is sent to customers on time, even though the photocopier is broken

Table 4.1. Basic and key skills in England.
Source: © OCR, *Skills for Life* Brochure 2006.

read and write and to use numbers with confidence. They are assessed with Level 2 Functional Skills (English and mathematics) and are seen as a gateway qualification into work for those young people who have not secured a grade C or above at GCSE (Ofqual, 2015). The equivalent skills qualifications across the UK are Essential Skills in Wales and Northern Ireland and Core Skills in Scotland. *— focused more on practical rather than academic*

The skills of finding, evaluating, sharing and presenting online information should be high on the list of things schools need to teach children and young people. One of the challenges we all face in this digital age is finding accurate, trustworthy and relevant information. We are all so busy that there is a natural tendency to accept information at face value. The top listing in Google's search results typically receives 33 per cent of the traffic, compared to 18 per cent for the second position and less than 3 per cent for the tenth page of results (Lee, 2013). How often do we go beyond the first few pages of an Internet search? How regularly do we read the 'About us' information on a website? How many of us check sample sizes in education research projects? The Internet, undoubtedly one of the greatest inventions in history, has brought inaccurate content and online misinformation into our classrooms. Few students verify the accuracy of what they read online and around two-thirds of primary and secondary schools do not teach online critical reading skills (Bartlett and Miller, 2011).

Schools are often pressed into teaching other skills, depending on the prevailing social, political and economic imperatives of the moment – and the list can seem endless. In their additional roles as surrogate parents and social workers, for instance, teachers are expected to develop a range of wider personal and social skills that are rarely acknowledged by policy-makers (Webb and Vulliamy, 2002). These vary from parenting classes (BBC, 2006; Garner, 2009) to Bear Grylls urging schools to teach survival skills (Kendrick, 2014).

From a compliance point of view, clearly the priority for schools is to teach the skills set out in statutory documentation or recommended by the government. These can be substantial. For example, in England's most recent national curriculum in 2013, despite heavy criticism for its strong knowledge content, there are more than eighty explicit references to skills. To take one example only, in order to teach English in the primary school, teachers are expected to cover decoding skills, early skills of inference, handwriting skills (Year 1), speedy word reading skills and phonic skills (Year 2), skills in reading non-fiction plus wider skills in spoken language (Years 3 and 4) and skills of information retrieval (Years 5 and 6).

The assessment and reporting requirements that accompany the teaching of particular skills are often more concerning than the teaching of the skills themselves. So, for instance, while the development of early reading skills is undoubtedly a priority for pupils in Key Stage 1 (5–7 years), there was far less consensus among teachers over the introduction of the test for phonic decoding skills for 6-year-olds. In one survey of 2,000 teachers, 67 per cent were against the idea (NASUWT, 2011: 4). Moreover, one of the difficulties when schools are directed to focus on particular skills and approaches is that this can be at the expense of others, even though teachers want learners to experience a rich, broad curriculum. As Graham Donaldson (2015: 8) explained in a review of the curriculum in Wales: 'A reluctance to let go of aspects in the curriculum that are of limited relevance while at the same time adding fresh expectations can place schools and teachers under increasing pressure.' Flutter and Rudduck (2004) point out that by the time children get to secondary school, if not well before, they are hungry for 'real' learning, when they can get stuck into tasks and problems that have meaning and relevance, rather than go over the same old exercises that have been done time after time. The authors suggest a new three R's: responsibility, respect and 'real' things to explore.

Relevance is one of the principles that underpins effective curriculum design in many countries. This is the case, for example, with the *Curriculum for Excellence* in Scotland. In the United States, the Partnership for 21st Century Skills (P21) wants schools to teach a more relevant curriculum: 'The world is full of engaging, real-world challenges, problems and questions – why spend so much time on disconnected questions at the end of a textbook chapter?' (Trilling and Fadel, 2009: xxviii). Studies show that pupils value connections between classroom practice and real-life experiences but teachers need to make these very explicit (Jamison, 2001; Reiss, 2001; Harland et al., 2003).

However, the cry for relevance is a contentious one. While there are many commentators, policy-makers, school psychologists, teachers and teacher educators who strongly endorse a skills agenda in schools, this is seen in some quarters as watering down the academic aspects of the curriculum. Christodoulou (2014) questions the rhetoric around twenty-first-century skills and the implication that there is something outdated about twentieth-century skills – skills such as critical thinking have been around for a very long time. Shirley Lawes and other contributors to *The Corruption of the Curriculum* (Lawes et al., 2007), question the continual fiddling with the curriculum in the name of relevance. They do not accept the argument that educationalists should relate subjects directly to the language and ideas with which pupils are familiar in their everyday lives. They flinch at the thought of pandering to the latest fad (e.g. learning styles, happiness lessons, Circle Time, thinking skills, global citizenship, British values), which they see as distractions from the core business of schools – namely, to transmit essential knowledge and socialise children so they are aware of what is acceptable behaviour in society.

These commentators want to see schools provide an academically strong liberal education, with pupils introduced to the great 'movers and shakers' in our heritage and culture. This means moving pupils into unknown territory, away from their familiar and everyday experiences towards an awareness and appreciation of great human achievements in art, poetry, writing and so forth – for example, to read stories from classical literature (which by definition has stood the test of time). There are frequent reports that many children are ignorant of the likes of Emily Brontë and Charles Dickens but they are familiar with *The Diary of a Wimpy Kid* and Harry Potter. As Furedi (2009: 144) puts it: 'education brings knowledge that is external to a child's experience into the classroom'.

This type of thinking values knowledge and subject teaching and is sceptical of the ubiquitous skills agenda which rebrands almost everything as a skill, including personal attributes such as resilience and self-control. According to this line of thinking, education is not 'edutainment' and neither should it involve teachers worrying about how to make lessons fun with gimmicks, when their main priority should be to ensure that the teaching points are understood. These traditionalists do not want to see the dumbing down of lessons, for example, by reverting to popular culture at every opportunity. They baulk at the thought of teaching Shakespeare through rap music or simplifying the Bard's words into teenage street-speak. As Martin Samuel (2006) wrote in *The Times*:

Instead of trying to shake future generations out of complacency, their ignorance and lack of interest is resumed. We no longer aspire to education but to maintenance. We babysit, really, until X Factor begins. We depict Shakespeare as boring and obscure, then wonder why teenagers produce exam papers full of gibberish and misunderstanding.

The question of making subjects relevant to children's experiences has long been debated. More than forty years ago, David Shayer wrote a book on the history of teaching English in school. He argued that it was 'certainly high time that we paid serious attention to our pupils' likes and dislikes and to their actual capacity for literary experience, and this "relevance" approach is excellent as far as it goes' (Shayer, 1972: 173). Shayer pointed out that, faced with the non-reading pupil, teachers are justified in using any reading materials if it will 'get him into reading'. He was quick to commend the efforts of colleagues who used science fiction, crime novels, ghost stories, westerns, romances, spy or war stories. But he issued a warning that is still very valid today:

The trouble with the 'modern' and the 'relevant' is that it dates so quickly; today's best seller may well be a meagre has-been in two years' time when its essential triviality has had time to emerge, and what children need today more than anything else is a sense of permanence and continuity, of the valuable which remains valuable whatever the vicissitudes of popular taste or journalistic fashion. (Shayer, 1972: 173–174)

Despite misgivings about making the curriculum relevant and the focus on skills, the big idea in this chapter does not have to be a divisive one. Good teachers know that motivation is central to learning and see the value of novelty in their everyday practice. They recognise the need to draw on learners' prior knowledge and experience and make links between what is happening in the wider world. But this does not have to lead to superficial learning. Rather, the goal is to introduce learners to new knowledge, insight and experiences. References to the here and now are a means to this end. This is not about 'dumbing down' content; rather, it is a matter of skilled teachers seeking to bridge present understanding with new learning. This might, for example, include using graphic novel versions of classics such as Jules Verne's *Twenty Thousand Leagues Under the Sea* or Daniel Defoe's *Robinson Crusoe* as entry (rather than end) points into the literary canon.

Sometimes teachers make cosmetic links between lesson content and the wider world. Take mathematics as an example: many teachers have demonstrated creative ways of making the subject relevant so that it reflects everyday life. This includes drawing on children's experiences or knowledge of numbers, patterns, shapes and measures that they see around them, for example, when travelling to school. It might include reference to DIY projects at home, to football or other sports. But as Boaler (2009) points out, there is a danger of teachers thinking that they are highlighting 'real maths' when they are actually providing 'fake maths' in 'ridiculous contexts'. Children are frequently asked to work on problems involving the price of food or clothes, or how many people can fit into a lift, which bear no resemblance to what happens in real life. For instance: 'A restaurant charges £2.50 for one eighth of a quiche. How much does a whole quiche cost?' As Boaler observes, everyone knows that if extra people turn up more quiche is ordered or individuals go without a slice, but this is ignored in the 'Mathsland' of classrooms. What concerns Boaler is the long-term effect that these make-believe contexts have on children's attitude to mathematics – a subject that becomes increasingly mysterious. Her advice is to use real-life contexts where students learn to consider variables rather than ignore them.

The school grounds and the wider neighbourhood provide many genuine opportunities to develop mathematical investigations in contexts that mean something to children. Drama and role play enable children to explore the human side to mathematics – for example, interactions at a market stall, bank, supermarket, car wash, travel agency or baby clinic, all of which present a wealth of opportunities for pupils to apply their mathematical skills. For professional mathematicians, the important skills are identifying patterns, estimating, visualising and representing ideas symbolically. This is why using a prompt such as 'What if ...?' is a powerful lever into mathematical thinking and illustrates the creative element in the subject.

The importance of context is illustrated through the well-known studies of Brazilian street children using mathematical thinking. The researchers set street market sellers and schoolchildren the same problem:

In the market

Customer (researcher): I'm going to take four coconuts. How much is that?

Child (aged 12): There will be one hundred five, plus thirty, that's one thirty-five ... one coconut is thirty-five ... that is ... one forty!

In school

Child solves the problem 35 x 4, explaining out loud: 'Four times five is twenty, carry the two, two plus three is five, times four is twenty.' [Answer written: 200] (Nunes et al., 1993: 24)

The researchers found that 98 per cent of the responses in the informal situation were correct, compared to 74 per cent in the formal school context. The figure dropped to 37 per cent when dealing with arithmetical problems. Perhaps of greater significance than the differences in success rate is the fact that children approached mathematics in different ways – mental methods tied to the actual numbers, communicated orally, worked better than abstract paper-and-pencil methods. Children can easily lose the feel for what is reasonable when working on paper, hence the importance of estimating.

One of the myths surrounding skills-based education is that once learners acquire a skill they can transfer it to any context. On the contrary, cognitive science tells us that learning is situated. This means that when someone learns something it is shaped by all kinds of contextual factors – how they were feeling, the nature of the task, the time of day, the physical surroundings and so forth. Teachers cannot use a checklist to tick off when a piece of learning occurs and then assume the learner has 'got it' and can transfer this to any future context. A child may have read fluently in an English lesson last week but struggle with a text of similar challenge in a history lesson today. Children forget things or lose interest. Adults forget much of their school learning but this does not mean that they did not learn things properly in the first place. Rather, it simply means that the learning is linked to the school context. Such learning can come flooding back when one reads books such as the 'I Used to Know That' series (e.g. Taggart, 2011) or when memories are prompted by an old school report or photograph.

Who is behind it?

The subject of skills is such a broad one that it is challenging to highlight key figures who have contributed to their rise to prominence. Policy-makers have always had an eye on knowledge and skills when devising educational systems. Rab Butler (1902–1982), the architect behind the Education Act of 1944, envisaged meeting the needs of a post-industrial workforce when it was anticipated that 80 per cent of people would work in manual jobs and 20 per cent in clerical and professional positions. So the vast majority of children attended secondary modern schools where the focus was on developing practical skills that would lead to apprenticeships or employment. Children in grammar schools pursued a traditional academic skill set.

The modern economy has moved on from mass production to one of constant innovation, requiring very different skills. While literacy and numeracy remain essential, businesses want people who can work as a team, use information technologies and think in flexible and creative ways. This is because of the demands to produce new services and products and to keep pace with ever changing market conditions. Many of the UK's key industries are to be found in communication, information, entertainment, science and technology. Creative industries such as advertising, designer fashion, software and computer services, media and the arts are also very much on the rise.

Globally, there is a reasonable consensus today over the kinds of skills young people need for living in the twenty-first century. The World Health Organization (WHO) identifies ten core life skills: problem solving, critical thinking, communication, decision making, creative thinking, interpersonal relationships, self-awareness, empathy, coping with stress and coping with emotions (WHO, 1999). These skills enable us to explore alternatives, weigh up the pros and cons of a situation and reach rational decisions when it comes to solving problems. Ultimately, the success of any programme designed to develop life skills is whether behaviour changes for the better. The intended outcomes might be, for example, youngsters who demonstrate prosocial attitudes such as respect for others, the ability to cope with anxiety, improved conflict resolution and less impulsive behaviour.

Many writers have argued that schooling needs to be more connected to real-world learning. Bill Lucas and Guy Claxton established the

Centre for Real-World Learning in 2008. Both are leading proponents of experiential hands-on learning. They have coined the phrase 'expansive education' to describe new ways of thinking about schools (Lucas et al., 2013). This begins with questioning the premise of what schools are for. While they acknowledge the merit in the two common aims of education – to introduce children to the best of our cultural traditions and prepare them for employment – they think education is about more than this. They see education as giving pupils the confidence and capacity to flourish. To do this, schools need to take advantage of the rich opportunities in young people's lives beyond the school gates. In the context of vocational learning, the authors point out that this can be 'immediately fulfilling … more so than so-called "brain-work"' (Lucas et al., 2013: 20).

It is certainly the case that there are differences in how we learn within and beyond school. Learners have far more control over where, when, why and how they learn outside the classroom than in school. Longstanding research by Lauren Resnick (1987) has showed that whereas schools focus on individual performance and developing symbolic thinking and learning rules, outside school learning often occurs in teams or groups and in relation to first-hand objects and experiences. She cites various examples, including builders, factory workers and those trying to lose weight. In the case of the latter, one man was observed solving the problem of measuring out three-quarters of two-thirds of a cup of cottage cheese. Instead of multiplying the fractions, he used a measuring cup to find two-thirds of a cup of cottage cheese. Then he patted the cheese into an approximately round pancake, divided it into quarters and used three of the quarters. In this case, the cottage cheese itself was part of the calculation. He had broken the problem into two parts, each of which could be solved by direct action on the cottage cheese. There was no reference to abstract arithmetic. Resnick argues that schools discourage children from bringing into school their informally acquired knowledge, yet this knowledge can contribute significantly to children's progress in the classroom.

Claxton (2008: 93) notes that in real-life learning people use techniques such as the following:

» Watching closely how other people do things (e.g. run meetings, plant bulbs, cope with confrontation) and see if they can effectively copy what role models are doing.

» Going off by themselves, practising the 'hard parts' and then trying to fit this back into the overall performance that needs improving.

» Making scruffy notes and diagrams to help planning and thinking which no one will ever assess.

» Checking half-baked ideas and possibilities by trying them out on someone who they trust not to laugh at them.

» Running through things in their heads and imagining how different scenarios may play out.

» Imagining themselves doing something better than they currently can and then using that 'home movie' as a guide to help them practise.

On the surface, teachers can readily identify with the techniques of observing, trial and error, taking notes, rehearsing ideas and imagining. But their approach is often different from what happens outside the classroom. School learning is more formulaic, structured and directed, while the vocabulary is a lot more formal: objectives, assessment, success criteria, instruction and so on. While this may be necessary for planning purposes, children's experience of learning can easily become mechanistic, routine, lifeless and out of touch with the real world. It can descend into a near monotonous diet of recording answers on worksheets, answering set questions and never venturing beyond the intended learning outcomes. In other words, teachers can play it safe by focusing on the management of learning and avoiding risks, especially when being observed.

In order to bridge the gap between school learning and the real world, numerous organisations have picked up on the need for schools to exploit the potential of learning outside the classroom. For example, the Real World Learning campaign partnership believes there is no substitute for learning out of the classroom. It sees real-world learning as experiencing nature and culture first hand, rather than from a blackboard, textbook or computer screen. In practice, this means providing learners with regular opportunities to enjoy the experience of hunting for bugs, getting lost in a historic maze, marvelling at the size of a dinosaur's teeth or appreciating the darkness of a cave or forest. Such experiential learning challenges the assumption of learning as a process of dissemination from expert to novice.

One of the key things schools and teachers can do in order to get the best out of their students is to provide authentic or real-life learning experiences. This means:

» Practising skills by engaging with real-life issues.
» Valuing knowledge construction rather than transmission.
» Getting learners actively involved in solving problems.
» Using enquiry-based approaches to learning such as project work and problem-based learning (PBL).
» Learning beyond the school.
» Encouraging learners to work together.
» Developing opportunities for critical reflection.

Problem-based learning

A good example of an approach that supports authentic learning is problem-based learning, which originated with Howard Barrows (1928–2011) and other medical educators in the 1960s. Barrows was interested in assessing the clinical skills of doctors using simulated patients. He later established the Problem-Based Learning Institute to take PBL into secondary schools. It is now widely used in fields such as dentistry, engineering and teacher education. Torp and Sage (2002) describe PBL as focused, experiential learning organised around the investigation and resolution of messy, real-world problems. As Savin-Baden (2003) explains, PBL starts with a scenario, question or problem, to which learners respond by asking further questions, gathering information and participating in group discussion and evaluation. PBL is underpinned by social constructivist learning theory in which students are seen to be active learners, creating their own knowledge and meaning by working alongside peers in the study of real-life scenarios.

PBL is a 'process-driven' model of learning. The emphasis is on developing students' ability to reason, including making informed decisions, hypothesising and considering alternative viewpoints. Rather than seeking one 'correct' answer, pupils entertain the possibility of several answers and begin to see the complexities of the world. The trigger points are drawn from everyday contexts. So, for younger pupils, a teacher might set up a scenario where library books or other resources are scattered on the floor and then invite them to think about how these might be best arranged so they can be found quickly and also appear neat and tidy. Or the teacher may read a story in which they are asked to explore an incident or dilemma from the viewpoints of different characters and then invited to take on the role of 'Agony Aunt' or personal counsellor. PBL scenarios can be linked to subjects or themes – for instance, pupils may be presented with a scenario where they are allocated a grant of £500 to spend on developing a school garden so that it meets the needs of all pupils. They might begin by discussing what they know about the scenario and any relevant questions (e.g. Does the grant have to be spent in a given time period? What happens if pupils disagree on how the money should be spent? Where should the garden be located? Are there any pupils with particular needs, such as partially sighted pupils?). Groups might then work together to explore options, draw up designs and research where to buy resources to ensure value for money.

In a typical PBL scenario, learners work through a cycle of stages involving reading and defining the problem, establishing the facts of the case, getting to grips with the main issues, summarising collective understanding, setting out what needs to be researched further, reporting and challenging findings and presenting informed conclusions. The emphasis is not on finding the 'right' answer but developing a range of skills in the process. The stages are cyclical rather than linear – learners might present information but then return to the scenario to review whether they could approach the problem in a different way.

PBL is widely used at all levels of education in the United States – elementary and high schools as well as universities. Lambros (2004) points out that in some US schools, PBL begins with a student reading aloud a problem while others in the group follow along and offer support in dealing with any unfamiliar words. They then create a series of lists:

» The first is a list of *facts*. This helps to identify what they know.
» The second is a list called *need to know*. Here learners list all the information they would like to have to improve their understanding of the problem.
» The third is a *learning issues* list. This consists of the things learners need to research or explore in order to move forward.
» The next list identifies *possible solutions*. In other words, all the ideas the group suggest, however implausible, to solve the problem.

» This leads to another list setting out *new learning issues*. This is necessary because each idea needs to be researched and tested in order to rule in or out the possible solution.

» Finally, a list of *defendable solutions* is drawn up. This should include only those ideas that the group feels are strong enough to withstand criticism.

Approaches such as PBL call for a shift in the relationship between teacher and learner. The former becomes less of an instructor and more of a guide, facilitator or 'critical friend'; the latter becomes more independent, active, responsible and self-directing.

Despite the rather seductive common-sense appeal of PBL, in terms of making school learning relevant to everyday life, the evidence of PBL's impact in improving learning is mixed. Hattie (2009) says that PBL can have a positive influence for deeper learning, with its emphasis on meaning and understanding, but negative effects for acquiring facts (surface knowledge). Studies of PBL in secondary schools in Sweden and the United States also report contradictory outcomes in terms of its effectiveness as a teaching approach. On the one hand, gains are noted in terms of teamwork and problem-solving skills, the creation of a 'positive mood' in the classroom and the development of life skills such as planning, independent and interdependent thinking and reasoning skills. However, 'weaker students' find aspects of planning and teamwork too challenging and, in some cases, this can demotivate them (Pagander and Read, 2014). PBL also presents numerous logistical challenges, including monitoring the contribution of individuals in group work, devising engaging scenarios and managing, evaluating and assessing the learning, particularly in larger classes.

In sum, the evidence suggests that PBL is an approach that has relative merit when teachers want to develop specific skills such as collaboration and problem solving, but teachers need to ensure that they do not neglect surface learning first (Hattie, 2015). In my own experience of using PBL with trainee teachers over many years, the approach proves more motivating than traditional lectures to most students and introduces them to skills that are not usually prominent in teacher education courses, such as time and resource management, leadership, negotiation and collaboration.

Why is it important, and what can you do?

The importance of equipping learners with essential skills should be self-evident, beginning with literacy and numeracy. On average, each secondary school takes in around eighteen 11-year-olds who can't read properly, half of them with a reading age of 7 (Cassen and McNally, 2015). According to the Literacy Trust, around one in five adults are considered 'functionally illiterate' which means they struggle to read anything that is not familiar to them. It also means they would not be able to work in many jobs and would struggle to support their children with reading homework. They have literacy levels at or below those expected of an 11-year-old. They have been deprived not only of functional skills but also the deeper joy of reading for pleasure. The situation is worse for numeracy: around four in five adults have a low level of numeracy – roughly defined as the adult skills equivalent of being below GCSE grade C level.[1] Put bluntly, almost all of these adults went through the school system but were failed by teachers.

Good literacy and numeracy skills are essential if pupils are to participate fully in civic life. They are more likely to secure a decent job, enjoy a comfortable standard of living and deal with everyday challenges. The all-round benefits of being literate and numerate are significant. A report by the Northern Ireland Audit Office (2013: 10) shows that those with poor literacy and numeracy skills are:

» Four times more likely to be unemployed.
» If employed, more likely to be in a low-paid, low-skilled job.
» More likely to suffer from ill-health or depression.
» More likely to be dependent on state benefits.
» More likely to be in poor housing.

One of the longstanding aims of schools has been to prepare pupils for the world of work. In the early history of state education, the focus was very much on teaching literacy and numeracy. These skills remain high priorities, especially when employers report shortcomings in these areas, but school leavers need to be more than effective communicators and

---

1 See http://www.literacytrust.org.uk/adult_literacy/illiterate_adults_in_england.

know how to handle numbers. Organisations such as the Confederation of British Industry (CBI) have argued for some time that young people are short on 'employability skills' such as teamworking, problem solving and the application of numeracy. There are regular surveys of businesses that also decry the lack of basic social skills among school leavers – for example, a survey by Barclays Bank found that four in ten youngsters (in a survey of 2,000 14- to 25-year-olds) had no idea of when it was inappropriate to use their mobile phone, and hence no understanding of workplace etiquette (Paton, 2014c). The CBI report that nearly nine out of ten employers consider attitude and character as being the most important attributes of a job candidate (CBI, 2013). A popular saying in business is 'recruit for attitude, train for skill'. The fact that more and more employers prefer 'soft' skills to technical ones has been identified by the Oxford Royale Academy (2014) as one of the key trends that will matter to young people as they move towards the job market.

So what can teachers do to narrow the skills gap between school and work? Historically, governments have supported vocational education programmes and apprenticeship schemes in secondary schools and further education. The last twenty years of the nineteenth century has been called 'the golden age' of vocational training in England, with growing support for science and technical education. In the early twentieth century, it has been calculated that there were typically 350,000–400,000 apprentices in any given year, mostly in building, engineering, shipbuilding and printing (More, 1980). Despite this, by the end of the twentieth century concerns remained about the conditions of apprenticeships where youngsters were seen as cheap labour in place of adult workers. In the 1980s, initiatives such as the Youth Opportunities Programme (YOP) and the Youth Training Scheme (YTS) were criticised because youngsters did not gain marketable qualifications; hence the introduction of National Vocational Qualifications (NVQs) at different levels (from basic to postgraduate) to raise the status of apprenticeships. The Young Apprenticeships programme for 14–16-year-olds, introduced in 2004, has enabled pupils in compulsory education to spend up to two days a week in a workplace to learn on-the-job skills. The notion of apprenticeship can also be seen in teacher training, where school-based training has increased through initiatives such as the Graduate Teacher Programme and Teach First.

The premise behind vocational education is, of course, that this will equip school leavers with essential skills so they can take their place in the workforce. Over recent decades, both primary and secondary schools have been expected to provide lessons in entrepreneurial skills or 'enterprise education', which involves developing a range of skills such as risk management, innovation, financial capability and creativity (DCSF, 2010). The Enterprise Village website (www.enterprisevillage. org.uk) provides professional development opportunities for teachers and includes news, training events, case studies and resources. Despite these developments, Lord Baker, who introduced the national curriculum in 1988, believes that technical skills are being squeezed out by an overemphasis on academic subjects (Gurney-Read, 2015).

There is no doubt that the incentive of working with real money and problems can prove very motivating for children. In one primary school, 500 pupils were each given £1 and asked to devise ways of making their money grow by producing products or providing services to sell at a school market day. A local business and secondary school provided the funding. The original aim was to double their money to donate to a learners' charity. The two-week project developed positive attitudes and skills such as taking initiative, communication, solving problems, making informed decisions and reviewing and reflecting on outcomes. The pupils' money-making endeavours included the following:

» Year 6 boys pooled their resources and set up a car washing service for teachers on the two market days.
» Some learners undertook activities such as face painting and nail polishing or made products such as bracelets, bookmarks and cards.
» Many learners produced and sold food products such as homemade smoothies, popcorn, fruit kebabs and lemonade.

In total, the pupils raised £1,250 to donate to charity, with the original £500 grant being kept for future enterprise projects (Specialist Schools and Academies Trust, 2010: 8).

One of the greatest challenges policy-makers and educators face is responding to the fact that no matter how effective the education system, this does not guarantee secure, stable and highly paid employment for all school leavers and graduates. Simple economics tells us that there will always be fluctuations in the economy and a need for street cleaners, waiters and shop assistants. But more fundamental than this is knowing that there is no automatic association between qualifications and the work people do – one official estimate is that half of graduates are working in non-graduate jobs (Allen, 2013).

For these reasons, some economists, educationalists and politicians are beginning to question the purpose of schooling. Rather than charging the education system, with the remit to prepare children for work that may not yet exist, they are beginning to look at schools in a more holistic light. Kidd (2014) discusses the philosophical shift from accepting that not everyone may earn well to a worldview that values learning as being within the reach of all. She implores teachers to 'bring events and ideas into teaching as they happen' and frame all knowledge with the question, 'Who in the world needs to know this stuff and why?' (Kidd, 2014: 38). Her vision is for children to enjoy learning *now*, to be immersed in the love of learning new things and not to worry about how the information might help them pass examinations or prepare them for the world of work.

Primary and secondary teachers have an important role in helping pupils to understand why people work and the different jobs they do. Clearly this needs to be handled sensitively, particularly in areas of high unemployment. Teesville Primary School is situated on the eastern outskirts of Middlesbrough, a town that has among the highest unemployment rates in the UK. Yet 'pupils are steeped in becoming work-ready from their first day, with visits to workplaces and universities and lessons to raise aspiration and self-confidence' (Woolcock, 2015). Schools in the area have a strong focus on developing children's emotional health alongside literacy and numeracy. They seek to develop resilience, resourcefulness and a can-do attitude, so deprivation is not accepted as a barrier to educational achievement.

The four skills highlighted by the US-based Partnership for 21st Century Skills – critical thinking, communication, creativity and collaboration – are equally important here in the UK. Table 4.2 provides a few examples of possible activities to promote these skills. Sometimes very small changes can make an impact. When one teacher introduced the expectation that all group members should add the word 'because' to their answers, he found the more dominant individuals began to interrupt less as they had to justify their vocal responses, while other pupils took the opportunity to shine and voice their views (Hill, 2008). This is a good illustration of nudge theory, which suggests that behaviour can be corrected through a series of small steps or subtle nudges to encourage people to make the right choice rather than prohibiting behaviour through rules (Thaler and Sunstein, 2009).

In 2010, the coalition government set up the Behavioural Insights Team – or 'Nudge Unit', as it was dubbed. It aims to tackle some of the most intractable problems in society (from tax fraud to illegal immigration) through behavioural psychology. In education, trials have tested different approaches to encourage teenagers to attend university during a time of austerity and mounting student debt. The researchers found that a talk emphasising the lifestyle benefits of going to university was far more effective than sending a letter outlining the benefits of university education (Wright, 2015). In the long term, the key to improving the skill set of learners is to establish clear policies and consistent practices that are adopted throughout the school, to share what works well with colleagues and set the skills in the wider context of real-life learning so that pupils are stimulated and engaged.

If learners are to develop the kinds of skills reviewed in this chapter, they need regular opportunities to practise these in real-life contexts. There are lots of programmes and organisations that support real-world learning under various guises. Place-Based Education in the United States aims to deepen children's and young people's understanding of their local community. They are provided with opportunities to apply their school knowledge to real-world problems. One of the straplines is 'No Child Left Inside'. Closer to home, Learning through Landscapes has supported many schools in developing the use of their grounds to create stimulating learning experiences, while Open Futures focuses on encouraging children to grow and eat their own food. A common theme is promoting learners' direct engagement with nature. Richard Gerver, a former head teacher, describes how he and his staff embarked on the Grangeton Project to turn the school into a town where children could apply their learning in a real 'adult world'. The town included a council made up of elected representatives, an environmental team, a franchise of healthy eating shops, a French café which served freshly prepared snacks at lunchtime, a school museum, craft centre and its own media centre

Skills	Possible activities
Critical thinking	• Pose a new question a day using the who, what, when, where, why and how of any issue. • Ask learners to regularly use simple evaluation ideas such as plus, minus and interesting (PMI), where they say one positive and negative feature and one point of interest. • Consider dramatising stories using 'courtroom' scenes with individuals playing different parts (e.g. prosecutor, witness, defence lawyer, reporter, artist) perhaps linked to a story such as *The Three Little Pigs*. • Ask learners to sort facts and opinions by analysing newspaper articles. • Compare two reports of the same event (e.g. football match).
Communication	• Try to provide real-life audiences for learners to talk to and write to (e.g. pupils in other schools, governors, councillors, local businesses). • Play 'barrier' listening games in and out of school. • Model the joys of reading (e.g. magazines, poetry, newspapers, online blogs, extracts from books). • Teach the children sign language. • Use drama techniques such as freeze-frame to develop commentary skills. • Explore vocabulary in the lyrics of songs, nursery rhymes, etc. • Ask children to produce a television or radio broadcast of a football or netball game or contemporary issue. • Introduce novelty features when communicating in school (e.g. taking the register by varying voice control). • Present opportunities for learners to talk for three minutes about a subject they are passionate about and provide feedback on the quality of their talks. • Systematically build up learners' vocabulary through games, puzzles, spelling lists, apps and other technologies.

Skills	Possible activities
Creativity	• Model curiosity and constant questioning: why does that happen? What if I tried this instead? What if I change one thing (e.g. colour, size, shape, weight)? • Act the 'big kid' at times by playing around with ideas, resources and ways of working. • Encourage risk taking using different materials or resources, new routines and approaches (e.g. painting with your toes). • Create a classroom and outdoor environment that appeals to all the senses (e.g. quiet areas, stones, pebbles, clay). • Build up a bank of resources to stimulate creative ideas (e.g. funny words, pictures, sounds, music, place names, design briefs, natural objects and materials).
Collaboration	• Use reciprocal reading with groups where individuals are allocated one of these roles: leader (decides who does what and introduces the text), predictor (encourages all to make predictions in text), clarifier (asks the group to clarify confusing words), summariser (identifies the most important ideas) and questioner (asks questions). • The same idea can be applied in other areas of the curriculum – for example, in mathematics, see the activities suggested by the NRICH Project based at the University of Cambridge (http://nrich.maths.org/7908). • Ensure that, as a regular habit, groups review how well they collaborated – make the success criteria clear.

Table 4.2. Possible activities to develop the four C's.

which produced a newspaper, daily radio programme and various films (Gerver, 2010).

Every school neighbourhood opens up opportunities for learners to apply their skills. In history lessons, there is no better way for pupils to learn about enquiry skills than to handle first-hand sources at a local archive or museum. If we want children to grow up caring about their environment they need to experience fieldwork and place-making activities such as den building. In science, opportunities can be created to visit different habitats during the year, such as woodlands, rivers and coastlines. In mathematics, teachers can set up 'number hunts' in the environment. There are plenty of opportunities to illustrate real-life contexts for teaching the different genres of writing, such as persuasive emails to the local council or supermarket. The rich heritage of the UK can be explored through the built and natural environments. Grigg and Lewis (2016) suggest hundreds of ideas to promote out-of-class learning using the likes of allotments, libraries, museums, galleries and parks.

There are practical things teachers and schools can do to make their teaching relevant and engaging, including:

» Using hands-on experiences during classroom lessons (e.g. opportunities to touch objects, paint, conduct experiments, act out mini scenes).

» Inviting guest speakers into the classroom to model how they are using information or skills taught in school in their lives.

» Providing opportunities for learners to pursue open-ended, enquiry-based projects focusing on real contemporary events and issues, such as a sports tournament (for physical education), anniversary (history), global disaster (geography), celebration or festival (religious education).

» Highlighting local applications in topics studied.

» Using a real-world problem to trigger questions and discussion (e.g. in the home: designing a new bedroom or garden, how to stop burglars entering the house, planning a house of the future, designing a space-saving kitchen).

» Using a range of stimulating resources (e.g. photographs, stories, newspaper articles, audio recordings, film clips, artefacts).

» Making the most of regular fieldwork and out-of-class visits.

By using these kinds of strategies, teachers can promote a broad range of skills. Weinstein et al. (2000) suggest a model of learning based on 'skill, will and self-regulation'. Skill includes reading and listening, problem solving and retrieving information. Will includes beliefs about learning, setting goals, the motivation to learn and creating and maintaining a positive mindset. Finally, self-regulation includes managing time, concentrating, handling stress and adopting a systematic approach to learning. This is developed further in Chapter 5 under the next big idea – cultivating the right dispositions for learning.

Conclusion

A well-rounded education includes the acquisition of knowledge *and* skills. Individuals are able to do things well once they know and understand what they are doing and then practise a particular skill deliberately and frequently. We acquire, develop, use and lose skills over the course of a lifetime. One of the challenges facing educational systems is identifying the skills needed to supply advanced economies. Unfortunately, there is a mismatch between the skills school leavers and university graduates possess and those required by employers. Around one in five vacancies in the UK are due to inadequate skills (Sellgren, 2014). Too many pupils are leaving school without the necessary literacy and numeracy skills – in 2014, 36 per cent failed to achieve a C in GCSE English and 42 per cent did not achieve this standard in numeracy (CBI, 2014).

The development of science, technology, engineering and mathematical (STEM) skills remains critical for economic success, so the recruitment of suitably qualified teachers in these subjects is an obvious priority. Organisations such as the National STEM Learning Centre (www.stem.org.uk) make an important contribution to supporting schools in their professional development of existing staff, through resources, networking and training as well as the recruitment of new teachers in these shortage subjects. The government has also introduced new vocational qualifications to sit alongside the more traditional academic A levels at 18, geared towards those wanting to specialise in technical careers such as engineering and computer science. But the challenges facing the educational system are not confined to addressing shortcomings in skills. As the next chapter indicates, unless school leavers have developed the right attitudes to work and life in general, then securing high academic standards will not be sufficient for individuals or society at large to flourish.

Summary

» Skills are the ability to do things. They vary in complexity and some cluster together, such as the ability to listen, speak, read and write (communicate).

» The kinds of skills taught in school have remained largely the same over the years, revolving around literacy, numeracy, social and vocational skills.

» Many commentators would like to see schools give more attention to a much broader range of skills, including critical thinking, creativity, communication and collaboration.

» To develop skills effectively, careful consideration needs to be given to the nature and range of classroom activities.

» Learners need regular opportunities to practise skills in real-life contexts. Problem-based learning is an example of how this can be achieved.

Points for reflection and action

» What kinds of skills do you wish you had been taught at school but weren't? What about time management, self-defence or how to negotiate?

» A recent poll by Interflora suggested that the five skills grandparents teach children are cooking, etiquette, sewing, knitting and mending, confidence and a love of history.[2] How relevant are these skills today?

2 See http://www.interflora.co.uk/content/the-wisdom-of-grandparents/.

Chapter 5

Dispositions

Effective learning depends upon cultivating positive dispositions

What is the big idea?

We all know people who have a cheerful outlook on life who we might describe as having a 'sunny disposition'. They are inclined to see the positive in even the most challenging of situations. Research from different fields suggests that it certainly pays to be optimistic – happy people have strong immune systems, make more money and have more fulfilling relationships (Furnham, 2010). For those who have a disposition more akin to Karl Pilkington, television presenter and author of *The Moaning of Life* (2014), all hope is not lost. While studies of twins suggest that we are born with predispositions for happiness, just as we are for depression, environmental factors also play a key role. The early family home environment, in particular, can 'set up' dispositions in later life. These formative influences, including schooling, shape children's attitudes and outlook.

The inclusion of what have been dubbed 'happiness lessons' in schools has been controversial. Supporters such as Richard Layard point to extensive international research (involving 270,000 children), which indicates a 10 per cent gain in children's social skills and academic performance from following well-being programmes (Donnelly, 2015). In a world where one in ten young people suffer mental anxiety and depression, there are strong grounds to extend specialist support. Anthony Seldon, headmaster at Wellington College, introduced happiness lessons in 2006. More recently, he has stressed the importance of going beyond happiness to find deeper meaning and joy. Among his simple suggestions for a good life is not therapy, mediation or religious practice, but finding ten interrupted minutes each day to explore personal feelings and beliefs about an aspect of our lives, and then writing down these thoughts (Seldon, 2015).

The big idea in this chapter is not about positive psychology or developing reactive counselling services for young people – what Guy Claxton (2008: 14) calls a 'Band-Aid' response. Rather, it is to highlight the fundamental issue of how schools can cultivate the right dispositions to learning so that learners feel safe, secure and confident to take on challenges. The short answer is to provide a stimulating curriculum, high quality teaching that is in tune with each learner and school leadership that builds a sense of community, clear vision and shared values. If successful, learners will routinely set their own personal goals, solve problems more effectively and handle everyday pressures. Above all, they will enjoy learning and see it as valuable for its own sake, rather than something that is only validated through paper qualifications.

In previous chapters the importance of knowledge and skills have been highlighted in a well-rounded education, but these are not sufficient by themselves. Educators must also give attention to modelling and developing dispositions so that learners can achieve their full potential. The word 'disposition' is generally defined as someone's inherent qualities of mind and character. It describes what people are likely to do in given situations, their tendency or inclination to act. Katz (1993: 16) describes a disposition as, 'a pattern of behaviour exhibited frequently … in the absence of coercion … constituting a habit of mind under some conscious and voluntary control … intentional and oriented to broad goals'.

According to Ennis (1996), dispositions are not automatic but exercised with discretion. Learners may have the capacity to do something, but for whatever reason refrain from doing so or not do so to their potential. There is a difference between the skill of being able to read a selected text fluently, having the inclination to do so and getting into the habit of reading purposefully and for enjoyment. The extent to which someone is disposed to do something depends on many intrinsic and external motivators – how tired they feel, personal drive, the time of day, the location, the presence and influence of others and so forth. At times, we all feel disinclined to do certain things, even though we have the necessary knowledge and skills. We simply may not be in the right frame of mind or mood to paint the house, tidy the garden or run an errand.

While it is the case that we are all born with certain innate dispositions – such as curiosity in exploring our immediate environment, playfulness or the urge to bond – these vary from one individual to the next. Intellectual and social dispositions, such as solving problems or being friendly, can be developed. The gardening metaphor is important in an educational context because it signifies the guiding and nurturing role of the adult so that learners get the most from learning experiences. But not all dispositions are socially acceptable or desirable. Toddlers who are bossy in the preschool setting learn that this is not something that adults generally approve of. On the other hand, social dispositions such as the tendency to cooperate and share things are looked on favourably.

The literature on learner dispositions centres on the premise that the extent to which learners *believe* they are able to change over time, their *attitudes* towards learning and the *values* they hold are critical to how well they learn. In short, these beliefs, attitudes and values provide the intrinsic motivation necessary for learning. Interestingly, some societies seem to cultivate happier individuals than others. Students in Latin nations are generally happier than those in the Pacific Rim countries. If students develop the disposition of staying focused and engaged with challenging tasks (i.e. persistence), we know that this is a good predictor of how well they will do in examinations. Across OECD countries, children from low-income families generally have less positive dispositions than their more affluent peers. This chapter considers the particular kinds of dispositions that are widely recognised as valuable for learning in the twenty-first century, rather than learners' general disposition, personality or character.

It has become fashionable over recent years to compare the academic performance of students in the UK with those abroad, usually by reference to positioning in league tables based on results in the Programme for International Student Assessment (PISA). These assessments show that Pacific Rim students generally outperform those in the UK. The Chinese educational system, for example, is praised for its efficiency and outputs in terms of academic standards. As Yong Zhao (2014: 9) points out, however, what is less well publicised is the country's failure to support individual strengths, 'cultivating a diversity of talents and fostering the capacity and confidence to create'. He adds that while people admire the Chinese educational system for emphasising a hard work ethic instead of inherited intelligence, this is the authorities' strategy to evade responsibilities for 'levelling the playing field for those with diverse abilities and talents'.

Lauren Resnick, one of the leading figures in the field of intelligence research, explains that 'one's intelligence is the sum of one's habits of mind' (cited by Claxton, 2008: 62). In other words, the most intelligent people are those who, when faced with new problems, consider alternatives, seek and clarify information, ask questions and make connections – in short, they try to figure things out. They do not give in, walk away, jump in with the first answer in their heads or accept what they are told. Resnick's research shows that those children often labelled as 'bright' are prone to struggle and go to pieces when confronted with something they don't immediately know how to do. They 'implode' and feel less worthy of their tag. On the other hand, students described as 'weak' do not try or quit quickly when faced with what looks like a difficult task. Why bother investing time and effort in something that is already perceived to be too hard?

The key issue is both the level of inherent challenge in tasks and how learners view them. Unfortunately, teachers can slip into thinking that they need to protect children's self-esteem (i.e. keep them happy) by ensuring that learning is always fun and the risk of failure is eradicated. This is the backdrop to the media-fuelled debate over the so-called 'dumbing down' of curriculum content and standards. Research into the relationship between self-esteem and academic performance shows that most learner satisfaction comes from completing 'hard' work – the feel-good factor *follows* hard work and not the other way round.

Who is behind it?

Francis Galton (1822–1911), cousin of Charles Darwin (1809–1882), was the first to coin the phrase 'nature versus nurture' to describe the debate over whether we are born with certain characteristics that shape who we become or, as 'blank slates', whether we learn everything from experience. For much of the twentieth century, psychologists argued the case. In the 1940s, Arnold Gesell (1880–1961) suggested that we go through the same developmental changes that allow inherited abilities and characteristics to emerge through a process called maturation. He believed that the environment determined the occasion and intensity of behaviour but not the basic progression of human development. He metaphorically summed up the causal relationship between development and culture: 'Culture accumulates; it does not grow. The glove goes on the hand; the hand determines the glove' (Gesell, 1940: 358). But by the 1950s his ideas were falling increasingly out of fashion.

Psychologists such as John B. Watson (1878–1958) and B. F. Skinner (1904–1990) argued that individuals do not inherit traits; rather, these are shaped by the environment and training received. Watson, who established behaviourism as a school of psychology, shifted the emphasis away from studying the mind to measuring behaviour and how people respond in given situations. Skinner famously likened the influence of the environment on human behaviour to how a sculptor shapes a lump of clay. Adults mould children into shapes, which then 'set' at specific ages.

The nature versus nurture debate has gradually drawn to a close over the last fifty or so years. As Ridley (2004: 3) puts it: 'Everybody with an ounce of common sense knows that human beings are a product of the transaction between the two.' Jean Piaget (1896–1980), the most influential developmental theorist of the twentieth century, sensibly suggested that nature and nurture have pretty much the same degree of influence on child development (Smith, 2002). His conclusions have since been borne out by studies of identical twins around the world over the last fifty years (Tan, 2015). In all, more than 2,700 studies involving 14.5 million twins have been collated. The results indicate a narrow victory for the environmentalists (51%) over the geneticists (49%). In other words, educators and others can now rest soundly in the knowledge that they can make a major contribution to developing children's innate dispositions, mindset and intelligence.

Professor Lilian Katz has been researching young children's dispositions for more than thirty years. She has concluded that dispositions are unlikely to be developed through didactic teaching approaches but by being around people who exhibit them (Katz, 1988). What is important is providing the opportunity for children to demonstrate desired behaviours and to acknowledge and celebrate these when they occur. According to Katz, the most appropriate means of developing dispositions is through the use of project work in which children can investigate topics of interest or concern to them. For Katz and others, good project work encourages young children to apply their emerging skills to open-ended, informal activities, with the intention of improving their understanding of the world they live in (Katz and Chard, 2000). They advocate the Project Approach to develop learning 'the stuff of real life' (http://projectapproach.org) and offer guidance on each stage of its development:

» **Phase 1:** Getting started. The topic should be closely related to at least a few of the children's everyday experiences so they can raise relevant questions. It should allow for the development of literacy, numeracy and wider skills and be rich enough to be sustained for at least a week.
» **Phase 2:** Field work. Preliminary discussions are held between teacher and children and a concept web drawn up as a focal point. The children should then undertake direct investigation which usually includes handling objects, observing closely, recording findings, undertaking visits, constructing models, predicting, discussions and drama activities.
» **Phase 3:** Culminating and debriefing events. Results are prepared and presented in various forms, including displays, talks, drama and guided tours.

In the UK, the project approach is particularly associated with primary schools in the pre-national curriculum era. Pinder (1987), a former head teacher in London, provides examples of successful projects including a year-long campaign to revitalise a local stretch of the Regent's Canal in north London. Through their studies, the children learned about canal horses, toads and other wildlife, the historical contribution of navvies, interpreting archival materials such as contemporary prints and newspapers, water safety, model making to scale, canoeing and teamwork skills such as self-catering on a canal barge. Perhaps above all, they discovered that ordinary people like themselves and their families could improve the environment. Today, the canal and its towpath is frequently used for pleasure cruising and is a busy cycle route for London commuters.

So why is it that project-based learning has had such a poor press? Critics lampoon the haphazard nature of such work and what they perceive as the neglect of essential knowledge. Moreover, empirical studies seemingly have not supported project-based learning and similar enquiry-led approaches such as PBL (discussed in the previous chapter). John Hattie's meta-research ranks these as below average in terms of impact (Hattie, 2009), but there is a danger of taking this at face value. Hattie talks up the importance of feedback, formative assessment, challenge and creating trusting relationships, but all of these highly effective elements in teaching should be present in well-planned project-based learning environments. Undoubtedly, project work can be a disaster in the hands of practitioners who struggle to cope with open-ended, 'messy' tasks and who adopt a light touch view of planning. However, experienced primary teachers know the value of projects in building on young children's interests, but also recognise that they require careful preparation and organisation. The most successful ones, in terms of learning gains, tend to be those that lead to public exhibitions of some kind so that children, parents and others can see the results. However, they are not driven by the outcomes (products) but by the quality of learning en route. This is why it is important to design projects with specific learning goals and opportunities for self-monitoring and regular feedback. Critical and creative thinking skills are not taught in isolation from content.

It is also not the case that project work necessarily takes up too much time. Some schools plan to use projects a couple of times a year, rather than every term, and save time by adapting projects from existing schemes, collaborating with other schools or repeating the project in later years. Finally, project-based learning does not mean abandoning other approaches (e.g. direct instruction – see Chapter 7). Vega (2012) provides a useful overview of the research supporting project-based learning which, when well implemented, can increase knowledge retention and improve students' learning dispositions, among other benefits.

Art Costa and Bena Kallick are key figures in the field of learner dispositions or what they call 'habits of mind'. These are defined as a mix of 'skills, attitudes, cues, past experiences, and proclivities' (Costa and Kallick, 2008: 17) that humans display when behaving intelligently. They quote the words of Horace Mann (1796–1859), an American educator, to illustrate the strength of a habit: 'a cable; we weave a thread of it each day, and at last we cannot break it' (Costa and Kallick, 2008: 16). The goal is to get learners into the habit of behaving intelligently; constant repetition of actions strengthens habits. The authors are interested in how successful learners solve complex problems, especially when confronted with demanding new situations. Costa and Kallick (2014: 23–24) have so far identified sixteen habits of mind that successful people demonstrate:

1. Persistence – stick to it!
2. Managing impulsivity – take your time!
3. Listening with empathy – understand others!
4. Thinking flexibly – look at it another way!
5. Thinking about thinking – know your knowing!
6. Taking responsible risks – venture out!
7. Finding humour – laugh a little!
8. Thinking interdependently – work/learn together!
9. Open to continuous learning – learning from experiences!
10. Striving for accuracy and precision – check it again!
11. Questioning and posing problems – how do you know?
12. Applying past knowledge to new situations – use what you learn!
13. Thinking and communicating with clarity and precision – be clear!
14. Gathering data through all senses – use your natural pathways!
15. Creating, imagining and innovation – try a different way!
16. Responding with wonderment and awe – have fun figuring it out!

Without going into the detail of these habits, it is sufficient to say that most teachers will recognise that these are areas in which their learners need support. Every class is likely to have learners who give up too easily when they don't know the answer to a problem. They declare, 'It's too hard!' or 'I can't do this!' These are students who need to develop persistence and a range of problem-solving strategies. Classes also contain pupils who blurt out the first answer in their heads. They struggle to control what they have to say. Those who manage their impulsivity and exercise self-discipline make greater strides in learning than those who do not. Many teachers complain that children do not listen closely enough to what they are told. According to Costa and Kallick (2008), we spend 55 per cent of our lives listening but it is the least taught skill in school. The skills of listening without interrupting, waiting patiently for a response, checking understanding, to self-monitor as someone else speaks and to disagree sensitively are complex and demanding to master and need extensive practice.

One of the things that distinguishes humans from other animals is our capacity for metacognition – we are able to stand back and reflect on what we say, believe, think and do. Yet studies show that although we all have this capacity, not everyone exercises it – some people do not take time out to wonder why they are doing what they are doing, to question their own performance. Teachers will know of individual learners who, when asked to explain the strategies they use to solve problems, are unable to do so. Moreover, some deploy the same strategies and do not take risks or try out new approaches. They may fear failure or ridicule. Asking questions, thinking in creative ways, using a full range of senses and displaying a thirst for new knowledge are all dispositions that are in short supply in the school population.

Successful teachers often draw on these habits in everyday practice. So, for example, when a teacher stops a lesson to discuss a key teaching point, she may be thinking flexibly (by diverting from the lesson plan), listening with empathy (to what the pupils have to say) and questioning (posing an open-ended question). When teaching habits of mind, the focus is on improving pupils' dispositions and skills when they are in uncertain situations or don't know the answers to problems. The goal is to build pupils' confidence so they feel more inclined to ask questions, take risks and work alongside others.

Costa and Kallick reject accusations that these are 'soft skills' wrapped up in emotions, beliefs and attitudes – that is, separate from cognitive thinking. They argue that the most successful thinkers draw on dispositions when confronted with problematic situations. The dispositions act as an internal compass, prompting individuals to think about what they can do when they do not immediately know the answer to a problem. So, if someone is asked to bake a cake for the first time, the following might apply:

» **Thinking interdependently** – who might be able to help bake the cake or offer advice?

» **Striving for precision and accuracy** – what are the measurements of the cake?

» **Thinking flexibly** – what alternatives can be used if short of certain ingredients?

» **Asking questions** – what kind (e.g. fruit, sponge, ice cream, etc.) and size (e.g. cup or wedding) of cake is needed? What equipment will I need?

» **Finding humour** – how can I decorate the cake to bring a smile to the recipient?

For teachers, it is useful to see how dispositions relate to the national curriculum requirements. In England, while these do not explicitly mention dispositions, the importance of developing pupils' positive attitudes to learning is made clear, for instance, in developing stamina for writing (DfE, 2014: 32). Moreover, the *Teachers' Standards* (DfE, 2011a: 10) expects teachers to 'set goals that stretch and challenge pupils of all backgrounds, abilities and dispositions'. In Wales, equipping young people with the dispositions they need is a central element of plans for a new curriculum (Donaldson, 2015). Similarly, in Scotland, dispositions are very much part of the curriculum rhetoric: 'Children have a natural disposition to wonder, to be curious, to pose questions, to experiment, to suggest, to invent and to explain. Staff have an essential role in extending and developing this' (Scottish Executive, 2007: 13).

Many other writers have followed on from Costa and Kallick in their endorsement of cultivating dispositions, albeit under different names. Deakin Crick and Goldspink (2014) identify seven 'learning power dimensions', such as critical curiosity (an orientation to want to 'get beneath the surface') and resilience (the readiness and openness to persevere in the face of challenge). In the UK, the most prominent advocates have been Guy Claxton and Bill Lucas (Claxton, 2002; Lucas et al., 2013; Claxton and Lucas, 2015). Claxton's Building Learning Power (BLP) programme is very much the British cousin to habits of mind in the United States. Claxton likens these dispositions to learning muscles and the classroom to a mind gym. His learning power equation seeks to sum up the necessary elements to successful learning: 'Unlock learning behaviours + build learning habits = a powerful learning character'.[1] Teachers are encouraged to talk up and share the language of learning while creating a classroom culture which fosters confidence, curiosity and independence, so that young people are equipped with the habits *and* qualifications to do well. BLP has been adopted in many schools and has spurred lots of action research projects (see Chapter 11), although there has been little independent evaluation.

---

1 See http://www.buildinglearningpower.com/#row2.

Based on extensive research over several decades, Carol Dweck (2006) shows that those who are successful in school and later life are 'mastery-oriented' and focus on achieving learning, as opposed to performance goals. They treat feedback as a means to an end and are eager to learn from their mistakes. They are less concerned about how their performance compares or appears to others. 'Failure' – for example, in terms of low scores or not completing a task – is seen as a temporary state and something that can be improved on, put into perspective or at least explained by factors beyond their control. However, many learners are not so inclined to respond to feedback in such a constructive manner. They take negative feedback as a personal shortcoming, reflecting their limited abilities and success as conditional ('Yes but …'). Dweck contrasts these approaches in terms of displaying a growth or fixed mindset. The good news for teachers and learners is that it is possible to cultivate a growth mindset through, for example, effective feedback. Dweck argues that simple strategies such as the 'Not yet' tag (e.g. 'You are not able to do this yet but I'm sure tomorrow …') can be very powerful. Unfortunately, simply praising learners for effort over ability is not the silver bullet to improving learning. Alfie Kohn (2015) points out that this simplistic approach can 'communicate that they're really not very capable and therefore unlikely to succeed at future tasks ("If you're complimenting me just for trying hard, I must really be a loser")'. Classroom life is complex and, for Kohn, what matters most is questioning the quality of pedagogy, the curriculum and whether assessment is authentic, rather than being side-tracked into thinking that telling learners to try harder will make a big difference.

Why is it important, and what can you do?

One of the most important implications from reviewing the work of Dweck and other researchers (e.g. Sternberg, 1983; Perkins, 1995; Lucas and Claxton, 2011) is that teachers need to build children's confidence and self-belief in what they are capable of achieving by applying themselves and putting in the effort. For their part, although something of a cliché, teachers need to create stimulating classroom environments and deliver engaging lessons.

It is also increasingly recognised around the world that education systems need to move beyond equipping young people with the skills of literacy and numeracy to include the cultivation of dispositions (Perkins, 2014). Employers want people who can think on their feet, show resilience and resourcefulness. A CBI (2014) survey found that businesses are looking first and foremost for graduates with the right attitude and aptitudes for the workplace, with nine in ten employers valuing these above other factors such as degree subject. Developing the right dispositions is not simply in the interests of employers. Children need to develop strong minds in order to cope with life's challenges and uncertainties, whether moving school or home, handling relationship issues or settling into a new role. In short, cultivating dispositions is important because it is the basis of children becoming ready, willing and able to learn and adjust to life beyond school.

Unfortunately, too many children and young people lack the dispositions they need to be successful at school and in life. Across OECD countries, almost two in three 15-year-olds confessed that they tend to 'put off difficult problems', almost one in two reported that they tend to 'give up easily when confronted with a problem', and only one in three said that they 'liked to solve complex problems' (OECD, 2014: 78). While teachers can provide lots of opportunities for learners to practise skills and stress the importance of hard work, these alone are not enough for learners to achieve their potential. Learners need to believe that they can succeed, develop the drive to have a go and the fortitude and stamina to cope with failure. Teachers can encourage learners to see mistakes as learning opportunities and, more generally, to create a climate in which learning is seen as progression through a series of steps determined largely by applying dispositional thinking (see Figure 5.1).

There is growing evidence that links the cultivation of dispositions to how well pupils do at school. Research in neuroscience, reported by Paul Tough (2012) in his book *How Children Succeed*, highlights a strong relationship between children's capacity to succeed and their persistence and self-management. Significant research carried out by the Effective Pre-School, Primary and Secondary Education Project (EPPSE) investigated the academic and social-behavioural development of approximately 3,000 children from the age of 3-plus years. It found that student dispositions are significantly associated with their academic attainment, in particular

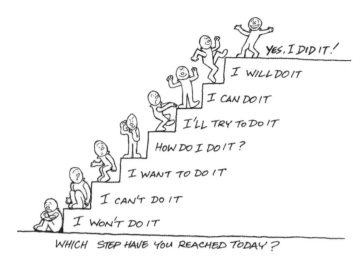

Figure 5.1. Steps towards success.

Source: http://everydaypowerblog.com/2014/05/25/
motivational-quotes-for-kids/.

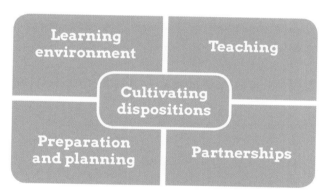

**Figure 5.2. Aspects of school provision that
contribute to cultivating dispositions.**

their 'English and maths academic self concept' and 'enjoyment of school'
(Sammons et al., 2012).

In order to cultivate dispositions, schools need to consider all aspects of
their provision, including the learning environment, teachers' preparation
and planning, teaching–learning interactions and partnerships within
and beyond the school (see Figure 5.2).

Learning environment

Classroom and corridor displays should include examples of pupils' work in progress (e.g. drafts, sketches and annotations as well as final pieces) so that progression through learning is clear. Some schools have learning walls that feature photographs of learners collaborating, listening and persisting and demonstrating the habits of mind in action. Mobile displays could feature the key vocabulary associated with learning and thinking using child-friendly icons. Posters and other visuals can be displayed and used as reference points so that learners can see what 'good' learning looks like (what makes a good listener, writer, artist, historian, etc.). Many teachers provide inspirational quotes and images appropriate to the age range. These should be drawn from different walks of life so that learners see the universality of dispositions – for example:

'Our greatest weakness lies in giving up. The most certain way to succeed is always to try just one more time' – Thomas Edison

'If someone tells you, "You can't" they really mean, "I can't"' – Sean Stephenson

'All things are difficult before they are easy' – Thomas Fuller

'Success is falling nine times and getting up ten' – Jon Bon Jovi

'When the world pushes you to your knees, you're in the perfect position to pray' – Rumi

'Don't let what you can't do stop you from doing what you can do' – John Wooden

'We all can dance when we find music that we love' – Giles Andreae

'No one is perfect ... that's why pencils have erasers' – Wolfgang Riebe

Costa and Kallick (2008) refer to 'word splashes' for each disposition – for example, for finding humour this includes funny, comic, clown, comedian, laughable, playful, bizarre, pun and satirical. These words can be displayed around the classroom and added to by learners as and when they encounter new terms. In one school I have visited, the foyer was surrounded with children's jokes and riddles displayed on giant lollypop sticks, creating a pleasant first impression of a happy school.

The wider school grounds can also be used as a stimulus for children's dispositions, particularly curiosity, in terms of gathering data through all senses and responding with awe and wonder. There is plenty of guidance available for schools to develop their grounds through organisations such as Learning through Landscapes (www.ltl.org.uk) and Eco-Schools England (www.eco-schools.org.uk).

Preparation and planning

Merely listing dispositions is not enough to cultivate their use among learners. Teachers need to define the behaviours associated with the dispositions – for example, when painting in an art lesson, they should expect learners to describe the colour, shades, tones, brushstrokes and other techniques associated with striving for accuracy. Dispositions can be a specific focus when preparing resources and planning units of work and lessons. Real-world opportunities can be created so that learners are able to demonstrate their dispositional thinking – for example, writing to real audiences beyond the school or interviewing visiting speakers. Support staff can be deployed strategically to work alongside learners who are struggling with particular dispositions. Learners can be invited to co-plan lessons, thereby developing further opportunities for collaboration.

Dispositions take time to develop. Tasks need to be set so that learners can try to apply dispositional thinking in a range of contexts. So, for example, if a teacher decides that the focus should be on developing learners' questioning skills then they should be asked to compose questions for different purposes and audiences. They might set questions for a quiz night in school, to ask a visiting politician, as a guide to a storybook for younger children or for a formal examination. Costa and Kallick's (2008) 'three-story intellect' model is a useful aide for teachers when constructing tasks and questions of increasing challenge (see Figure 5.3). Loosely based on Bloom's taxonomy of educational objectives, the model moves learners from gathering data (inputs) to analysing (process) and applying (outputs) what they have gathered. On the 'first floor' tasks and questions are constructed so that learners describe, define, name and list things. On the 'second floor' they compare, sort, explain, sequence and analyse. Finally, on the 'top floor' they imagine, speculate, judge and evaluate.

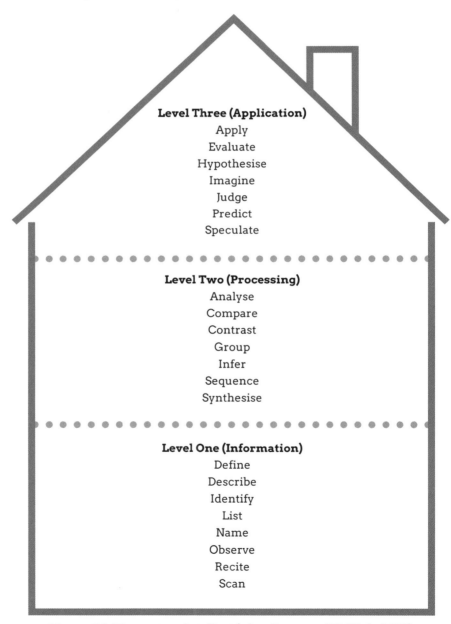

Level Three (Application)
Apply
Evaluate
Hypothesise
Imagine
Judge
Predict
Speculate

Level Two (Processing)
Analyse
Compare
Contrast
Group
Infer
Sequence
Synthesise

Level One (Information)
Define
Describe
Identify
List
Name
Observe
Recite
Scan

Figure 5.3. Three-story intellect (after Costa and Kallick, 2008).

Partnerships

Discussions with parents and carers should centre on how they can support their children through praising effort and creating opportunities for them to work on dispositions at home. Parents can be invited to document and report on when they notice children demonstrating positive behaviours. Many parents, particularly those from low-income backgrounds, are hesitant to come into school, perhaps because of their own experiences as a child or because they lack confidence in communicating with teachers. But parents and grandparents represent a significant pool of talent for schools to tap into, given their diverse experiences. Wider partnerships within the community could extend opportunities for children to demonstrate dispositions such as persistence, striving for accuracy and responding with awe and wonder – for example, fundraising for a local charity, working alongside the local archaeological society, library, bank, shopkeepers or wildlife centre.

Teaching

Teachers and the support staff should seek to model specific dispositions, such as perseverance, both in the school and, indirectly, through references to the wider world. It is important to capture moments when this happens, rewarding and celebrating this – for example, by holding a 'learning hero' assembly. In everyday teaching, it can be helpful to regularly use question prompts linked to the relevant dispositions. Meier (1995: 41), a former principal of a secondary school in Harlem, identified five habits of mind and turned these into questions for her students:

» **Significance** – why is it important?
» **Perspective** – what is the point of view?
» **Evidence** – how do you know?
» **Connection** – how does it apply?
» **Supposition** – what if it were different?

These are very useful questions for teachers to reflect on when planning units of work. For example, at the heart of historical and scientific enquiries lies the question, how do you know? Similarly, 'What is the point of view?', invites learners to consider the viewpoints of different characters in literature, current news in geography and how the past is interpreted. For younger children, puppets or teddy bears can be used to embody different dispositions (e.g. Persistent Percy, Flexible Felix, Adventurous Amy).

Marzano et al. (2001) outline the problem-solving steps for teachers to model:

1. Identify the goal you are trying to accomplish.
2. Describe the barriers that prevent you from achieving this.
3. Identify possible solutions.
4. Hypothesise which solution you think is likely to be the most effective.
5. Try your solution.
6. Explain whether your hypothesis was correct and decide whether you want to test another hypothesis.

Initially, teachers might state the goal and provide the resources. They may also offer key words or a writing frame to support the thinking process, such as:

The challenge is to ...
I think if I try ...
Then ... will happen.

However, as learners gain confidence they should be given more independence in how they approach tasks.

Teachers should try to use specific thinking terms, or what Costa and Kallick (2008) call 'mindful language' – for example, rather than say 'Let's look at these pictures', use 'Let's *compare* these pictures'; instead of saying 'What do you think might happen if ...?', try 'What do you *speculate* might happen if ...?' In providing feedback to learners, nudges, prompts and exclamations can focus on dispositions – for example, 'How else could you do that?' (thinking flexibly), 'Go on, I dare you to have a go' (taking responsible risks) and 'Look very carefully' (using all the senses). Progression in the development of dispositions can be made explicit through, for example, the use of skills ladders. Learners can also be encouraged to use journals to record the learning challenges they face and how they are overcoming them.

Person	Field	Challenges
Jim Carrey (1962–)	Acting	At the age of 14, he lived in a camper van when his father lost his job.
Vincent Van Gogh (1853–1890)	Painting	He only sold one of his 900 paintings during his lifetime – his talent was recognised only after his death.
The Beatles (1960s–)	Music	The first record company they approached declared: 'We don't like their sound and guitar music is on its way out.'
Ludwig van Beethoven (1770–1827)	Music	He began to lose his hearing in his early twenties, eventually becoming completely deaf. He is still regarded as one of the greatest composers in history.
J. K. Rowling (1965–)	Literature	A single mum who had many book proposals rejected before the Harry Potter phenomenon took off and she became among the world's most famous children's authors.
Nelson Mandela (1918–2013)	Politics	He overcame prejudice to train as a lawyer and, although imprisoned, was a key player in bringing apartheid to an end, eventually becoming the president of South Africa.
Helen Keller (1880–1968)	Literature and politics	She became deaf and blind as a toddler but still learned to read and write. She became the first deaf-blind person to gain a university degree.
Olaudah Equiano (1745–1797)	Literature	He was enslaved at the age of 11 and transported to the United States. He later wrote *The Interesting Narrative of the Life of Olaudah Equiano*, which proved a turning point in public opinion against slavery, leading to the Slave Trade Act 1807 in the UK.

Table 5.1. Individuals who have succeeded against the odds.

Modelling is a very powerful teaching strategy. There is a strong correlation between positive teacher dispositions and students' success (Stronge, 2010). Teachers and classroom assistants can model being a learner in lots of ways – for example, by talking about a new skill they are learning, perhaps at night school or during the holiday and the challenges this brings. At times, it is important for learners to see teachers practise what they preach, perhaps by writing their own poems, reading aloud, applying numeracy in real life or painting a picture.

In every subject and area of life there are much-respected individuals who have fought against the odds to achieve success (see Table 5.1). Some have come from very humble beginnings and faced many knock-backs, but demonstrated perseverance and determination, often with the support of a particular friend, teacher or coach. Reading extracts from their life stories can inspire pupils. Michael Finnigan's book, *They Did You Can* (2011), discusses how leading sports figures such as Gordon Banks, Philip Neville, Jonathan Davies, Clive Woodward, Dame Mary Peters and Beth Tweddle achieved their fame using two things: a raw gift and a great attitude. Local people whose stories demonstrate courage, high aspirations and hard work can also inspire children.

Another approach to developing dispositional thinking is to induct pupils into the working practices of skilled specialists. For example, wall displays could advertise working as a scientist with pictures of iconic figures (e.g. Albert Einstein) surrounded with prompts showing ideal dispositions for science, such as being curious, investigating, collecting and recording precise data, cooperation, communication, seeking answers, asking new questions and persistence.

Conclusion

Traditionally in the UK, the school system has focused on sorting children and young people according to their abilities. Those who did not do so well at school were perceived to be not as 'bright' as those who did. Today, individuals are still grouped according to ability in classrooms around the country under various labels. Children soon learn the codes for their ability groups, whether 'elephants', 'tigers' or 'hippos'. Neuroscience, psychology and classroom observations tell us that innate ability should not set a limit on what learners can achieve through effort, practice and good teaching.

Many of our greatest thinkers and creative talents were written off at school: Nick Park, founder of Aardman Animations and creator of Wallace and Gromit, was described in his primary school report as 'inclined to dream. Could do better if he tried'; 9-year-old Winston Churchill was reported to have 'no ambition'; 17-year-old John Lennon was said to be 'certainly on the road to failure'; and it was observed about the television presenter Jeremy Paxman, 'It is a pity that the threat of failure in his exams has not helped him to grow out of a tediously lackadaisical uncooperativeness' (cited by Hurley, 2002: 56). Professor Tanya Byron was told alongside her parents at a meeting with her teacher that 'Tanya will never be a high flyer' (cited by Claxton and Lucas, 2015: iii). My personal experience was similar – at the end of primary school, the teacher asked what I wanted to be. I explained that I wanted to be a postman or teacher (I had delivered newspapers and assumed that it was a natural graduation to become a postman), to which I was told, 'You're not clever enough to be a teacher.'

Teachers need to believe in all children's capacities and to instil confidence and self-belief among their charges. This does not mean giving children false hopes or telling them that their work, effort or behaviour is good when it is not. But it does mean having high expectations, seeing intelligence as expandable and focusing on effort rather than talent. Research tells us that primary schoolchildren's aspirations reflect their sense of hope for the future more than their assessment of ability and constraints. Their early aspirations can be seen as a very good proxy for dispositions such as resilience or hopelessness and self-perceptions regarding competence (Cicchetti and Rogosch, 2009).

Summary

» Children and young people's learning should be not be fixed by their ability or intelligence. What matters most is the quality of teaching and how learners respond to this.

» Carol Dweck highlights that the most successful learners have a 'growth mindset', believing that hard work and perseverance rather than innate talent can help them to improve their learning.

» Cultivating the right dispositions is essential if school learners are to become productive and well-adjusted members of society.

» Art Costa and Bena Kallick suggest that there are common habits of mind that the most successful people in life demonstrate, such as perseverance and flexible thinking.

» Schools need to spend more time and energy in nurturing these habits of mind.

Points for reflection and action

» Choose a disposition and find out more about why this is important for learners. For example, for persistence, read and reflect on the '10 Unbelievable Stories of Persistence' (http://www.oddee.com/item_98975.aspx), including the Korean grandmother who passed her driving test after 960 attempts, the professional ballerina who lost her right arm in a car accident and the cat named Dusty who stole 600 items in three years.

» Watch the video of the ex-footballer Ian Wright meeting Syd Pigden, one of his former teachers (https://www.youtube.com/watch?v=omPdemwaNzQ). What does this say about the lasting influence of teachers?

Chapter 6

Ethics

Teachers' conduct should be guided by a moral purpose

What is the big idea?

Between 1911 and 1951, students entering university teacher-training departments were required to make a pledge that they would follow the teaching profession in exchange for receiving state grants to support their training. It was essentially seen as a moral obligation. Unfortunately, some less scrupulous youngsters took advantage of the grants and headed off to university with no real commitment to teach. In 1944, the McNair Report on the supply, recruitment and training of teachers conceded: 'Everyone knows that the present system brings a number of unsuitable candidates into the profession and that it involves in some cases a moral strain which ought not to be imposed on young people' (McNair, 1944: 91).

Today, most of those who enter teacher training do not make a pledge, although participants on the Teach First route are expected to commit to a two-year leadership development programme, working in schools to tackle educational inequalities. Teach First recruitment makes a strong appeal to graduates' sense of moral purpose – specifically to make a difference in schools in socially disadvantaged areas. After a decade of success, the organisation proclaims: 'in a world that is all too often characterised by apathy or cynicism, a successful enterprise can be built on moral purpose' (Hill, 2012: 27).

But what is moral purpose, and what does professional morality entail? In its simplest form, morality is about the difference between right and wrong. It is derived from the Latin word *moralitas* meaning proper behaviour. Ethics, or moral philosophy, is concerned with judging whether an action is morally good or bad. By its very nature, teaching is a moral activity. Teachers with a strong moral purpose are able to discern the morally right course of action and follow it, however challenging this may be.

The chapter on ethics covers two inter-related themes: teachers' professional conduct and their role in children's moral education. This is difficult territory, partly because of the dangers of moralising and engaging with issues that are controversial and divide opinion. Moral relativists are quick to raise questions about whose values and moral purposes should take priority. Haydon (2011) discusses the widespread 'confusion' that exists over moral education and the idea of morality in society at large. Is morality about ideals we should aspire to, so we should not worry whether we fall short? Or is morality a set of minimal constraints on what each of us can do, so that we do not unduly interfere with others (not harming each other, keeping contractual obligations, etc.)? Or is morality interpreted as following religious codes or universal truths?

For those in education, is it necessary to be a morally 'good' person to be an effective teacher? In China, where Confucian tradition puts a great emphasis on the morality of teachers, the Ministry of Education declares: 'moral conduct shall become the foremost factor in testing, appointing, employing and evaluating teachers' (Peng et al., 2014: 79). Teachers are expected to possess moral integrity ahead of teaching expertise. In rural parts of the country, many low-paid teachers do their work out of a moral duty to society.

There are lots of questions about the relationship between a teacher's personal lifestyle, values, beliefs and classroom practice. Should teachers be free to express their own views on matters such as politics, religion and sexual conduct? What about teachers who are members of far right but legal organisations such as the British National Party? Should they be forced to resign, or should their legitimate political rights be acknowledged?

Perhaps in any discussion about the role of teachers in children's moral development, the first question should be: can moral values be taught? There are philosophical objections to teaching any lessons on morality because teaching implies expertise and any notion of moral expertise is dubious. Perhaps monks, rather than teachers, are best placed to educate children in the virtues of honesty and sobriety. Further, education invariably involves assessment, but how can teachers genuinely assess children's moral development? For these kinds of reasons, there are those who suggest that moral education is caught rather than taught, and that it is better for schools to employ good role models who practise the moral characteristics that we want children to emulate (see Winch and Gingell, 1999). This, in itself, raises further questions about the extent to which a teacher's personal conduct outside school should have a bearing on their professional life.

Teachers in the UK are expected to fulfil their responsibilities according to professional codes of conduct. The General Teaching Councils in Wales, Scotland and Northern Ireland and the Teaching Council in England set out general principles relating to, for instance, confidentiality, care and respecting the rights of others (General Teaching Council for Wales, 2009; DfE, 2011a; General Teaching Council for Scotland, 2012; Teaching Council, 2012). Teachers are expected to uphold public trust in the profession and maintain high standards of ethics and behaviour. This extends beyond the school gates to, for example, educational visits and other school related business. It also covers behaviour more generally, such as showing tolerance and respect for the rights of others and 'at all times observing proper boundaries appropriate to a teacher's professional position' (DfE, 2011a: 14).

Teaching codes deliberately avoid prescriptive solutions to moral and ethical dilemmas. Campbell (2003) is sceptical of codes because they are rarely useful in concrete cases and she argues that moral principles need to be 'a living force' in the teacher's mind. However, codes of conduct are essential to establish norms in the profession and build the general public's confidence in teaching. Even so, in England more than 10,000 teachers signed a petition in protest at the insistence in the *Teachers' Standards* (DfE, 2011a) that teachers uphold 'public trust' in the profession outside school by maintaining 'reasonable standards in their own behaviour'. They see this as an intrusion into their private lives. According to one teacher, the code was 'practically demanding sainthood' (Clark, 2009). This is overstating the case. Those who enter the profession need to recognise that they are 'moral agents' who should set an example by the way they dress, speak to pupils and the effort they put into work (National Curriculum Council, 1993).

The big idea in this chapter is that all teachers should seek to conduct themselves to a high professional standard within an ethical framework and with moral purpose. Moral purpose in teaching requires a commitment to show kindness, compassion and care. To behave in a moral way requires both the intention to do so and the freedom to make moral decisions. If a school receives notice of an inspection and teachers then feverishly mark children's books, filling in any gaps with comments, then this decision cannot be regarded as a moral one. The fact that this may lead to a positive outcome – for example, in belatedly helping pupils to move forward in their learning or securing a good inspection judgement – is not the point. What matters, from a moral perspective, is the teachers' intention.

Moral purpose begins with the conviction that teachers can make a positive difference to the lives of *all* children and young people. It does not accept, for instance, that factors beyond the school's influence, such as children's social and economic background, are justifiable reasons why children from low-income families cannot do as well as those from wealthier ones. Too many children and young people are not achieving their potential. Whatever one's political views, few would disagree with Michael Gove's assessment:

How can it be right that more than a fifth of children left primary school without having reached a basic level of literacy and numeracy? We wouldn't accept a fifth of hospital operations going wrong or a fifth of flights ending badly. So why should we accept a system in which school standards were still too low? (cited by Forsyth, 2014)

The attainment gap between children from low-income families and their more privileged peers is illustrated by the backgrounds of those admitted to Oxford and Cambridge universities. Although only 7 per cent of British children overall attend fee-paying schools, and 15 per cent at sixth form, they make up 39 per cent of Cambridge undergraduates. At Oxford the figures are even starker: 43 per cent attended private schools (Koppel, 2014). Traditionalists argue that addressing unfairness and social imbalance may undermine academic achievement. However, the fact is that privately educated students are over-represented at our top universities. While universities have a remit to widen participation of under-represented groups in higher education, both primary and secondary state schools need to do more to address the impact of poverty on educational attainment. Evidence from the most successful schools shows that all staff (including non-teaching assistants and governors) hold a strong moral conviction that poverty should not be an excuse for underachievement. They share this belief with students and their families (Egan, 2012).

Gove was one of the main supporters of the pupil premium – additional funding introduced in 2011 to support pupils eligible for free school meals and those who have been looked after continuously for six months. Although it is still too early to say what difference the pupil premium has had on attainment, the grant is an example of how resources are allocated centrally with a moral purpose. However, at school level the spending of the grant has thrown up a range of ethical issues. These include variability in how schools define 'disadvantage' – while most use the official criteria relating to pupils eligible for free school meals and looked-after children, others have identified children in particular circumstances, such as those not having English as a first language, having a parent in the armed forces or being a child of refugees or asylum seekers.

Carpenter et al. (2013) found that in the case study schools studied by the Centre for Equity in Education, disadvantage was defined in a much broader educational way than set out by the government's economic focus. As one head explained, the key question in determining whether children are disadvantaged or not is, 'Are they equipped for school and ready for learning?' Other school leaders emphasised the need to focus on all children experiencing difficulties. As one head argued: 'We don't look for the stamp on the forehead that says, "You're a poor person, and therefore you get this kind of provision." ... It's the effectiveness of what we're doing in terms of teaching and learning that is the determinant, not how many pounds they've got in their pockets' (Carpenter et al., 2013: 29). Clearly, then, the well-intentioned pupil premium has raised tensions and moral dilemmas for school leaders. Some are uneasy about spending the funding on children who fall outside the official categories by which it was allocated. As one head teacher explained, it calls for bravery because, 'I know that's not what it's for, but that's what I did' (Carpenter et al., 2013: 29).

Moral and character education

Despite the challenges associated with moral education, paradoxically, there is widespread agreement over its importance. Teachers have a clear responsibility for children's moral education. In 1995, they were told by the School Curriculum and Assessment Authority (1993–1997), in no uncertain terms, that school values should include: telling the truth, keeping promises, respecting the rights and property of others, acting considerately towards others, helping the less fortunate and weaker than oneself, taking personal responsibility for one's actions and self-discipline (SCAA, 1995). Schools should also reject bullying, cheating, deceit, cruelty, irresponsibility and dishonesty. These were presented as moral absolutes. Academics such as Jane Erricker have taken issue with this interpretation. She argues that such guidance 'lists every mode of behaviour that nice, middle-class, British parents would want their children to conform to', but it pays no attention to the 'way the child is feeling at any particular time' (Erricker, 2000: 87).

Erricker goes on to draw on her own research experience to suggest that working-class children often struggle to adjust to these values when at school. They are then chastised and soon become dispirited. Yet, their own experiences often involve taking on challenging emotional and practical responsibilities that 'protected' middle-class teachers have no knowledge of; experiences that arise from complicated, unstable and possibly abusive family situations. In these contexts, she found that young children are able to make considered moral decisions. Research published in the United States suggests that working-class parents are more likely to emphasise the role of politeness, respect and deference to authority, although in classrooms middle-class children are more likely to be noticed by teachers because they are more likely to raise their hands, ask questions and not be afraid to ask for help (Paton, 2012). Erricker's main point is that children are not fools and they know that moral absolutes are not what most people follow in real life. It is certainly the case that children (irrespective of class) are surrounded by cheating, lying and violent conduct – trawl through any daily newspaper to find examples. It is clearly important to acknowledge that moral education is aspirational and that if it is to make a difference to how children and young people behave, then engagement in real-life contexts, where decisions are less black and white, is important.

Under the terms of the Education Act 2002, state-funded schools must provide for the spiritual, moral, cultural, physical and intellectual development of their pupils. Sir Michael Barber, one of the leading educational figures in the UK, has put forward a formula to sum up the moral purpose of education, E (K + T + L), where K stands for knowledge, T for thinking and L for leadership. These are wrapped up within an ethical framework (E). Barber (2009: 16) suggests:

To thrive in vast, diverse cities, share the planet with other living things, preserve the wildernesses, generate economic growth without waste, resolve conflicts peacefully and deploy wisdom and judgment at moments of crisis. It is not 'all relative'; these are matters of right and wrong on which the quality of life, and perhaps life on Earth itself, ultimately depend.

Moral education involves motivating individuals to behave morally, developing their knowledge of ethical codes and conventions agreed by society and their ability to make judgements on moral issues. Teachers have a key role to play in children's moral development, but there certainly needs to be greater clarity over what form this should take. Is this a matter of instructing children in certain moral rules and universal truths? Or does it involve teaching children to reason on the ethics of particular situations and reach their own decisions? Or perhaps it should be more about the cultivation of virtues and character traits?

All of these approaches have merit, but it is the latter that has caught the eye of politicians, the Church of England, employers and civic leaders, now publicly supporting projects that build 'grit and resilience' among schoolchildren (Paton, 2014b). Character education has been defined as school-based activities that seek to shape the behaviour of pupils by influencing the values believed to bring about such behaviour (Lockwood, 1997). But this is not the same as behaviour control or indoctrination because, as Arthur (2003) points out, the goal of character education is much broader and ambitious. It holds out the hope of what an individual can become, as opposed to what they are naturally.

Character formation, as an approach to moral education, has been around for a very long time. In Victorian schools, the emphasis was on inculcating the values associated with 'muscular Christianity', including duty to God, the Queen and the Empire. Well-established organisations such as the Scouts and Guides and schemes such as the Duke of Edinburgh Award have always considered character building as part of their remit. The renewed interest has seen the setting up of a new subject association called the Association for Character Education (www.character-education.org. uk) and government financial support for programmes including those aimed at children typically excluded from mainstream schools. These programmes are reported to improve behaviour, engagement, attendance and attainment (Clay and Thomas, 2014). A major research study by the Jubilee Centre for Character and Virtues, covering 10,000 students and 255 teachers across the UK, suggests that cultivating virtues has a positive impact on academic performance (Arthur et al., 2015). Although most teachers believe that they place a high priority on moral teaching, the student responses to the survey indicate a disparity in terms of outcomes. The students were presented with moral dilemma tests and many answered purely from a self-interest point of view. Interestingly, contrary to the traditional view that sport builds character, the researchers found that students who claimed to participate in sporting activities did not perform better than those who said they did not practise sports. The one change that researchers recommended in order to improve character education was to provide more 'free space' so that students could do things they really liked, without having to think about exam scores.

What has brought about this renewed interest in character education? In part, it arises out of employer concerns over school leavers who lack the resilience, drive and flexible thinking needed in the modern workplace. But, to a large degree, it is in response to what Arthur (2003: 3) calls 'a litany of alarm', with anxieties over the scale of teenage pregnancies, young male suicide rates, sexual abuse, drug addictions, school truancy, mental health problems and emotional insecurities. Since Arthur wrote *Education with Character* in 2003, the threats posed by radicalisation and extremist ideologies, along with rapid developments in digital technologies, have added further impetus to character education.

The dangers of radicalisation, where children are introduced to extreme political, social or religious ideals, should not be underestimated. It was recently illustrated by the 'Trojan Horse' scandal in 2014, when Islamic extremism was reported to have infiltrated thirteen schools in Birmingham. Members of staff were alleged to have put up posters warning children that if they didn't pray they would 'go to hell', Christmas was cancelled and girls were taught that women who refused to have sex with their husbands would be 'punished' by angels 'from dusk to dawn' (Swinford, 2014). Concerns have not been limited to a few Muslim schools. In October 2014, Ofsted placed Sir John Cass's Foundation and Red Coat Church of England Secondary School (in Stepney, London) in its 'special measures' category, partly because senior leaders were not doing enough to guide sixth-formers on the dangers associated with social media and the promotion of extremist views. This was despite the fact that teaching and student behaviour were reported to be good. However, school leaders had not taken decisive action following reports from the police in 2013/2014 about extremist views, including one posting stating that any sixth-form students who attended a 'leavers' party' and engaged in 'free-mixing' or 'listening to music' would face 'severe consequences later' (Ofsted, 2014b: 5). This particular school has since improved significantly to become outstanding (Ofsted, 2015), but such stories illustrate why teachers need to be mindful of the dangers to children's well-being posed by political or religious extremists on social media.

The threat of extremism is not confined to radical Islamist groups such as Isis. Far-right groups such as the English Defence League and criminal gangs also pose a danger to young people. Although it is very rare for schoolchildren to become involved in extremist activity, they can be exposed to radical views via the Internet from an early age. It is generally agreed that children with low aspirations are more vulnerable to radicalisation and adopting extremist views. This is why it is important for schools to build all pupils' confidence, self-belief, respect and tolerance, as well as setting high academic expectations.

Successive governments have introduced guidance and practical materials to support schools in educating children and young people about the dangers of extremism (DCSF, 2008d; DfE, 2014). The government's Prevent strategy was introduced to counter terrorism, with the aim of preventing people from becoming terrorists or supporting violent extremism. The strategy points out that schools should 'look at terrorism in the round and not just at Al Qa'ida' (HM Government, 2011: 25), so that pupils understand how, historically, people have been recruited from many faith groups to extremist causes. Schools have been provided with advice on how to encourage children and young people to challenge prejudices such as Islamophobia and anti-Semitism, think for themselves and debate moral issues. In more recent times, the Conservative government has adopted a tougher approach to extremism, with David Cameron arguing that there was no time for 'kid gloves' when faced with the threat to Britain's values of democracy, equality and tolerance (Espinoza, 2015b). Ironically, in defence of the same values, liberals fear that in a democratic society there is a danger of removing the right to free speech and preventing discussions on controversial topics in schools and universities. Cardiff and Cambridge student unions tried to ban the likes of Germaine Greer and Nigel Farage from speaking in 2015 on the grounds that the former had caused offence to transsexuals and the latter was an extremist (Espinoza, 2015b). There have been warnings from teaching unions that teachers may stay clear of discussing divisive issues, which would undermine rather than defend free speech.

Schools are certainly caught up in these political debates and are expected to be at the front line in tackling extremism. Under the Counter-Terrorism and Security Act 2015, all schools have a statutory duty to 'prevent people from being drawn into terrorism'. School leaders are required to make a risk assessment of children being drawn into terrorism and to effectively police pupils' access to the Internet so they do not view extremist material online. This is demanding territory for schools. Children's innocent comments can be easily misinterpreted. When a 10-year-old boy from Accrington, in Lancashire, mistakenly wrote in an English lesson that he lived in a 'terrorist house' rather than a 'terraced house', police arrived at his home the following day and examined the family laptop (Robertson, 2016). In another story, a 4-year-old's drawing of his dad holding a cucumber was mistaken for a knife. Nursery staff feared the worst when they heard the child describe the vegetable as a 'cooker bomb' and reported the matter to social workers, who took no action (Fox, 2016).

Teachers are not experts in monitoring teenagers for signs of radicalisation and are naturally anxious over how best to tackle difficult issues and undertake new responsibilities. There are big questions to ask about the role of schools in the new world of counter-extremism and whether their influence, compared to the persuasive voices on the Internet, counts for anything substantial. How do teachers distinguish between extremism and narrow-mindedness or religious dogmatism? At what point should a pupil who airs a strong personal conviction, albeit in a non-violent way, be considered an extremist? Teachers are clearly mindful of those teenagers, such as Talha Asmal from Dewsbury, who attended state schools before heading off to Syria and Iraq to fight for Isis.

Who is behind it?

In ancient societies, ideas about rightness and wrongness were generally governed by religious or supernatural beliefs. The great religious traditions of Hinduism, Buddhism, Judaism, Christianity and Islam shaped how people's actions were viewed and the laws that governed their behaviour. Each of these world faiths has a strong ethical and intellectual dimension. This is best summed up through the Golden Rule, variations of which can be found in most religions and secular philosophies:

Brahmanism: 'This is the sum of Dharma [duty]: Do naught unto others which would cause you pain if done to you'. Mahabharata 5:1517

Buddhism: 'Hurt not others in ways that you yourself would find hurtful.' Udana-Varga 5:18

Christianity: 'Do to others whatever you would like them to do to you. This is the essence of all that is taught in the law and the prophets.' Matthew 7:12 (New Living Translation)

Confucianism: 'Do not do to others what you do not want them to do to you.' Analects 15:23

Hinduism: 'One should not behave towards others in a way which is disagreeable to oneself.' Mencius VII.A.4

Humanism: 'Don't do things you wouldn't want to have done to you.' British Humanist Society

Islam: 'None of you truly believes until he loves for his brother what he loves for himself.' Hadith attributed to Muhammad

Judaism: 'Thou shalt love thy neighbour as thyself.' Leviticus 19:18

Sikhism: 'Don't create enmity with anyone as God is within everyone.'
Guru Arjan Devji 259

The ancient Greeks, fathers of Western philosophy, had much to say about ethical behaviour. Plato believed that ethics is about behaviour that we *ought* to do. This theme was picked up by the naturalist Charles Darwin who observed: 'Of all the differences between man and the lower animals, the moral sense or conscience is by far the most important … It is summed up in that short but imperious word ought, so full of high significance' (Darwin, 1871: 70).

However, the challenge remains in deciding what to do when options appear to be equally favourable or unfavourable. Another ancient Greek philosopher, Protagoras, developed the notion that there was always more than one side to every argument and ideas about right and wrong depend on each person's perception and wider cultural values. This marked the beginnings of moral relativism. Aristotle, who first used the word ethics, recommended adopting a middle course between two extremes and this became known as 'the golden mean' (see Table 6.1).

For Aristotle, the good life was achieved by striking a balance between virtues and vices: too much and too little are always wrong. So, in terms of spending money, the goal is to become generous because this is the mean between wastefulness and stinginess, while relating to strangers requires friendliness as this lies between being ingratiating and surly. In simple terms, the advice was to avoid extremes and seek moderation in all things. The role of educators was to cultivate virtues and focus on character formation.

Babies enter the world with moral potential. By the age of 3, they are able to ask questions about why people do things and are beginning to understand ideas of what is fair and unfair (e.g. sharing toys). Children's moral development and the role of schools in promoting this has always attracted interest, particularly from religious bodies and the state, which have been the main historic patrons of education in the UK. Defining where moral education sits in the curriculum has proved challenging. Should it permeate school life, feature as part of a subject on the curriculum, as a separate entity, form a crosscutting theme or be associated with particular partnerships (say with parents and the community), programmes or

Feeling	Excess	Mean	Deficiency
Pleasure	Self-indulgence	Temperance	Insensibility
Honour	Vanity	Magnanimity	Pusillanimity
Anger	Irascibility	Patience	Lack of spirit
Shame	Shyness	Modesty	Shamelessness
Self-expression	Boastfulness	Truthfulness	Mock modesty
Confidence	Rashness	Courage	Cowardice

Table 6.1 Examples of Aristotle's virtues and vices within the Golden Mean.

initiatives? The nature of moral education has also varied, from being tied closely to religious instruction in faith schools to a broader coverage in subjects such as personal, social, health and citizenship education (PSHCE), which was introduced as a statutory subject in the secondary national curriculum in 2002. Here, moral education is associated with concepts such as democracy, justice, rights and responsibilities and respect for diversity. The emphasis is on encouraging children's moral reasoning over these key concepts and issues. In recent times, the discourse has shifted back to character education, focused on the development of virtuous traits and habits.

Through the ages, moral philosophers and others have had plenty to say about the ethical role of the teacher. Émile Durkheim (1858–1917), one of the founding fathers of the sociology of education, saw the purpose of education as maintaining the moral consensus in a secular society. In terms of socialisation, he thought that teachers should embody and introduce children to common moral values so that they could internalise these and contribute to the proper functioning of society. The assumption is that there is a static set of easily identifiable values which teachers can model and transmit. Writing in the heady 1960s on the role of the teacher, Eric Hoyle (1969) highlighted the dilemmas teachers faced in seeking to model the 'right' values, especially when the teacher does not agree with them. John Dewey (1859–1952) pointed out: 'everything the teacher does, as well as the manner in which he does it, incites the child to respond in some way or other, and tends to set the child's attitude in some way or other' (Dewey, 1910: 48). Dewey was among many who understood the importance of the teacher as a role model in terms of 'morals, manners, habits of speech and social bearing'.

Dewey's emphasis on promoting democratic education has led to considerable interest in the dynamics of power within schools. The modern German philosopher and sociologist Jürgen Habermas (1991) conceived of 'ideal speech' through which participants attempt to reach consensus via open dialogue. This means that decisions are not based on role, status or authority. Rather, what mattered was competence in communicating – listening with empathy, reasoning and persuasive argument. One of the major challenges for the ethical educator is how to move beyond such rhetoric so that learners are genuinely included in the big decisions that affect school life. This must go beyond representative voices, such as school council members, to include the less articulate and less visible learners.

Richard Peters (1919–2011), former professor of philosophy at the Institute of Education in London, is regarded as the founding father of philosophy in education. He wrote *Ethics and Education* (1966) in which he sought to bring clarity to the aims of education. For Peters, education implied something worthwhile being transmitted in a morally acceptable manner, so conditioning and indoctrination would not be acceptable. He discussed the ethical question, 'Why do this rather than that?', in the context of justifying worthwhile classroom activities. This is a key question for all in education to reflect on, irrespective of their role, experience or qualification. Peters maintained that it was illogical to say that a man [sic] had been educated unless he had changed for the better. His legacy included the setting up of the Philosophy of Education Society and the *Journal of Philosophy of Education,* the leading journal in the field.

The most influential modern-day British philosophers in education include John White, Richard Pring and Paul Standish. Among their writings, White (2012) addresses the fundamental question of what education is for and who decides. Should educational aims be decided centrally by the government, or left to head teachers or individual teachers? What about parental opinion? Pring (2005) argues that education should be left in the hands of 'moral educators' rather than managers, trainers or those who 'deliver' the curriculum. He is concerned that this message is being lost in the technical language of education and that practices are losing their moral perspective. Standish et al. (2000) argue that much of what happens in the name of improving formal education is nihilistic or devoid of a moral basis, such as the school effectiveness movement and its preoccupation with advancing academic standards.

The theoretical basis for moral education in the modern age draws largely on two contrasting theories: social learning theory and cognitive theories of development. Social learning theory views teachers and schools as agents of socialisation, providing models of 'positive' values for children to imitate. The emphasis is on creating an appropriate environment – for example, in terms of language, rules, displays and routines. In a sense, pupils are seen to be very much recipients of the principles and fundamental beliefs that schools and society at large value. It is assumed that the role of the teacher is to influence children's moral development, consciously or otherwise – for example, in their attitudes, relationships and teaching manner. Social and cultural factors, rather than an individual's capacity to reason on moral issues, are seen as the keys to understanding children's moral development (Haidt, 2001).

The psychologist John Bowlby (1907–1990) emphasised the importance of establishing deep, trusting relationships between infants and one main (maternal) attachment figure. Such secure relationships promote social development (e.g. sharing), language skills and, significantly, later in life better empathy and 'theory of mind' (the ability to infer other people's thoughts). In short, infants with strong attachments grow up to do well at school and lead more contented lives. One of his most famous studies involved forty-four young thieves who had been referred to a child guidance clinic (Bowlby, 1944). He wanted to explore the long-term effects of maternal deprivation to see whether the delinquents had experienced deprivation as children. He set up a control group of forty-four children who had been referred to the clinic for emotional problems but not as criminals. Bowlby found that half of the juvenile thieves had been separated from their mothers for more than six months during their first five years of life, compared to only two in the control group. He also found that a third of the thieves showed no care or feelings for others (chillingly dubbed 'affectionless psychopaths'), whereas all members of the control group showed empathy.

Although the study has been criticised for ignoring other possible factors, such as diet, parental income and education, early childhood experts agree over the importance of building strong relationships as the basis for children's moral development. They focus on the experience of attachment to move the discourse away from moral judgements based entirely on logic and the pursuit of objective truths towards one where what matters most is morality based on care, compassion and love. Studies have shown that young children are perfectly capable of making moral decisions and showing empathy for others.

In contrast to social learning theory, cognitive theories of development emphasise the role of moral reasoning. Building on the work of Piaget, in the 1960s the American psychologist and philosopher Lawrence Kohlberg (1927–1987) put forward a highly influential theory of moral development that established morality as a legitimate subject of scientific research. For Kohlberg, children's morality could only be understood by considering how they developed their powers of reasoning. Kohlberg proposed that children pass through three distinct phases in their moral development (Figure 6.1), from a 'pre-conventional' stage when they simply 'follow the rules' to a 'post-conventional' stage when they engage critically with socially accepted behaviour. He based the theory on observing how children justified their actions when placed in similar moral dilemmas. Kohlberg's classic scenario was of a husband who breaks into a chemist shop to steal an anti-cancer drug for his wife who is dying of cancer. The chemist refuses to sell the drug for less than US$2,000, even though it cost only US$200 to make. The children are invited to say whether the husband was right or wrong. For Kohlberg, the most advanced moral thinking occurs when both sides of an argument can be understood or judgements are influenced by the context, whereas novices base their reasoning simply on the rules.

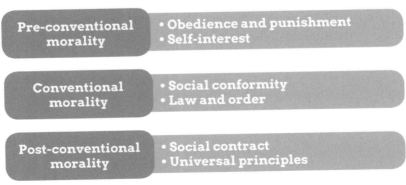

Figure 6.1. The stages of moral development (after Kohlberg, 1984).

Kohlberg concluded that children's moral development begins when they see rules as fixed and to be obeyed, or risk punishment. He did not think that young preschool children were capable of moving beyond the first stage in which they copied what adults did to invite praise or avoid anger. As they grow older, children begin to see that there are different views on what is right and wrong. But what matters to them most is 'what's in it for me?' – in other words, what rewards they can accumulate. At this stage of self-interest, rightness is about what is fair. The next developmental stage typically occurs in adolescence when young people see morality as social conformity and as going beyond making deals. They gain a sense of what 'good boys and girls' do and how they should live in terms of family and community expectations. They then begin to show an interest in how society functions as a whole, including the operation of law and order. Rightness here is seen in terms of contributing to society, groups or institutions. The final stages of moral development see young people understanding that values vary among groups in society but there are also universal principles that should be followed, such as respect for human rights, equality and justice.

Kohlberg's theory has inevitably attracted criticism over the years. Doubts have been cast over the cross-sectional (rather than longitudinal) research design, the validity of his sample (all boys aged between 10–16 years) and the hypothetical nature of the dilemmas (people might behave differently in real situations). Moreover, Kohlberg's theory has been attacked for its cultural bias towards Western liberal values. Perhaps the most significant criticism is that the theory is too rigid and linear, failing to acknowledge that children develop at different rates – not all children progress through the stages and a few slip back in their development.

Studies show that very young children (aged between 14–18 months) spontaneously want to help adults who drop something or need a door to be opened (Warneken and Tomasello, 2006, 2007, 2009). But when toddlers are rewarded for helping, perhaps with a sweet or coloured toy, the rewarded children don't help the adults on future occasions. It seems that very young children do not act to please their parents (Warneken and Tomasello, 2013). Those who are not given extrinsic rewards frequently help because they are intrinsically motivated to do so – provided they enjoy positive relationships (Music, 2014b). Interestingly, psychopaths who have taken Kohlberg's test have not necessarily achieved low scores.

This is probably because they are able to say one thing but act in a completely different way (Baron-Cohen, 2011).

All theories of moral development acknowledge the role adults play in shaping children's morality, including biological theories such as Marc Hauser's ideas about 'moral grammar' residing in the brain (Hauser, 2006).

Why is it important, and what can you do?

The importance of teachers as moral agents and the place of moral education in children's development are widely agreed on. As we have seen, most debate relates to how this works in practice. Global developments over recent years, including extremism, the ubiquitous Internet and a wide range of social problems, have refocused attention on what teachers and schools can contribute to the development of good, morally upright citizens.

Traditionally, the moral authority of teachers stood in place of parents during the school day (*in loco parentis*), a duty of care derived from the common law. The Children Act 1989 Section 3(5) defines duty of care to the effect that a person with care of a child may do what is reasonable in all circumstances for the purpose of safeguarding or promoting the welfare of the child. The modern view is that the teacher has independent authority by virtue of their status. The current legal position acknowledges that a teacher's duty of care to individual pupils is influenced by various factors, such as the subject being taught, available resources, the size of the class and the age of the children. Teachers are expected to take reasonable steps to avoid exposing pupils to dangers that are foreseeable and beyond those with which the particular pupils can reasonably be expected to cope. But this does not imply constant twenty-four hour direct supervision.

In the wake of concerns over radicalisation, teachers are expected to promote 'British values'. This is not straightforward. For one thing, it is debatable whether values such as democracy and tolerance of different faiths and beliefs are actually unique to Britain. Moreover, matters of identity – northerner, southerner, Londoner, English, Welsh, British, European, global citizen – are complex and often multilayered. Professional development certainly needs to explore and challenge stereotypical views of ethnic groups and focus on the humanity that brings people together.

In 2014, Former Education Secretary Michael Gove wrote to all schools and colleges in England urging them to be alert to signs of radicalisation and exploitation. He advised those who work with children and young people to assume that 'it could happen here'. In 2015, the Westminster government provided guidance (the Channel programme, part of the Prevent strategy) for those in danger of being drawn into terrorism (HM Government, 2015). The guidance includes a list of warning signs that an individual might be engaged with an extremist group, cause or ideology. These include changes in the style of dress in accord with the group, possession of materials or symbols associated with an extremist cause (e.g. the swastika for far-right groups) and attempts to recruit others to the cause, group or ideology.

Organisations such as the British Humanist Association have raised concerns over the teaching of sex and relationships in faith schools in ways that are discriminatory (e.g. against girls or homosexuals) or otherwise inadequate (e.g. promoting an abstinence-only education rather than discussing contraception or abortion). Dan Hodges (2014) would get rid of faith schools altogether because he argues that they promote narrow ideological views that do not prepare children for life in a modern, diverse Britain. Around a third of all state-funded schools are schools 'with a religious character' – the legal term for faith schools. The Church of England and the Roman Catholic Church provide the vast majority of these (around 98%). Government guidance recommends that in order to avoid insularity and conflict, faith schools should take into account the interests and sensibilities of the whole community. On the back of the Trojan Horse affair, the government decided to introduce a requirement that all schools should promote the British values of democracy, the rule of law, individual liberty and mutual respect and tolerance for those of different faiths and beliefs. This has proved contentious. Sir Edward Leigh, Conservative MP and president of the Catholic Union of Great Britain, argues that faith schools should stand tall and that the real British values are Christian values: love for God and neighbour, pursuit of truth, high aspiration and discipline (Espinoza, 2015a).

Religious beliefs certainly shape how people respond to moral conflicts. In some religions, such as Islam, morality is very much a community matter and it is considered appropriate for religious leaders to enforce moral behaviour. In the context of teaching at a university,

Halstead (2011) asked undergraduate students to write a contemporary list of seven deadly sins. The results indicated big differences between Muslim students and the rest (Christian, atheists and agnostics). For the Muslim students, there was a strong emphasis on behaviour condemned in the Quran, such as gambling, drinking alcohol and going behind one's parents' back. The non-Muslim students were more likely to include contemporary issues like racism, child abuse, homophobia, environmental damage and hypocrisy. The Muslim students drew on religious beliefs and traditional authority more so than the other students. Halstead suggests that moral education in schools presupposes certain 'Western' values that are not shared by all groups in society. He calls on teachers to be more aware of differences in moral language and cultural values if they want to fully engage *all* students.

Teachers' own conduct

History tells us that the moral examples set by parents and teachers – that is, who they are as people – matter more to children in the long term than what they teach. Consider the story of Albert Speer (1905–1981), Hitler's former friend, architect and munitions minister, who was once described as 'the Nazi who said sorry' (BBC, 1996). Reflecting on his crimes later in life, Speer confessed that although he had the 'best' education available at that time, it lacked any moral sense. Speer claims that he was unable to connect the statistics of manual workers whom he organised as slaves to the stories of the real people behind them. Speer's story illustrates how highly 'educated' individuals have been responsible for atrocities.

In our own times, we know that many of those recruited to Isis are not from low-income, poorly educated backgrounds. Rather, the likes of 'Jihadi John' (Mohammed Emwazi), the frontman in a number of grisly beheading videos, graduated from the University of Westminster with a computer science degree. Elsewhere, studies of the genocide in Rwanda show that well-educated professionals, including teachers and doctors, were responsible for some of the most heinous crimes. Yet those who risked their lives to save others were often the very poor (Heydenberk and Heydenberk, 2015). The story of Samuel Oliner is revealing here. He was a Jewish boy rescued by a Catholic peasant woman in Nazi-occupied Poland. Oliner became a sociologist and devoted his career to the study of altruism. He wanted to know what distinguished heroes from villains. His story highlights that it is the *quality* of relationships, rather than the level of education, that matters (Oliner, 2001, 2004). The good guys had been brought up with values such as independent thinking, care and respect for humanitarian principles such as justice, rather than values such as compliance and obedience. More recent studies (e.g. Killen and Smetana, 2013) have confirmed that the influence of the home and early childhood education is critical to a child's moral development, while teachers who highlight the intrinsic value of learning can help children to respond appropriately to others.

An understanding of ethics can help teachers to steer a sensible course through the challenges posed by teaching in the technological age where their conduct, or misconduct, which in previous times was known by a few, can be exposed to millions. In their role as moral educators, surely the biggest challenge is dealing with the threat to children and young people's well-being posed by digital technologies, particularly the Internet and social media. The most important moral imperative is to protect children and young people from physical and emotional harm. Children need to be safe and secure, both in the classroom and in the virtual world.

In terms of teachers' own conduct, very few cases of unethical behaviour are brought before the authorities. Nonetheless, it is essential to heed advice from trade unions and professional bodies, particularly in an age when texting, emailing and social media are so prevalent and are radically changing teacher–pupil relationships. Teachers can sometimes be put in awkward situations through no fault of their own or by simple oversight. Henley (2009) discusses the case of a 37-year-old male teacher, in a mixed west London secondary school, who received a text who it later transpired came from a pupil saying, 'Sir u r fit'. He didn't know who it was from and ignored the text. He then received a follow-up, 'Lets have fun lol'. He continued to ignore the text messages he received from different phone numbers over a month or so until they became abusive. In another case, an English teacher at a private school in the East Midlands was caught unawares when a girl took a picture of her on a camera phone when the teacher was bending down to pick something up. The picture then appeared on a social media site in a 'guess the bum' competition. Interestingly, although the girls were apologetic when found out, the teacher was not convinced that they thought they had done anything wrong. In a third case, a teacher responded at night to an enquiry from a sixth-form student about when an assignment should be handed in; he signed off and sent a reply as is his norm when sending emails with 'xx' before it dawned on him how this might be misinterpreted by parents and others. Fortunately, nothing came of this, but these cases illustrate the new territories teachers find themselves in and the care they need to take both in and out of school. The social distance and boundaries between teachers and pupils has narrowed as a consequence of technological change. It has created what one teacher calls a culture of 'new chumminess' (Henley, 2009).

The situation is complicated by the active encouragement of teachers to use the Internet and other technologies as educational resources – for instance, in supporting pupils with homework. Ethical dilemmas can easily arise when schools instruct teachers not to give out their personal mobile phone numbers to students and yet, during a trip, a teacher might decide to do so for fear of losing a child. The number then can be easily passed around.

There is certain conduct that is unacceptable in the profession. While friendly relationships between teachers and pupils are important in building mutual trust and an environment that is conducive to learning, there are clear lines to be drawn. It is an abuse of a teacher's professional status to:

» Enter into an improper association with a pupil.

» Show undue personal favour or disfavour towards a pupil.

» Commit such acts against a child which are illegal.

» Endeavour to exert an undue influence with regard to personal attitudes, opinions or behaviour which are in no way connected with the work of the school.[1]

These are the more obvious examples of unethical conduct. But most teachers face more mundane challenges, such as avoiding gossiping about students and their families or colleagues, being habitually late for meetings or appointments and generally not pulling their weight in terms

---

1 See the NUT Code of Professional Ethics at: https://www.teachers.org.uk/files/active/0/NUT-Code-of-Professional-Ethics.pdf.

of staff workload. The overriding consideration should be, 'What is the right thing to do?' Oser (1991) reports that teachers typically use the following strategies when faced with moral dilemmas:

1. **Avoiding** – 'solving' the problem by not facing it.
2. **Delegating** – the teacher delegates the responsibility to others such as the head.
3. **Single-handed decision making** – the teacher assumes responsibility and becomes the 'expert' who has the ability to settle the problem but often in an authoritarian manner.
4. **Discourse 1** – the teacher accepts responsibility for resolving the problem and explains how he/she has balanced justice, care and truthfulness in each situation.
5. **Discourse 2** – the teacher goes one step further and presupposes that everyone, including children, have an interest in and are capable of balancing justice, care and truthfulness.

An understanding of ethics is important in other areas of a practitioner's professional life, such as when conducting research and engaging with parents. The British Educational Research Association (BERA) provides guidelines on the responsibilities to participants, sponsors, the wider education community, fellow professionals and the general public (BERA, 2011). The overriding principles include avoiding harming others, gaining voluntary informed consent from participants, respecting privacy and being transparent about the research process and outcomes. For early years' practitioners, the British Association for Early Childhood Education's Code of Ethics provides guidance on researching early childhood (Early Education, 2011).

Being an ethical teacher is not only about one's personal conduct. It is also about relating to others. Teachers need to be considerate of the feelings and views of colleagues, show compassion when others are in difficulties, care about their professional reputation and that of the school and show courage to stand up for what is morally right, even when this is difficult to do so – for instance, reporting the misconduct of a colleague who is a close friend. The popular media are quick to pick up on teacher indiscretion – one study found that stories about teachers in civil and criminal cases occupied 29 per cent of newspaper coverage of all teacher-related issues in the tabloids compared to 7 per cent in 'quality newspapers' (Hargreaves et al., 2008). From examining newspaper reports, the authors conclude that there is a sense of the profession under siege – decent, hardworking, professional, committed teachers under attack from funding cuts, pay freezes, deterioration in pensions, discipline problems, changes in education policy, job-related stress and a decline in social values. Teachers in the UK are not held in high esteem compared to other professions or teaching in other countries. Within this broader context, it is challenging to maintain professionalism day in, day out, but the vast majority of practitioners do so. They understand that they are powerful role models in how they speak and act and take these responsibilities seriously.

Although rare, when teachers are found to have behaved in a seriously unethical manner the impact can be severe. Page (2013) refers to the emotional damage for individual pupils directly involved, other pupils being affected when their teacher is suddenly suspended, the additional burden on colleagues who may have to cover classes and the wider sensationalism in the press that affects the school. Given the strains on teachers, it is therefore remarkable how very few cases of unethical conduct in the profession are reported. The vast majority of teachers and other practitioners demonstrate a commitment to teaching because they want to work with children and believe passionately that they can make a difference by improving their life chances.

Teachers and moral education

We have known for many years that there is a close association between teachers' own moral conduct, shaped by their beliefs, values and experiences, and how they educate children (Hoyle, 1969). For ethical teachers, moral education is not confined to set lessons, fundraising activities and occasions such as assemblies. Rather, it is imbued in the life of the school. It is reflected in the playground, in the lunch hall, visual displays, school rules and regulations, staffroom discussions and school visits. Teachers need the ethical knowledge to guide what they say, think and do. Ethical teachers allow their consciences or 'inner voices' to guide their behaviour. They do not hide or seek to blame others when things go wrong. Rather, they step up to the mark and do not baulk at accountability and responsibility. When teachers think ethically, they are considering something or someone other than themselves.

At the core of ethical teaching is respecting universal human rights. Chris Riddell, the Children's Laureate, has produced an excellent introduction on human rights for children, *My Little Book of Big Freedoms: The Human Rights Act in Pictures* (2015). Organisations such as UNICEF have also made an important contribution to raising the profile of children's rights. For instance, the Rights Respecting Schools Award (RRSA) was introduced to acknowledge schools where the United Nations Convention on the Rights of the Child was at the heart of the school in terms of planning, practice and ethos. An independent three-year evaluation of the impact of RRSA reports 'life-changing experiences' (Sebba and Robinson, 2010). Gains include greater cohesion within the school community and improved skills in areas such as decision making and independence. On balance, there is no doubt that giving children and young people a genuine say in all aspects of school life is more of a help than a hindrance to creating a learning environment built on trust, respect and fairness rather than fear, power and inequality.

Most schools nowadays use a range of strategies to promote good social and moral values. These include peer support systems such as buddy schemes, counselling, mediation and conflict resolution approaches. Research shows that provided students are well trained, they are able to offer good support to peers troubled by experiences such as isolation, victimisation and rejection. The benefits extend also to the helpers and the wider school community. Cooperative learning, where there is an emphasis on group work to solve common problems, respectful dialogue and task sharing can result in more caring, supportive and committed relationships than competitive and individualistic learning (Slavin, 1987, 2011; Kagan and Kagan, 1994). So it is important to provide opportunities for pupils to work collaboratively, debate issues in a respectful manner, explore sources such as newspaper headlines which raise conflicting opinions and take on social responsibilities.

Many games lend themselves to promoting empathy and teamwork, including these for young children:

» **Count to ten** – the aim is to count to ten as a group randomly, one child calling out 'one', another 'two', another 'three' and so on. No two children are allowed to say a number at the same time. If this happens, everyone starts again. The idea is to encourage children to use body language such as eye contact and learn to wait.

» **Eye contact swaps** – two people establish eye contact across a circle. Without a word, each nods three times and then gets up and crosses the circle to sit in the other's seat. Only two individuals can stand up at any time. The point of the exercise is to encourage others to play and learn patience.

» **Pairs** – the children work in pairs with each given a card on which is a familiar conflict scenario (e.g. A and B both want the same reading book). They have to suggest as many solutions as possible (Goodall, 2007: 35–36).

Many schools have invested in values-based programmes and approaches such as Philosophy for Children (www.philosophy4children.co.uk), where there is a strong emphasis on sharing feelings, ideas, experiences and perspectives. New Labour's education strategy in the mid-2000s featured the Social and Emotional Aspects of Learning (SEAL) programme, now stored on the National Archives website (e.g. DfES, 2005, 2007). It was designed to improve academic standards, behaviour and attendance. Evaluations of SEAL reported mixed success, however, with primary schools doing better than secondary schools – largely because of implementation issues. Research indicates that values-based programmes, such as Roots of Empathy, reduce levels of aggression among children and make them more responsive to the feelings of others (Scott, 2010). Many teachers seek to resolve difficulties within their own classrooms in a way that exposes all the pupils to a shared experience of resolving difficulties, with an emphasis on cooperation and responsibility for action (Oser and Althof, 1993). Other researchers have found that private talk, or one-to-one dialogue, is the most prevalent strategy used by teachers to resolve moral dilemmas (Maslovaty, 2000).

Every lesson has a moral dimension. The content itself might involve questions about right and wrong, fairness, bias, prejudice or tolerance. In history, this could involve discussions over what sources tell us (and do not tell us), who recorded the information and why, whether they are incomplete in some way or could be challenged by other sources. In science lessons, there are moral issues concerning the collection and presentation of data (e.g. anonymity, confidentiality, accuracy) and the treatment of subjects. It can be useful to audit schemes of work and library resources with a view to noting how inclusive planning and resources provision is – for example, in history, how much coverage is given to under-represented groups such as women, children and those from ethnic minority backgrounds?

There is considerable advice available to practitioners on how to handle moral and ethical dilemmas within the curriculum. Organisations such as Oxfam (2006), the Historical Association (2007) and the Association for Science Education (www.ase.org.uk) provide guidance on teaching controversial issues in areas such as religion, politics, evolution, climate change and personal lifestyle. In history lessons, for instance, it is important for learners to understand that people's actions need to be judged by the values of the age in which they lived. In RE lessons, asking the question, 'What would I do?', is a useful strategy to prompt learners to think about the complexities and choices people face. It can be insightful to look at a situation from different perspectives, such as bystander, victim, perpetrator and rescuer. There are plenty of stories in local and national news that provide opportunities for classroom discussion and debate, including housing, immigration, environmental damage, poverty, mobile phones and social media.

Foremost, teachers and learners need to understand why an issue is controversial. Often it is because there is a lack of consensus, the evidence to support a viewpoint is debatable or the consequences of particular actions raise ethical or moral concerns. The Ajegbo report *Diversity & Citizenship: A Curriculum Review* (DCSF, 2007a) pointed out that pupils are very interested in debates on controversial but deeply relevant issues. The process challenges misinformed views and helps to build understanding and appreciation. External groups such as theatre companies can also prove effective in setting up dilemmas to inform discussions.

Teaching is certainly among the most ethically demanding professions. It is one thing to agree on virtues such as respect, tolerance, honesty and fairness, but another for all staff in a school to apply these consistently. Oser (1991) suggests that moral conflicts in educational settings arise when teachers struggle to meet the moral claims of justice, care and truthfulness. Other writers have upheld, in particular, care as a critical aspect of making moral judgements (Noddings, 1992; Tirri, 1999).

Each day teachers face moral decisions about how they respond to situations. Here are a few examples from teachers I have spoken to:

» One girl in the class has poor personal hygiene. To be frank, she smells. I wasn't sure how to tell her.

» I hesitated but gave out my personal telephone number to a Year 10 student because she said she needed someone to talk to when not at school.

» A Year 12 student asked for an extension to hand in her homework. I said it would be okay because I believed she had genuine reasons, although she hadn't followed the school procedure.

» The school policy is for pupils not to bring mobile phones into the classroom. I really think we are missing opportunities to use such technologies for learning but I'm not sure what I can do.

» The head asked me to cover for another teacher, a friend, who reported sick. I know she wasn't unwell and had taken the day off to take her son to university.

The nature of these kinds of dilemmas inevitably involves a wrestling of the mind. But as Lyons (1990: 168) has noted, 'many of the dilemmas of teaching are not solvable and must simply be managed rather than resolved'.

There should be a moral dimension to what teachers do, from planning lessons to organising educational visits, from allocating roles in the school play to relating to colleagues, parents and the wider community. Children and young people, as well as colleagues and parents, have a right to be treated fairly, honestly and with respect. They place their trust and confidence in the teachers who are responsible for caring for them. Children know when teachers (and others) have a genuine interest in their well-being and soon pick up on hypocrisy.

Conclusion

This chapter highlights the importance of a strong moral purpose in all that teachers do. This includes a commitment to narrowing the gap between the achievement of high and low performers in school. It also means providing an environment that is conducive to learning and growth. But teaching within an ethical framework is challenging

– for example, balancing the needs of an individual against the class, respecting confidentiality or weighing up personal feelings over what is right for children against school policies and practices and government directives.

Moreover, teachers should not rely on others or ethical codes to determine how they should behave. They are responsible for moderating their own behaviour. As Campbell (2003) argues, in the interests of ethical professionalism, teachers need to assume and exercise moral responsibility, individually and collectively. While gathering evidence for his review of teacher training, Sir Andrew Carter commented on the 'tremendous sense of moral purpose that is a distinguishing characteristic of this noble profession' (Carter, 2015: 4). The vast majority of educators know that the moral dimension to what they do is fundamental to children's all-round development.

Summary

» Teaching is a profession governed by a code of ethics.
» The vast majority of staff in school act in an ethical manner, in keeping with their professional standing.
» Teaching does raise ethical issues that, by their very nature, are not straightforward to resolve.
» Religion is never far from discussions over ethics.
» Much has been said about the moral purpose of education. Essentially this means doing what is right for children and young people.
» To be well educated certainly involves more than academic achievement. It calls for moral sensitivity to others.

Points for reflection and action

» What is the most challenging ethical dilemma you have faced in your professional practice? How did you respond?
» If a pupil asked you to keep something confidential, how would you respond? Are there any situations where you would respect pupil confidentiality?

» Do you know what signs of radicalisation and abuse to look out for in students?

» During 2015, in Atlanta, USA, twenty teachers were imprisoned for altering the test scores of their pupils. One principal wore gloves to erase answers and write in new ones. Another teacher justified her actions before the judge by saying that she believed this was necessary, in order to improve the chances of pupils staying on at school and participating more fully in American society (see http://www.nytimes.com/2015/04/15/us/atlanta-school-workers-sentenced-in-test-score-cheating-case.html?_r=0). Was she right?

Chapter 7

Instruction

Direct instruction is a tried-and-tested means of effective teaching

What is the big idea?

If you ever observe young children 'playing school' then, for many observers, this illustrates what direct instruction means. The teacher is in the prominent position, telling children what to do, explaining things, setting out the resources and correcting when necessary. However, direct instruction is often misunderstood or misrepresented and, as John Hattie (2009: 205) points out, 'has a bad name for the wrong reasons'. Criticisms of direct instruction come from all quarters. These include the rather bizarre accusations that it is part of a Christian right-wing conspiracy, concerns over the reliability of supporting evidence, claims that it increases student stress, that produces compliant children who have very little opportunity for participation and ideological fears that it amounts to indoctrination (e.g. Berliner, 1996; Hayes, 1999). Much of this is dross. Direct instruction is a tried-and-tested approach that significantly moves learners on in their learning. In any event, the big idea here is not that direct instruction should be used on *all* occasions, but that it has an important place alongside other approaches within the teacher's repertoire.

Direct instruction is based on using carefully structured lessons and a clearly defined teaching sequence (see Figure 7.1). It is based on the following principles:

» All children can be taught.
» All children can improve academically and in terms of self-image.
» All teachers can succeed if provided with adequate training and materials.
» Low performers and disadvantaged learners must be taught at a faster rate than typically occurs, if they are to catch up with their higher performing peers.
» All details of instruction must be controlled to minimise the chance of students' misinterpreting the information being taught and to maximise the reinforcing effect of instruction.

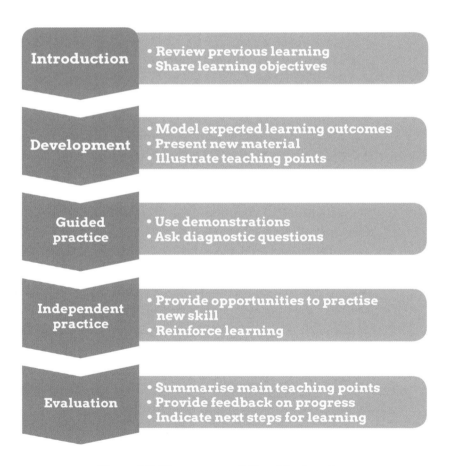

Figure 7.1. The process of direct instruction.

Introduction

The introduction of a lesson is an important time for teachers to set the scene, to 'hook' learners in and to make the purpose of the session clear. Under the direct instruction model, most teachers begin by reviewing previous learning. It is critical to ensure that pupils have fully understood material previously taught before moving on to new learning. If they do not, then the lesson should be retaught. The review itself can take various forms, such as quizzes, verbal games or question-and-answer interchange using checklists, summaries, picture or sound prompts, including rhymes and songs and visual diagrams. Homework assigned in the previous lesson should also be checked before moving on.

Many teachers now, as a routine, share learning objectives (i.e. intended outcomes, goals or targets) with the class. This is an important feature of assessment for learning (see Chapter 9). Clearly defined objectives provide focus and direction. As Gunter et al. (2007: 43) point out, 'without a clearly defined end, a person can be swimming toward any number of beaches'. Learning or instructional objectives are framed in terms of what learners should *know, understand* and be able to *do*, and this knowledge, understanding and doing (KUD) formula operates across all subjects. When expressed in this manner, it makes assessment more straightforward. Approaching the curriculum in this way is called 'backward design' (Wiggins and McTighe, 2005) – teachers begin planning with the end point in mind (the enduring understandings or big ideas) and work back from this point to collect evidence to show this understanding (e.g. through tests or observations), to choose appropriate resources and to plan the teaching methods.

An important cautionary note regarding learning objectives is that if they are too narrowly conceived they can have a negative effect on outcomes other than those specified in the objectives. What this means is that as learners concentrate on achieving the set objectives, they may miss out on knowledge incidental to the concept or skill. This is the reason why some writers suggest that learners should have the opportunity to personalise teachers' goals (e.g. Marzano et al., 2001). A useful thing to remember is to express learning objectives in terms of verbs (see Table 7.1) – to *describe* accurately what happened at the end of the story, to *know* the features of a motte-and-bailey castle, to *design* a new mobile toy for a baby, to *compare* arguments for and against the opening of a new road.

Level	Examples of associated verbs	Examples of questions
Knowledge	Define, match, name, list, spell, show, recall, tell	What is the name of ...? When did this happen? Who were the main ...? Can you list four ...? Who did this? How do you spell ...?
Comprehension	Compare, contrast, explain, classify, rephrase, summarise	What are the differences between ...? Can you explain ...? What is meant by ...? What is the main point here?
Application	Apply, build, choose, construct, develop, interview, organise, plan, select, solve, use, model, identify	How would you use ...? What examples can you find to ...? How would you solve ... using what you have learned? How would you organise ... to show ...? How would you show your understanding of ...? What approach would you use to ...? What questions would you ask in an interview with ...?
Analysis	Analyse, categorise, classify, compare, contrast, discover, dissect, divide, examine, inspect, simplify, survey, test	What are the parts or features of ...? How is ... related to ...? Why do you think ...? What is the theme of ...? What motive is there in ...? Can you list the parts of ...? What inference can you make? What conclusions can you draw about ...?

Level	Examples of associated verbs	Examples of questions
Synthesis	Choose, combine, compile, compose, construct, create, design, develop, estimate, formulate, imagine, invent, originate, plan, predict, propose	What changes would you make to solve ...? How would you improve ...? What would happen if ...? Can you elaborate? Can you propose an alternative to ...? Can you invent ...? How would you adapt ... to create a different ...? Can you predict the outcome if ...?
Evaluation	Assess, award, conclude, criticise, defend, determine, dispute, evaluate, interpret, judge, justify, mark, measure, rate, recommend, agree, explain, appraise	Do you agree with the actions ...? Or with the outcomes ...? What is your opinion of ...? How would you prove ... and disprove ...? Can you assess the value or importance of ...? Would it be better if ...? Why did they (the character) choose ...? What would you recommend? How would you rate ...?

Table 7.1. Verbs for writing learning objectives and questions based on Bloom's taxonomy.

It is more demanding to write objectives for learners' emotional development because they deal with attitudes and feelings which are relatively difficult to observe and measure. In a sense, behaviours are specified indirectly and the 'evidence' of their achievement is taken from what a learner does or says. So, in a lesson on developing positive attitudes towards healthy eating, an objective might be along the lines of appreciating the importance of a nutritious diet. The observable behaviours (not necessarily in the lesson) might include whether learners respond enthusiastically to the messages, choose a healthy option for school dinner, avoid junk food themselves or persuade their parents to buy healthier food.

Development

Modelling is a very powerful technique in teaching. Showing learners the kinds of things expected at the end of the lesson takes the mystery out of learning and helps to minimise the 'guess-what's-inside-my-head' routine practised by some teachers. So, for instance, if the main activity is for learners to bake a cake, write a 'get well' card or compose a haiku, then seeing examples can alleviate learner anxieties. This does not mean taking the creativity out of learning and it is not intended to produce clone-like end products. The BBC's long-running children's programme *Blue Peter*, and its strapline 'Here's one we made earlier' – the subject of a 2014 exhibition at The Lowry in Salford – illustrates the power of modelling.

Even when adults do not deliberately teach by example, children model themselves on those around them. They pick up both verbal and non-verbal behaviours. This is also the case beyond the school gates, as any observation of children at play reveals – they are quick to celebrate a goal in the manner of their football heroes or perform a song in the style of the latest pop star. Deliberate use of modelling is very much part of behaviourism, with its emphasis on rewarding desirable behaviour and sanctioning the less desirable.

Guided practice

The point of guided practice is to ensure that pupils are ready to work on their own. To this end, teachers who follow the direct instruction model make use of telling and demonstrations. Whenever a new tool or piece of equipment is introduced (e.g. scissors), children should be told the 'ground rules' of how to handle them correctly. Rogoff (1990) uses the term 'guided participation' to describe an apprenticeship approach where children learn from observing and practising alongside adults who model the desired behaviours and values of, for example, artists, mathematicians and geographers. There are times when it is practically difficult or impossible for children to find things out for themselves – for instance, they can guess but do not know the names of objects or people without being told and are unlikely to know the appropriate social conventions when visiting a particular place for the first time. Telling and demonstrating are also effective strategies in terms of promoting a healthy lifestyle, such as washing your hands after using the toilet or before preparing food.

Hand in hand with telling is the use of demonstrations. These show learners how to do things, such as the correct way of using materials and tools or how to accomplish a particular task. Sometimes teachers need to take the lead and show how something is done correctly, perhaps when children have forgotten something or when they need to learn a new skill. Effective demonstrators use clear language and break up the task into small, sequential steps. They deliver a running commentary on the demonstration and then provide lots of opportunities for pupils to practise the new skill or technique.

Throughout the different stages of the direct instruction model, teachers use diagnostic questions to see where pupils are at in relation to achieving the learning objectives. These questions are not usually wide open, viewpoint questions; rather, they are designed to converge on particular answers. Teachers also signal their intent by letting pupils know that they will be asked questions on the topic in hand, along the lines of: 'In two minutes, I want to review what you have done and so think about what you will say. I will ask you about …' To encourage pupils who are usually reluctant to speak out in class, one suggestion is to ask everyone to jot down their answers on a sticky note or piece of paper and pass them to the front of the class. These can then be read aloud, and if the pupils who never speak out are correct, they can be invited to read out the answers. Once this becomes a routine, pupils gain confidence to contribute orally.

Independent practice

Once learners have understood the content or skill, they need time to reinforce this on their own or in small groups. So, for instance, if learners appear to have grasped the skill of scanning for key information in a history book, they should then work independently to demonstrate the skill in another context such as scanning a magazine or television schedule. The role of the teacher at this stage is to circulate among the children, checking that no one is repeating a mistake or making errors. Pupils should have opportunities to check their own progress – for example, comparing their responses (e.g. with the correct answers) or using calculators, dictionaries and other reference materials. Wall charts and other visuals can provide useful prompts and reminders on, for instance, key vocabulary and the kinds of strategies learners can follow when they get 'stuck'.

One of the controversial aspects of direct instruction is the pace of lessons. On the one hand, fast-paced sessions provide momentum and sustain pupils' interest. Through daily practice, pupils have regular opportunities to consolidate their understanding of a particular concept until they 'get it'. The expectation is that lessons designed to teach basic skills are paced in such a way that during weekly and monthly reviews of progress, around 90–95 per cent of pupils should be able to respond correctly (Muijs and Reynolds, 2011: 41). However, the quick pace of lessons is not conducive to promoting higher order thinking or when learners need time to reflect on content.

Evaluation

Although it is customary to provide feedback *after* a learning experience, there is good reason to use feedback *before* and *during* sessions. Feedback before a session enables the learner to recognise areas for development and how these can be addressed. The immediacy of feedback during the learning experience means that learners can work on what is fresh in their minds. Good teachers provide continual feedback through verbal and non-verbal means, such as a smile or gesture to show approval. But feedback is most effective when it focuses on what children need to do next in order to move their learning forward or in more depth. Under the direct instruction model, corrective feedback is important – teachers make it clear what is wrong and how to put it right. They use mistakes as positive teaching points and encourage learners to justify their approaches or choice of resources. When presenting their work, learners are encouraged to provide feedback to each other using the learning goals as a measure.

Who is behind it?

The model of direct instruction originated with Siegfried Engelmann (b. 1931), an American professor of education, and his colleagues in the 1960s (Engelmann and Carnine, 1982). Their study, known as Project

Follow Through, was the largest controlled comparative study of teaching techniques in history. Between 1967 and 1995, more than 700,000 children in 170 disadvantaged communities across the United States participated in this US$1 billion study to discover the best practices for teaching underprivileged students. They found that carefully scripted instructional programmes were very effective with low-achieving pupils from poor socio-economic backgrounds. Although there were criticisms of how the data was captured, subsequent studies have confirmed that direct instruction raises standards in basic skills (Hattie, 2009).

Direct instruction draws on a behavioural theory of learning and the work of the psychologist B. F. Skinner (1963). He showed that rats could be trained to do certain things, like push a lever, through a process of conditioning. Every time the rat performed as desired it received a reward, thereby reinforcing the behaviour. Although educators naturally recoil from comparing children's learning to experiments with rats, nonetheless Skinner and others have shown that carefully planned training programmes can be highly effective in changing behaviours.

Robert Gagné (1916–2002), an American educational psychologist, has contributed significantly to the literature on direct instruction. Gagné (1985) suggests that direct instruction works well where motor skills or prerequisite intellectual skills are involved, such as learning grammatical rules and mathematical principles. He provided a framework to enable instructors to create lessons where every part was based on evidence-based principles of what works effectively. Gagné recommended that learners follow a particular sequence until they have mastered the intended outcome. This begins with gaining the attention of learners, sharing learning objectives, displaying the content and then moves on to feedback and transferring knowledge to other contexts. Robert Marzano, chief executive of Marzano Research, is another key contributor in the field of direct instruction. He argues that no amount of research will provide 'an airtight model of instruction' (Marzano et al., 2001).

One of the criticisms of direct instruction is that it is formulaic and can limit teachers to rigidly following a three- or four-part lesson. This same criticism was levelled against the national literacy and numeracy strategies (1998–2011), one of the most ambitious applications of direct instruction in recent times. The strategies were introduced to address underperformance in pupils' literacy and numeracy skills by providing a tight and clear framework for teachers' planning. The literacy hour meant: fifteen minutes of whole-class reading or writing; fifteen minutes on word and sentence work; twenty minutes of group work; and a ten-minute plenary. The structure of the numeracy hour was slightly less prescriptive and was based on a whole-class 'starter' activity, the main lesson and a plenary. The Department for Education and Employment advised teachers to 'spend as much time as possible in direct teaching and questioning of the whole class, a group of pupils, or individuals' (see Muijs and Reynolds, 2011: 48). Critics claimed that it led to a 'tick box' mentality where nothing was covered very well and 'only the quick survived' (Burkard, 2004: 6). But evaluations indicated that the strategies did contribute to higher standards of attainment and improvements in the quality of teachers' planning (DfE, 2011b). The strategies were particularly useful for inexperienced and weaker teachers who needed the additional support in structuring their lessons to ensure there was progression in the learning.

There are numerous myths associated with direct instruction. One of the most enduring is that it is the same as lecturing or didactic teaching. It is not. It is very much an umbrella concept that has at its core the quality of interaction between teacher and learners. It calls on a wide range of skills, including setting goals, communicating effectively, modelling, questioning, flexible thinking, reinforcement and feedback. Its aim is for learners to retain knowledge and achieve 'mastery' learning, where they continue to work at a task until they successfully demonstrate the intended learning outcomes.

Direct instruction (also called explicit or instructivist teaching) is one of the approaches that irritates progressive educationalists eager to 'follow the child'. Supporters point to the indisputable evidence that it works. It has twice the impact in learning gains than enquiry-based approaches (Hattie, 2009). It enables teachers to communicate information in an efficient (i.e. use of time and other resources) and effective (i.e. in terms of impact) manner. Whole-class teaching methods feature strongly, with teachers demonstrating, illustrating and summarising key points. Group and individual work reinforce learning.

Why is it important, and what can you do?

The evidence indicates that the key elements of direct instruction – such as sharing the purpose of the lesson, whole-class questioning, modelling and summarising – all contribute to effective teaching and learning (Muijs and Reynolds, 2011). But this does not mean that teachers need to slavishly follow this approach in all circumstances. For example, teachers might opt to start a topic using an enquiry-based approach – the children might enter the room to find there are floury footprints everywhere and the bin has been turned over. What has happened? Or the class might visit a local park, castle or other attraction to begin an investigation. But it is also the case that during an enquiry-based approach there are times for simply telling learners what to do. The decision as to which approach, or the relative balance of approaches, to use in any particular context depends on many factors, including the teacher's subject knowledge and the intended outcomes. Direct instruction works well when focusing on the transfer of knowledge but it is less effective when it comes to developing higher order skills and independent learning. Its structure also appeals to low-achieving pupils from disadvantaged backgrounds. Direct instruction is not a soft option – it requires very secure knowledge of both the subject and the learners in order to avoid potential pitfalls, such as chalk-and-talk style lecturing from the front of the classroom which allows little room for pupils to contribute.

In order to ensure consistency in the quality of teaching, there are well-evidenced strategies that should be applied throughout schools. Marzano et al. (2001) have identified nine key strategies that have a high likelihood of making a difference for students' achievement, based on a synthesis of research over several decades:

1. Identifying similarities and differences – e.g. using Venn diagrams.
2. Summarising and note taking – e.g. focusing on topic sentences, reciprocal teaching.
3. Reinforcing effort and providing recognition – e.g. providing feedback on effort, illustrating the connection between effort and achievement, using 'pause, prompt and praise'.
4. Homework and practice – e.g. through tasks focused on practising particular skills and with teachers' comments as feedback.

5. Non-linguistic representations – e.g. making physical models, drawing pictures and pictographs.
6. Cooperative learning – e.g. through mixed-ability groups and informal groupings such as 'turn to your neighbour'.
7. Setting objectives and providing feedback – e.g. personalising learning goals, correcting misconceptions, providing criteria-referenced feedback, self-assessment.
8. Generating and testing hypotheses – e.g. through historical investigations, inventions and problem-solving tasks.
9. Cues, questions and advance organisers – e.g. providing prompts about things, people, actions and events, using question stems, skimming information.

While most of these are supported across the educational research community, others are more contentious, such as the use of homework, mixed-ability groupings and praise. Ultimately, the key point is *how* these strategies are used and the quality of interaction between teachers and pupils. Moreover, these strategies do not mean that instruction should be rigid or didactic. Marzano and colleagues recommend that educators use the nine strategies across a unit of work in three phases. At the beginning, teachers are encouraged to set learning goals using 'I can' statements so they become more personal. These can be recorded in a learning journal and the pupils invited to discuss in pairs how they could achieve these. During the unit, pupils are expected to keep track of their progress towards meeting the goals and the effort they expend (e.g. recorded using a simple rating scale). They make sense of new knowledge by using strategies such as comparing this to what they already know, taking notes and creating visual representations. They actively contribute to summarising what they have learned. Homework is set to enable learners to practise and reinforce learning. Finally, at the end of the unit, learners are expected to contribute to an evaluation of the new knowledge and skills they have acquired.

Conclusion

The ultimate aim of direct instruction is to accelerate the performance of learners or, as Hattie (2009: 206) puts it, 'teach more in less clock time'.

The evidence points clearly to the effectiveness of direct instruction. But, like all approaches, it has limitations. Some tasks require more teacher direction than others. Expert teachers know that education is about developing children's independence and eagerness to learn. While they may acquire knowledge and skills more quickly through direct instruction than other approaches, learners also need to have time and space to become reflective and creative thinkers.

Most of the research evidence supports direct teaching of *new* ideas, rather than leaving children to discover things for themselves (Coe et al., 2014). According to research done in the United States, the most effective mathematics teachers use direct instruction techniques for twenty-three minutes during a typical forty-minute session. In contrast, the least effective teachers spend only eleven minutes presenting new materials and tend to give much shorter presentations and explanations, preferring to move on to distributing worksheets and telling pupils to get on and solve problems (Rosenshine, 2012). Obviously learners need to build on what they already know and have opportunities to investigate, but good teachers use a variety of approaches because classrooms are complex, multilayered places.

Summary

» Direct instruction is a structured approach to teaching with an emphasis on adults telling, showing and reinforcing learning.

» It is based on the principles that children can succeed, if they are provided with appropriate training and materials.

» The approach originated in the United States in the 1960s when Siegfried Engelmann worked with low-achieving pupils from poor socio-economic communities.

» The results, along with further research, show that direct instruction is a highly effective approach to transmitting information, but it is less effective in promoting independent, creative and critical thinking.

» The implications for practitioners are to provide a clear structure to sessions, regularly review learners' progress through questioning and model learning through demonstrations.

Points for reflection and action

» Try to observe a lesson that follows a direct instruction approach. Examples can be found online (for instance at: http://engagedlearning. co.uk/?p=1950). Reflect on the strengths and criticisms levelled against the approach.

» According to John Hattie, staff discussions only focus on teaching for about one minute a month and even less about their impact – most of their talk is about students, the curriculum and assessment. Listen to his BBC Radio 4 podcast: http://www.bbc.co.uk/programmes/b04dmxwl. Why does Hattie make this point?

» Videotape one of your teaching sessions and focus on the quality of your demonstrations. How well did you:
  - Use clear and inclusive language.
  - Break the task into small, sequential steps.
  - Check the understanding of all learners.

Chapter 8

Curriculum

*The curriculum is all the learning and assessment activities
in school, both planned and unintentional, that contribute
to agreed educational goals*

What is the big idea?

There have probably been more books, articles and reports written about
the curriculum than any other subject in education. Educationalists get
passionate about the national curriculum, the core curriculum, the spiral
curriculum, the cubic curriculum, the International Primary Curriculum,
curriculum policies, curriculum development, the hidden curriculum,
extracurricular activities, community curriculum and curriculum design.
For learners, whenever they hear the word 'curriculum' they tend to equate
it with assessment matters – 'passing exams, getting grades' and the like –
an association which increases with age (Lord and Jones, 2006: 4).

It is common to see the curriculum in terms of what has to be taught,
the prescribed content or the list of subjects to be 'covered' – a syllabus.
Those who stress the academic function of schools are reluctant to include
*extra*curricular experiences, visits or informal contacts between teachers
and children as part of the curriculum. However, the big idea here is to
take a more holistic view. Skilbeck (1976: 65) described the curriculum
as 'those activities planned and provided for in the pursuit of educational
ends and purposes'. The implication is that teachers need to reflect
upon what, how and why they teach, including the values and qualities
that schools seek to cultivate in young people. Similarly, Her Majesty's

Inspectorate (DES, 1985) has suggested that a school's curriculum consists of everything that is designed to promote the intellectual, social, personal and physical development of its pupils. This includes not only the formal programme of lessons, but also extracurricular activities and features that contribute to the school ethos, such as values and quality of relationships. This is a very broad-brush view of the curriculum but one that rightly emphasises that schools influence what pupils learn in lots of ways beyond formal lessons. School social hierarchies, uniforms and regulations are all designed to instil certain values and behaviours, such as obedience and deference.

But it does not mean that the curriculum applies to everything that goes on in school, which would make such matters as the colour of the school walls a question for curriculum designers. If, on the other hand, children are asked to undertake a makeover of, say, the school toilets – including sourcing materials, working out costings, establishing timeframes, canvassing preferences among the school population, completing health and safety checks and evaluating the outcomes – then these project management skills could become learning experiences. In such a project, children may pick up ideas and values that were not planned and these messages are also important for schools to consider.

Obviously, when it comes to managing the curriculum in practice, school leaders and teachers will inevitably focus on timetables, policy documents (containing aims and objectives), content, teaching approaches, resources and assessment opportunities. These are important matters, both in terms of the smooth running of the school and in seeking to provide a balanced, stimulating curriculum. One of the challenges, however, is to explore how children's actual learning experiences compare to this 'official' curriculum. This is where school self-evaluation systems play a key role in understanding the school experience from different perspectives (e.g. strength of learner voice).

Historically, schools have had considerable autonomy in devising their own curricula. It was only in 1960 that Sir David Eccles, the then minister of education, announced a change in government policy towards schools: it would in future go beyond providing resources to open up 'the secret garden of the curriculum' (Ross, 2000: 1). Aside from religious education, which between 1944 and 1988 was the only subject that had a statutory basis, schools could, in theory, teach what they wanted. In practice, many schools taught the same kinds of things, but in a major primary school survey, school inspectors (HMI, 1978) aired concerns over inconsistencies in curriculum breadth, balance and quality, particularly outside English and mathematics. The report was published during a period when the teaching profession was under growing scrutiny. Politicians were increasingly questioning the amount of autonomy given to schools in curriculum matters. This was the backdrop to the introduction of a national curriculum, which also included mandatory testing in Years 2 and 6. Richards (2001) argues that the national curriculum ended the 'curriculum lottery' that operated prior to 1988.

Subsequent revisions to the national curriculum have brought heated debates over what counts as worthwhile knowledge. The problem with a narrow content definition of the curriculum is that arguments inevitably arise over what should be left in or out. The Labour government commissioned an 'independent' review of the curriculum led by Sir Jim Rose (DCSF, 2009c). His report proved sympathetic to teachers' views that the curriculum was overloaded, but it did not, as the media reported, suggest 'abolishing subjects' as the way forward. Rather, Rose maintained that subjects were an essential means of organising knowledge but were not sufficient in themselves. While direct subject teaching was seen as 'vital', the review recommended combining this with cross-curricular studies – for example, using dance and drama to enhance language development. There was overwhelming support (92 per cent) from respondents for a move towards creating a primary curriculum based on six areas of learning:

» Understanding English, communication and languages.
» Mathematical understanding.
» Scientific and technological understanding.
» Historical, geographical and social understanding.
» Understanding physical development, health and well-being.
» Understanding the arts. (DCSF, 2009c: 16)

The Cambridge Primary Review of the curriculum, the most substantial since Plowden, provided a wealth of evidence on all aspects of primary school life (Alexander, 2010). Nearly 3,000 researchers, and over a thousand organisations and individuals, contributed to the review and more than 4,000 published sources were consulted. The ten themes cover purposes and values; learning and teaching; curriculum and assessment; quality and standards; diversity and inclusion; settings and professionals; parenting, caring and educating; children's lives beyond the school; structures and phases; and funding and governance. Among its seventy-five recommendations, the Cambridge Review called for a reinstatement of a broad and balanced curriculum and the removal of the artificial distinction between 'core' and 'foundation' subjects. Despite its comprehensiveness, ideologically it did not align with government thinking and, like the Rose Review, it has fallen by the wayside. Although the Labour government accepted the Rose Review and in 2011 began planning for a new curriculum, this was scrapped following the election of the coalition government. While teachers broadly welcomed the Cambridge Review, insofar as it recommended more flexibility in the curriculum and more scope for teachers' own initiative, it suffered from a lack of political support. As Peter Cunningham (2012: 37) points out, governments have short-term agendas, are conscious of their public image and 'are frequently impatient of the necessarily complex and provisional conclusions of social research'.

The curriculum is often subjected to political interference. In the 2000s, for instance, the Labour government was criticised for 'corrupting' the curriculum by trying to include everything from 'happiness lessons' to 'Britishness', from sex education initiatives to more lessons on obesity and healthy eating. Organisations such as Civitas complained about the 'dumbing down' of traditional academic disciplines. Writers pointed to the decline in map work in geography because of the emphasis on global ethics and the loss of chronology in British history lessons because teachers were expected to include multiple perspectives from minority groups. They concluded that 'an anti-educational curriculum' (Ledda, 2007: 13) had developed where educators were demanding that schools helped children to feel good about themselves rather than focus on teaching the likes of mathematics, reading and science effectively. Anthony Seldon, Master of Wellington College, writing nearly a decade ago, claimed: 'The curriculum in schools today resembles a dilapidated house on the outskirts of Mumbai' (cited by Lawes et al., 2007: 13).

No doubt such writers were delighted by the Conservative government's subject and knowledge-centred revised national curriculum introduced in 2013. It was announced as 'tough', with 5-year-olds expected to 'understand what algorithms are' and to 'create and debug simple programs', while 9-year-olds should know their 12 times tables (Richardson, 2014). By 14, children should have studied two Shakespearean plays. On the other hand, there were plenty of educationalists unhappy over what they perceived to be a narrow, elitist and outdated curriculum, which left no room for creativity and the development of transferable thinking skills.

These criticisms reflect the passions held about the curriculum, which is never a value-neutral thing. In simple terms, the debate centres on the degree of autonomy afforded to schools and individual teachers in deciding what to teach children. For some, the balance is not right; while a national curriculum might be acknowledged as a good thing, greater local discretion is needed. However, imposing a top-down curriculum on schools has at least four advantages:

1. It provides the necessary structure so there is, in theory, consistency across schools.
2. It avoids unnecessary duplication in that learners do not repeat what they have learned in previous years.
3. It is easier to monitor, assess and compare learner progress and teacher performance if they are all doing the same kinds of things.
4. It means that reporting to parents, governors and others becomes more standardised.

In essence, these are the arguments to justify a national curriculum. The most recent form of the national curriculum in England was introduced on the basis that it needed to be slimmed down and to focus on essential knowledge and skills. Schools now have more freedom to create a curriculum to complement the statutory requirements of the national curriculum. Research has shown that in the recent past, many primary schools replaced the national curriculum with their own, despite its statutory status, because they did not think it fully met the needs of their learners (Johnson, 2007).

Whatever the curriculum model, the key is to build it on solid principles. Most curricula in the UK and internationally draw on similar principles – for example, advocating breadth, balance and relevance (Hall and Øzerk, 2008). Scotland's *Curriculum for Excellence* (Scottish

Executive, 2007) has seven principles, Wales has ten (Donaldson, 2015), while the Expert Panel that advised on the national curriculum in England followed the principles of 'freedom, responsibility and fairness – to raise standards for all children' (DfE, 2011c: 6).

Who is behind it?

We owe the modern subject-based school curriculum to scholars in the medieval church and universities. Although the oldest surviving school in the world is said to be the King's School, Canterbury, founded in AD 597 by St Augustine (and later renamed under the reign of Henry VIII), our first glimpse of the curriculum emerges in the eighth century when the schoolmaster Alcuin of York offered what appears to have been a very broad curriculum. Through Latin, Alcuin taught law, poetry, grammar, music, natural history, geometry, arithmetic and scriptures. His students trained for a life in the Church and so the curriculum was heavily shaped by Christian values and theology. It was not until the eleventh and twelfth centuries with the establishment of universities that more specialist education in subjects such as law and medicine, as well as theology, began to develop. The medieval curriculum comprised the seven liberal arts, beginning with the trivium (grammar, dialectic, rhetoric) and followed by the quadrivium (arithmetic, geometry, music, astronomy). Robinson (2013) discusses the relevance of this curriculum as a *way* of learning rather than simply a list of subjects. He argues that knowing, questioning and communicating should continue to form the basis of schooling. Too much emphasis, Robinson maintains, is placed on education as a ticket to the world of work rather than attaining wisdom or living a good life.

By the eighteenth century, the curriculum was beginning to shape up in its modern form, particularly with the introduction of physical sciences. But thinking about the curriculum was along segregated lines, with different provision for different classes and with different subjects for boys and girls. The notion of a national curriculum for those attending state schools was introduced in the nineteenth century. The subjects – English language and literature, maths, science, history, geography, physical exercise, drawing, singing, manual training and housewifery for girls – is still largely recognisable in today's national curriculum. The twentieth century was characterised by periodical debates over how the curriculum should be organised. But the classical, elitist model focused on academic subjects has steadfastly remained in place.

Mainstream thinking in early and primary years' education in the UK reflected a spirit quite different from an industrial, scientific and results-driven model of curriculum planning. The child, rather than the curriculum, needed to be centre stage in education. These sentiments had been aired in the 1930s by the Board of Education in a remarkable series of reports under the chairmanship of Sir William Hadow. They were noteworthy for their vision and eloquence, expressed during the years of tough economic depression when the world of work was a priority. Hadow called for the primary curriculum to be 'vivid, realistic, a stream in motion, not a stagnant pool' (Hadow, 1931: xii–xiv).

Bridget Plowden, who chaired the 1967 report that bears her name, picked up this theme. She and her fellow committee members highlighted the need for a flexible curriculum where there was time and opportunity for children to learn by discovery. Plowden's influence can be seen in many later curriculum reports and commentaries. The school inspectorate's report, *A View of the Curriculum* (HMI, 1980: 2), argued that the curriculum should 'contribute to children's present well-being whatever the age and stage of growth and development they have reached'. The Schools Council working paper (1981: 26) put it succinctly: 'the curriculum needs to fit the child'.

The Plowden Report suggested that 'rigid division of the curriculum into subjects tends to interrupt children's trains of thought and of interest and to hinder them from realising the common elements in problem solving' (Plowden, 1967: 197). It recommended organising subjects around themes drawn from pupils' experience, such as 'weather', 'growing plants' or 'scenes in the road or street' (Plowden, 1967: 231), based on subjects from a wide range of 'disciplines' (e.g. language, mathematics, literature and history). In curriculum studies, theorists have continued to debate whether the curriculum should be organised around disciplines, modes of thinking or areas of experience. Hirst (1975) defended the importance of subjects and established forms of knowledge, a view echoed by recent Westminster government standpoints (Garner, 2014a). However, one of the main arguments against separate subjects is that this is not how children see the world and that an integrated approach offers a more holistic understanding.

Particularly in the early years, there has been widespread support for the notion of a negotiated curriculum where child-initiated questions and ideas are used as a basis for co-planning with teachers (see Hill et al., 2005). Negotiation is based on the principle of ownership: children will work harder and learn better if they can follow up their own ideas and ask their own questions. Children learn most effectively when they are motivated; however well teachers transmit information, they cannot impose understanding because it comes from within. In general, a negotiated curriculum does not align well with the direct instruction model reviewed in the previous chapter. But the need for balance has been recognised in the continuum of approaches to learning featured in the Early Years Foundation Stage and the Welsh Foundation Phase. Both see the need for adult direction at one end of the continuum and unstructured experiences at the other, with child-initiated play (i.e. adult support for an enabling environment and sensitive interaction) and adult guided activities in-between.

Another way to look at the curriculum is to consider the experience through the eyes of the learners themselves. The National Foundation for Educational Research (NFER) has conducted the most substantial piece of research on pupils' experience of the curriculum (Lord and Jones, 2006). Among the findings were the following:

» Decreasing enjoyment as pupils get older.
» A dip in Year 8 in terms of motivation and engagement, as pupils enter an 'educational limbo'.
» Across all ages 'practical' activity enthuses pupils.
» At secondary school, subjects with higher levels of practical activity (e.g. PE, ICT, art) are enjoyed most.
» Pupils consistently value teachers who explain clearly, listen, are fair and who are interesting.
» Pupils value a sense of responsibility and autonomy in their work.
» Pupils value connections between their curriculum and real life. They also value real-life relevance from those 'in the know', such as teachers with wide subject-based knowledge and professionals from within the field.

The formal curriculum is the one most people readily identify with – in its simplest form, it amounts to a list of subjects. Despite periodic outcries over what schools are teaching, the formal curriculum has changed very little over two centuries. There has not been any curriculum revolution since state support for schools began. However, while this may be the case for the names of subjects, there have been changes in what is taught under those headings. In part, this reflects the decisions made by schools responding to contemporary demands. Such decision making, according to Goodlad (1979), occurs at three different levels: decisions made by individual teachers at the instructional level, leaders who make decisions at institutional level and those decisions made at a societal level (e.g. by local and central authority policy-makers). Labaree (1999) has also distinguished between different forms of the curriculum: the 'rhetorical curriculum', the 'curriculum-in-use' and the 'received curriculum'. The first refers to what the authorities recommend is taught, the second refers to the actual content that is implemented in the classroom and the third equates to Goodlad's 'experiential curriculum' – what children actually learn.

It has long been recognised that children learn many things in and outside of school that are not part of the formal curriculum. The sociologist Phillip Jackson (1968) described the values that children pick up as forming the 'hidden curriculum' – a whole set of assumptions that include how to relate to others and the behaviours they imitate. In a negative sense, this can lead to pupils accepting that they are not very good at learning particular subjects because of the manner in which they are treated – for example, the body language of a teacher, the ridicule from peers or pressures to keep up with others. Often pupils enter subcultures in school that govern how they speak, act or dress, which are contrary to what the school wants. However, Wood (2011) points out that the hidden curriculum may not be as pervasive as imagined. Although schools may have established rules and routines, individual teachers and classes negotiate these and work out a modus operandi for living together. Pupils test the expectations set by teachers to see where the boundaries lie, which may lead teachers to revise their expectations.

Although there had been debates over the content of the curriculum before the modern era, it was not until the first half of the twentieth century that the unscientific nature of teachers' planning and the lack of clarity over what they were trying to achieve were questioned. In the

United States, Franklin Bobbitt (1876–1956), a professor of educational administration at the University of Chicago, wrote a seminal book called *The Curriculum* (1918). Bobbitt argued that teachers would plan more efficiently if they took lessons from industry where each worker was given a specific task to do, with set procedures to follow. Bobbitt and others saw schools as a major means of dealing with the social problems that could be found in the country's growing industrial towns. If school leavers were equipped with the knowledge and skills for specific work, this would provide greater stability and social order.

Another American educator, Ralph Tyler (1902–1994), raised questions about what was selected for the curriculum and how learning experiences could be evaluated – he is said to have been the first person to use the term 'evaluation'. What became known as the 'Tyler rationale' for curriculum planning received support from economists who saw that a clear statement of objectives was the quickest way to a proper evaluation of whether money invested in education was wisely spent. The likes of Bobbitt, Tyler and Benjamin Bloom were not satisfied that curriculum planning should start with deciding on a list of subjects and the content to be covered therein. Rather, they wanted to see a much sharper focus. The legacy of such a scientific approach to the curriculum, with its emphasis on results, can be seen all over the world with trainee and serving teachers expected to plan lessons around learning objectives and intended outcomes. These are then used as a basis for assessment. There is no doubt that this 'product' model of the curriculum has advantages, not least making it clear to all the learning intentions in lessons.

However, it did not take long before the assumptions behind an objectives-led approach to the curriculum were questioned. The big idea of the curriculum as a dynamic process began as a reaction to seeing it in purely instrumental terms. In the 1960s and 1970s, writers such as Hilda Taba (1962), Richard Peters (1965), Lawrence Stenhouse (1975) and Richard Pring (1976) raised philosophical and practical concerns about what they perceived was a 'closed', inflexible curriculum model. As Peters (1965: 110) famously declared: 'To be educated is not to have arrived at a destination; it is to travel with a different view.' Individual teachers know that the vibrant and uncertain nature of classroom life makes it difficult to condense learning into three or four tight measurable objectives. The pressures to meet these can mean that teachers ignore other potentially rich lines of enquiry that emerge from dialogue with learners. In short, education is as much art as it is science.

Since the early 1990s, the development of a national curriculum, followed by non-statutory schemes of work, has brought much needed consistency to teachers' planning. But, on the downside, teachers have lost the skill of curriculum design, with off-the-peg lessons and units widely available online. So, this is not about advocating a return to the 1960s and 1970s when the teaching profession had too much autonomy for its own good. But I believe we have gone too far towards a prescriptive curriculum and a nervous, constrained profession unwilling to take risks. There are promising signs: Ofsted and the government have both made it clear that lesson planning is not expected to follow a particular format. But the centralised, prescriptive content of the national curriculum remains a concern for some commentators. Teachers frequently comment about having too little time to fit everything in, a point acknowledged by curriculum reviews over recent years (DCSF, 2009c; Alexander, 2010; Donaldson, 2015).

Why is it important, and what can you do?

It is important to see the curriculum in broad terms because there can be a significant gap between what someone thinks the curriculum should be and what is actually experienced by learners. Hence, it is essential for teachers to regard the curriculum not as a rigid structure but as a flexible, organic and dynamic set of experiences. Even when the curriculum is scripted or handed down, there is usually some scope on how the details are interpreted.

The role of the teacher is clearly critical to implementing a curriculum that is enriching, stimulating and challenging. As Alexander (2010: 243) notes, 'a curriculum is only as good as those who teach it'. One of the underlying criticisms of schools has been that too many teachers do not challenge pupils enough. This theme has come through in many inspection reports where the slow pace of lessons, the choice of activities and the overuse of worksheets has left pupils bored, under-stimulated and underachieving (Pollard and Triggs, 2000). In part, this has been attributed to the performance culture in schools where teachers have focused on preparing children to do well in tests. There are also professional development issues, with tighter budgets limiting opportunities for teachers to sharpen their practices through further training.

A broad, exciting and relevant curriculum is particularly important for disadvantaged learners who may not otherwise access these experiences at home. Ofsted reports on schools, which succeed in challenging circumstances, show that an attractive curriculum is a key driver to motivating learners, improving behaviour and raising academic standards. These are schools that describe themselves, for example, as 'beset with alcohol and drugs in one direction and gangs in the other' (Ofsted, 2009a: 17). The emphasis is on providing an engaging curriculum and expert teaching. This includes personalising the curriculum to provide more choice and to meet the needs of individuals and specific groups. One school, for instance, arranges the timetable in discussion with parents/ carers of potentially disaffected and challenging students to enable them to benefit from curriculum enrichment activities such as residential events. The aim is that each year every student will have the opportunity to go on a course away from the school.

Seeing the curriculum as more than a list of subjects, lesson plans, units of work and assessment tasks means taking a broader view on the impact of what children are taught in school. It means, for example, considering the links between the curriculum, the immediate community and society at large. During the Great Depression of the 1930s, parents in the United States were so concerned about how to eat nutritionally, preserve food, cope with unemployment and keep costs down that they went to school with their children to learn how to survive (Alexander, 1972). In the UK, there is a long tradition of adults attending schools to up-skill themselves at vocational classes and to provide voluntary support to teachers in areas such as listening to children read, cooking, gardening and, in more recent times, digital technologies. Yet, there are also many parents (particularly from low-income, working-class backgrounds), who never or hardly set foot in their children's school, partly because they think back to their own experience (which may have been negative) or because of other commitments they lack the time or confidence to do so.

In 2007, schools in England were required to promote 'community cohesion' following riots and disturbances in 2001. This has meant that schools have had to reflect on how the curriculum could strengthen pupils' understanding of identity, heritage and community – for instance, through fieldwork, visits and interaction with people from different age groups and backgrounds. According to the Labour government's *Children's Plan*, it was also expected that all schools would become 'extended schools', which meant that schools were expected to provide access to 'a range of out of school opportunities' (DCSF, 2007b: 28). Since then, the notion has lost its impetus with a change of political direction and a period of austerity. An emphasis on 'parental choice', business models of school leadership, the development of specialist schools and academies, and demographic changes have all meant that the relationship between schools and their neighbourhoods is changing. Secondary school populations can be made up of children from outside the immediate area, making it more difficult to establish a community 'feel'. Moreover, while the idea of school leaders and teachers working closely with a range of specialists in multi-profession teams to enhance the curriculum and meet the needs of learners can only be a good move, in reality this has proven to be challenging in a period of tight funding.

Any curriculum should be based on what we know about learning. Most research highlights that the most effective learning is 'social and active', with opportunities for learners to make decisions and learn from mistakes (Ko and Sammons, 2013; Siraj and Taggart, 2014). Children need to be motivated, engaged and challenged. This is why some commentators (e.g. Johnson, 2007) push the importance of a curriculum that is as much about skills and learning dispositions as well as factual content.

When planning to implement the curriculum, there are several questions to consider relating to purpose, content, pedagogy and assessment:

» What are you trying to achieve? – e.g. rationale, aims, learning intentions.

» What do you want to teach? – e.g. the balance between formal, extracurricular, community-based elements.

» How will you teach and relate to learners? – e.g. direct instruction, play, use of technologies.

» What are the most effective teaching methods and strategies? – e.g. instruction, enquiry-based learning.

» How should the curriculum be organised? – e.g. subjects, themes, topics, challenges.

» How will success be measured? – e.g. attainment data, quality of learning experiences.

These points are important to reflect on, irrespective of whether the curriculum is seen in narrow terms, such as creating a syllabus for a particular subject, or in the broader terms put forward in this chapter. Ofsted (2009b) reports on how many schools are simplifying their approach to planning the curriculum. In one case, detailed mid-term plans were pared back and replaced by topics based on two questions: (1) What do we want children to get out of it? and (2) What do we want children to learn? School leaders can take these kinds of questions and compare their answers with those from teachers and pupils themselves. Establishing a consensus over what the school is for and the kind of learners it seeks to develop is central to the success of the school (see Chapter 12).

Streamlining planning can free teachers to discuss new approaches and give them a renewed focus on learning. The key message from reviewing the approach to the curriculum taken by outstanding schools is their confidence and imagination in taking the statutory curriculum and making it their own. There is a strong emphasis on basic skills but not at the expense of a narrow curriculum. There is no conflict between a prescribed curriculum and creative approaches. These schools recognise the importance of creativity. As the German philosopher Friedrich Nietzsche reminds us:

For dancing in any form cannot be excluded from a noble education; being able to dance with the feet, with concepts, with words: do I still have to say that one has to be able to dance with the pen – that writing has to be learned? (Nietzsche, 1990 [1889]: 39)

Conclusion

For many pupils and teachers, the curriculum is simply a race to cover what is expected on the official syllabus. Ironically, this reflects the original meaning of the word curriculum, derived from the Ancient Roman practice of chariot racing – a *currere* was a fast chariot or racing car, from which the idea of pursuing a course developed. In crude terms, this Darwinian view sees schooling as a process of separating winners from losers, with children having to jump over a series of assessment hurdles, the success of which determines their progress.

Throughout the twentieth century, the history of the curriculum in England and Wales has been characterised by a struggle to ensure all have equal access, culminating in the national curriculum. This has undergone numerous revisions but there have been calls to end the tinkering and start again to meet the needs of learners in the twenty-first century (Johnson, 2007; Alexander, 2010; Carswell, 2013). In Wales, the case for bringing the national curriculum to an end draws on a range of arguments, including the inhibiting impact of over-prescription on the teaching profession in dealing with emerging issues, the loss of creativity in schools and the failure to engage all learners, particularly those from disadvantaged backgrounds. In extreme cases, it has led primary schools to focus almost exclusively on literacy and numeracy and secondary schools to become preoccupied with preparation for qualifications (Jones, 2014; Donaldson, 2015). So the Welsh Assembly Government has decided to put its faith in the teaching profession and Donaldson's recommendations, so schools will be 'liberated' from a curriculum framed around subjects and timetables, from a top-down prescribed curriculum and a burdensome assessment regime.

In contrast, the curriculum fortunes in England over recent years have seen government rejection of the most comprehensive review of the primary curriculum in our lifetime, the *Cambridge Primary Review* (Alexander, 2010). Instead, teachers have had to grapple with new initiatives and directives and a target culture that has caused undue stress and demotivation (Garner, 2014b; Richardson, 2015). They received an imposed, albeit slimmed down, new national curriculum in 2013 but without any teacher input, unlike previous versions. Of course, a curriculum can be updated to reflect change and there are arguments in favour of ensuring that all children have access to the same core knowledge and skills. But a one-size-fits-all curriculum over the past twenty-five years or so has simply not ensured this – there are significant variations between learners' experience within a school, let alone between schools.

While this is largely to do with quality of teaching and how this is managed, teachers continue to spend too much of their precious time mediating yet another initiative or directive, rather than focusing on how to improve their teaching (Sergeant, 2009). But teaching, rather than structural things, is the single most important school-based factor that can make a difference to raising standards and creating joyful learning experiences. John Hattie (2015) describes the 'politics of distraction', suggesting that we are taking our eye off the most important things, like teaching and learning, by spending too much time trying to fix the infrastructure – the curriculum, assessment, buildings. As this chapter has shown, the curriculum should be seen as more than a set of discrete subjects to include all the learning and assessment experiences a school offers to pupils. This is important because, from the learners' perspective, their experience of schooling goes beyond the subjects they are taught. It includes the values they pick up about their potential to learn. Staff need to be mindful of this and be ready to make changes to the planned curriculum in the light of learners' experience and feedback.

Summary

» The curriculum can be described in different ways – this chapter defines it as all the planned learning and assessment experiences in school.

» The process of designing the curriculum is based on values – what knowledge and skills are considered worthwhile.

» Sociologists such as Philip Jackson and Basil Bernstein have long argued that the values that children pick up in school – the hidden curriculum – shape their success.

» There are different ways of organising the curriculum, including subjects, themes and areas of experience. The breadth and balance of the curriculum and what learners experience are more important than how it is organised.

» The success of any curriculum depends on how well it is implemented by teachers.

Points for reflection and action

» Think back to your schooldays. How has the curriculum changed since then, and why?

» Do you think the curriculum should be organised around problems, puzzles, projects and big questions, or core knowledge, skills and academic disciplines?

» The BBC asked members of the general public questions about topics that feature in the national curriculum introduced in 2013. Watch the video at: http://www.bbc.co.uk/news/education-28987787. How do their views compare to your own?

» Does it really matter what is in the school curriculum? Find out what John Hattie's views are on this.

Chapter 9

Feedback

Providing personalised, accurate, specific and timely
feedback is one of the keys to improving learning

What is the big idea?

Feedback is central to modern life, from completing online customer surveys to annual performance reviews. In business, the latter is wonderfully mocked in the appraisals episode of the BBC television comedy *The Office*, screened in 2002. The office manager David Brent sits down with Keith Bishop from accounts. He uses prompts from the standard questionnaire to find out Keith's strengths ('Accounts'), weaknesses ('Eczema') and training needs ('Don't know'). The ineffectiveness of the appraisal system has led some big businesses to move away from the crude ranking and grading of employees towards more fluid, ongoing forms of feedback. These include Amazon's Anytime Feedback Tool where employees comment on each other's performance and Adobe's 'check-ins' based on regular dialogue between line managers and workers.

Business terms such as 'performance', 'achievement', 'value added', 'goal setting', 'best practice', 'portfolio' and 'benchmarking' now shape conversations about assessment in education. The term 'feedback' itself originated in the world of engineering and mechanics. By the 1920s, it described the return of the output from a device to its input to modify performance. So, for example, when a central heating system exceeded a certain temperature it turned itself off and could restart when the temperature got below a certain level (Hattie and Yates,

2014a). Built in to the original notion of feedback then is a sense of self-control. This remains important – the ideal scenario is for feedback to motivate recipients so they get into the habit of critically reviewing their own work, spotting and correcting errors and seeing ways in which they can improve. After the Second World War, the term began to be used in industrial relations when discussing people and performance management. It was increasingly recognised that employees needed feedback to improve their performance.

But giving feedback is widely recognised as one of the most demanding skills across many professions, from business executives to doctors, from dance instructors to filmmakers. It is challenging because there is an inherent tension in the process between wanting to be supportive and encouraging but also accurate and fair. Those providing feedback are often caught between a coaching and assessing role. Invariably they try to do both and this results in the classic feedback trilogy of praise–criticism–praise. Research now suggests that the 'sandwich approach' can actually undermine the quality of feedback (Schwarz, 2013). It seems that while people believe that giving positive feedback is a way of gently easing in the negative message, it only creates the very anxiety that it seeks to avoid – both the feedback giver and receiver share the build-up of anxiety. For recipients, there is also the mixed feeling of wanting to improve and yet the need to feel appreciated. Schwarz and other writers argue that it is far better to get straight to the point and be transparent with people. Clearly this needs to be done sensitively and not in the style of Lord Sugar on *The Apprentice*! The emphasis should be on how to improve, not remove.

In an educational context, feedback is the giving of information about one's performance in order to reduce the gap between present and potential learning (Figure 9.1). Identifying the gap is one thing; doing something to close the gap is another. It is only if a positive outcome

Figure 9.1. Role of feedback in closing the gap between desired, current and potential learning.

in learning follows that the 'feedback loop' (Sadler, 1989) is completed. Feedback effectively signals what next steps are needed to move learning forward. Unless it does this, there is little point in providing feedback.

This process of feedback can be expressed as three simple questions:

1. What do I want to learn (desired learning, e.g. intentions, goals, objectives)?
2. How am I doing (current learning, e.g. acquired knowledge and skills)?
3. What do I need to do next (potential or further learning, e.g. next steps)?

Hattie and Timperley (2007) ask similar questions and relate these to notions of 'feed up, feed back and feed forward'. The process begins with feed up – clarifying where the learners are heading and what they need to learn, conveyed in terms of realistic goals. The feed back dimension is all about progress from a given starting point, while feed forward highlights where to go next – the possibilities of future learning.

Providing feedback is both emotionally and logistically challenging in terms of time, effort and resources (Ackerman and Gross, 2010). In the field of business and technology, this led to the development of immediate feedback techniques and programmes. One of these is FAST feedback, a notion that originated in US businesses in the late 1990s (Tulgan, 1999). Employers found that productivity and relationships with the workforce improved when they provided feedback that was on the right *frequency*, *accurate*, *specific* and *timely*. The FAST model closely aligns with what is known about effective feedback in schools. Its characteristics are now briefly reviewed.

Frequency

Despite claims from teachers that they provide plenty of feedback to individual learners, studies indicate that this is not the case, even when it involves expert teachers (Ingvarson and Hattie, 2008). When learners are asked about the feedback they receive, many say it is infrequent, and when calculated it amounts to little more than a few seconds each per day (Hattie and Yates, 2014a). Feedback that is provided in small amounts on a regular basis is more effective than an overload of information every so often. But frequency here is not describing the number of times feedback is given. Rather, it refers to how well teachers 'tune in' to the unique frequencies of learners, like tuning in to an old-fashioned radio. It is personalised feedback and demands that teachers know their class as *individuals*.

Effective feedback has to be set within the wider need to establish supportive, trusting relationships. Children are more likely to respond to feedback if they think teachers are taking a genuine interest in their well-being. For example, it is customary at the start of the school year to get to know classmates through sharing stories about hobbies, family and friends, music, sport, reading, art, birthdays and so forth. In primary school, children are often asked to make a 'me box' of objects that tell others about what matters to them. Teachers can also create a playlist of favourite songs based on submissions by each pupil which can be used at appropriate times, such as to signal transitions or the start of an activity. This level of attentiveness can be sustained through the year by making time for one-to-one conversations and by keeping learning logs.

There are many innovative ways to get to know children as individuals through the use of technology. Pupils can create word clouds or infographics about their lives using tools like Wordle, Infogr.am, Piktochart or Visual.ly. Google Voice messages allow students to leave messages sharing something about their lives. Teachers can learn about children's geographies using Google Map Personal Stories – this allows pins to be dropped in places that mean something to children. They can also use iPads and tablets to take photographs of their favourite spots around the school, while Google Earth can be used to create a narrative around these places. Applications such as Smore allow children to create posters and newsletters about themselves.

The old jazz song 'T'Ain't What You Do (It's the Way That You Do It)' illustrates that *how* something is said or done is often more important that the act itself. When giving feedback, a teacher's tone of voice and body language really matter. Voice control is particularly important in establishing a calm and purposeful learning environment for the feedback to be well received. When teachers are tense or agitated their voices tend to become high pitched, which signals their nervousness and lack of confidence. Actions such as folding arms, standing behind a desk, shuffling papers or looking at a watch when a child speaks, signal a lack of genuine interest. Facial gestures are important in conveying moods – frowns obviously denote disappointment or anger, while smiles express contentment and encouragement. Often during the course of a lesson, the quickest feedback is a smile, frown, nod or wink. In one study, undergraduate students at Harvard University gave speeches and did mock interviews with experimenters who were either nodding and smiling or shaking their heads and crossing their arms. The first group of students performed better than the second when they were later asked questions (Kassam et al., 2009). Placing a hand on the chin encourages learners to think about their answers, while hands out and palms up shows that the teacher is inviting a response. Eye contact is also essential to effective communication – it shows interest in what is being said.

The way feedback is presented can have an impact on how it is received, which means that sometimes even the most well-meaning feedback can come across the wrong way and reduce a learner's motivation. Learners generally do not respond well to feedback that they perceive is too controlling or competitive. This is why feedback should help learners to understand more about themselves than others, and to compete against their own previous bests rather than try to keep up with peers.

Accurate

Feedback needs to be accurate and based on facts rather than hearsay. Sometimes what children say, do or write can be misinterpreted, so teachers need to understand the context and double check with children what they mean. Therefore, in a class discussion, it is good practice for the teacher to use question stems to clarify any uncertainties before giving oral feedback – for example, 'Do you mean …?', 'Are you saying …?', 'Can you give an example?' Corrective feedback should pick up errors related to the learning objectives and indicate how these can be addressed. Inevitably teachers are also drawn to more general language issues such as misspellings and poor grammar when marking work in, say, geography or history. While it is important for pupils to apply their literacy skills across the curriculum, this has to be balanced against the particular focus for the lesson. Hence, if pupils are asked to write an account of a day in the life of a Victorian kitchen maid after visiting a stately home, the focus is likely to be on historical imagination and factual detail rather than the accuracy of spelling and punctuation.

In their everyday monitoring, teachers need to identify and correct fundamental errors. Jacob Kounin (1970), an American researcher, coined the term 'withitness' to describe teachers who could split their attention between the children they are with and the rest of the class. Monitoring is important because it enables teachers to give quick oral feedback on how individuals, groups and the whole class are progressing. Often, all that is required is a simple prompt such as, 'Explain to me what you are doing' or 'How are you getting on?' Given that the original meaning of the word 'assess' meant to 'sit alongside', it is entirely appropriate for teachers to plan their time so they spend a few minutes sitting beside and talking to individuals or a group. This requires careful time management skills and clear routines so that those groups who are not receiving adult support know what they can do if they are stuck, without troubling the teacher. They may, for example, be expected to move on to the next question or task, use reference books, checklists or other materials or ask someone else in the group. Wragg (2001: 37) makes the acerbic point that some secondary teachers patrol the room but do not scrutinise pupils' work, 'creating a draught rather than monitoring'.

Getting the right balance between positive and negative feedback is challenging. The evidence suggests that they do not have equal impact on learning. Too much negative feedback can lead to poor self-esteem and task avoidance. Research in building effective management teams found that high performance was achieved when the ratio for positive and negative feedback was at least three to one – three positive comments for every negative one – but did not exceed eleven to one (Losada and Heaphy, 2004). This has filtered through to the popular classroom feedback strategy of 'two stars and a wish' (two positives and one desirable).

Specific

Learners need specific rather than vague guidance. They need information on what exactly they did well and what they need to do to improve. It is also helpful to tell learners what they are doing differently than before. Hattie and Timperley (2007) point out that effective feedback focuses on a particular goal that learners are working towards. The information should enable learners to see specifically what they are doing right and wrong. Feedback comments such as 'Good girl' do not tell the learner what she did right; likewise, a statement such as 'Not quite there yet' does not shed light on what was wrong and how this can be improved next time. Moreover, terms such as 'excellent', 'good' and 'poor' are value-laden whereas specific comments about the quality and content of pupils' work are more helpful. Feedback that focuses on the learner rather than the learning is ineffective. While praise can boost self-esteem and give confidence in the short term, used alone it has no long-term impact on learning.

Timely

Children who play computer games are often fully immersed trying to better their previous scores. Gaming is a good example of just-in-time feedback. Players can try again and progress to the next level to win whatever reward is on offer. They are fully engaged and stimulated by the task. Feedback is most effective when it is given immediately or just after the learning, rather than at a later point in a few days' or weeks' time. Research shows that learners who get immediate feedback perform better than those whose feedback is delayed – so the sooner, the better (Irons, 2008). If teachers wait too long to give feedback, the moment is lost and the learner might not connect the feedback with the action. Some schools are now creating 'read comments' time for feedback at the start of each lesson. This enables learners to understand the progress they have made from their initial performance to where they are now. Studies show that use of this 'progress feedback' enhances both learning and motivation (Schunk and Ertmer, 1999).

All pupils should receive feedback on the progress they make from given starting points. There are times, however, when it is wise to wait a short while before giving feedback. For instance, teachers sometimes need rehearsal time to think through what they might say, particularly when offering feedback on personal and social development issues. Or, when observing learners who are fully engrossed in their activity, the feedback they naturally acquire through trial and error may prove more helpful than direct feedback from the teacher.

Who is behind it?

Several psychologists in the first half of the twentieth century started to consider the role of feedback in their studies of animal and human behaviour. The American psychologist Edward Thorndike (1874–1949) found that cats could escape purpose-built puzzle boxes by learning to negotiate various challenges, such as opening a door by pressing a button. The process was repeated time and time again using different cats. Thorndike noticed that the cats soon learned what to do to escape and receive food as a reward. From his observations, he proposed the 'law of effect' which states that a response to a situation, which results in a satisfying outcome, is more likely to be repeated; conversely, responses to situations that bring unsatisfying outcomes are less likely to be repeated. For Thorndike, learning was a matter of making connections and the role of reinforcement (feedback) was to strengthen the connection between action and outcome.

Other psychologists were interested in the role of technology in providing feedback to learners. In the 1920s, Sidney Pressey (1888–1979) created a teaching machine (resembling a typewriter) in which users pressed keys when answering multiple choice questions and received immediate feedback on whether they were right or wrong. Pressey's machines appeared during the Great Depression when there was no appetite for investing in technologies that might reduce the number of teachers. However, during the Second World War, US soldiers were trained using motion picture films and this gave impetus to the spread of audio-visual technologies in many schools. Moreover, Soviet advances in the Space Race put pressure on educators in the United States to keep up, particularly in the field of science, mathematics and technology. Teaching machines offering 'fast' education flooded the market.

The psychologist B. F. Skinner's interest in technology began when he visited his daughter's school to observe an arithmetic lesson. He noticed that all the students worked at the same pace and had to wait twenty-four hours to learn the accuracy of their responses to the problems set. Within a few days he had built his own machine, where students pulled levers to indicate their numerical answers. A light appeared when they answered correctly. Skinner wanted to go beyond testing student responses to giving them feedback, by teaching them new material in small steps. Rather than using a multiple-choice format, his machine enabled users to construct their own text and compare this to the right answer by sliding a panel to the side. From this breakthrough, the term 'programmed learning' was coined to describe information constructed in a logical and systematic manner (Skinner, 1958). Travelling salespeople were soon selling thousands of teaching machines, with predictions that half of the student population in the United States would be using one by 1965. Gradually, the development of the microcomputer in the late 1970s and early 1980s offered new opportunities for programmed or computer-assisted learning and quick feedback.

One of the core principles of programmed learning is that learners need to demonstrate mastery at a certain level (usually a threshold of 80 per cent) before advancing to the next level. This was the case with Benjamin Bloom's Learning for Mastery programme in the 1960s, where regular feedback was provided on how well learners met objectives. Bloom noted that teachers' traditional practice was to organise curriculum content into units and then assess students' progress on completion. He reasoned that it would be more valuable to integrate feedback as part of the teaching and learning process and then set specific corrective tasks (Bloom, 1971). Those who did not reach the threshold were retaught, while enrichment activities were provided for those who demonstrated competence so they could broaden their learning. Tests were used before and after to measure progress.

In more recent times, theorists have stressed the active role of students in the feedback process and have played down the stimulus-response connections advocated by behaviourism. When feedback is provided to students they filter messages and seek to make meaning, drawing on their prior knowledge and experiences rather than simply responding to stimuli in an automated manner. To make sense of things, learners go through a process of self-regulation in deciding what they want to achieve and devise strategies to do this.

While feedback has summative purposes in terms of summing up where pupils have reached in their learning, since the 1990s there has been growing recognition that there should be more to it than this. Between 1996 and 2010, a group of academics worked together as the Assessment

Reform Group (ARG) to provide a firm evidence base for policy-makers in the field of assessment. It defined assessment for learning (AfL) as: 'The process of seeking and interpreting evidence for use by learners and their teachers to decide where the learners are in their learning, where they need to go and how best to get there' (Assessment Reform Group, 2002; DCSF, 2008b: 3). ARG set out ten principles where assessment for learning:

1. Is part of effective planning.
2. Focuses on how pupils learn.
3. Is central to classroom practice.
4. Is a key professional skill.
5. Is sensitive and constructive.
6. Fosters motivation.
7. Promotes understanding of goals and criteria.
8. Helps learners know how to improve.
9. Develops the capacity for peer and self-assessment.
10. Recognises all educational achievement.

Underpinning these principles is the belief that everyone can make progress.

Two prominent members of the ARG, Paul Black and Dylan Wiliam, popularised the idea that assessment should be used to inform and shape learning, rather than simply describe what has been learned. They reviewed findings from 250 studies on assessment before recommending teachers should:

» Be clear about the learning objectives and success criteria.
» Use effective questioning.
» Encourage pupils to see errors as learning opportunities.
» Give constructive feedback.
» Encourage pupils to review their own work and that of others. (Black and Wiliam, 1998)

Pausing is an important sub-skill of questioning. Having asked a question, effective teachers allow learners time to think, reflect, rehearse what they are going to say and answer their questions. Mary Rowe (1978; 1987) an American researcher, coined the term 'wait time' to describe how much time teachers gave pupils to answer their questions in the context of teaching science. After analysing 800 tape recordings of lessons, she found that teachers waited only a second or less before they asked someone else, answered the question themselves or rephrased the question. But when she persuaded the teachers to extend the wait time to three seconds, she found that the quality and length of pupils' answers improved.

All learners make mistakes – these are intrinsic to the learning experience. Mistakes can be categorised as errors or misconceptions. Errors can occur for all sorts of reasons, from a slip of the pencil to a lapse in concentration. These errors are usually recognised when learners are asked to review their work. Their progress in learning is not usually hindered. However, there are times when learners do not understand the ideas presented and they develop misconceptions. In mathematics, for example, they may think that to multiply by 10, you just add a zero (not always the case, e.g. 23.2 x 10) or they may think that a number with three digits is always bigger than a number with two (e.g. 3.76 is bigger than 4.5).[1] Teaching children to estimate answers is a useful way of helping them to limit the number of careless mistakes.

In terms of providing written feedback, it is simply unmanageable for every piece of work generated by learners to be marked in detail. Hence, Shirley Clarke (2003) advocates the use of selective 'quality marking', using specific prompts:

» A reminder prompt – e.g. 'Don't forget to look at ...'
» A scaffold prompt – e.g. 'Can you find another way?'
» An example prompt – e.g. 'Choose one of these or your own.'

Teachers need to decide which pieces of work to give detailed attention and which they are simply going to acknowledge. Learners can also select what they consider to be their best contributions in a unit of work.

Written feedback can take a mixed form of questions, encouragements and pointers. Simply saying what needs to be improved is not sufficient – learners also need to know *how* to improve to inform future performance. Constructive feedback is often best given on a one-to-one

---

1   For a useful list of common mathematical errors see: http://www.counton.org/resources/misconceptions.

basis, with a focus on learners' personal development rather than comparison to others. This is particularly so for younger, less able or less confident pupils. Some schools expect teachers to record verbal feedback (VF) alongside the work in pupils' books as a record of the feedback provided.

Marking pupils' work can be very time consuming and hence many schools use marking codes and symbols to make the best use of teachers' time. However, it is important for teachers to go beyond ticks and crosses because these can demotivate and, if given without a comment, can imply that they do not take much interest in what is written. The inclusion of short phrases such as, 'I agree with this', 'Spot on' or 'Interesting point', take a little longer to add but can prove motivating. Many teachers try to make time to develop a brief written dialogue with learners by encouraging them to respond to questions or prompts. This can turn into a three-way dialogue involving other pupils or parents. These additional audiences can add interest and perspective.

Traditionally feedback takes a one-directional format – the teacher gives information to the learner about his or her performance. However, Pollock (2012) calls feedback the 'hinge' between teaching and learning. It allows for the transfer of information from the teacher to the learner and back again. Teachers should therefore receive feedback from learners and use this as a basis for future planning. According to Hattie (2009: 173): 'The mistake I made was seeing feedback as something *teachers provided to students* – it was only when I discovered that feedback was most powerful when it is from the *student to the teacher* that I started to understand it better.'

So what do we know about pupils' views of feedback? MacBeath et al. (2008) found that pupils were concerned about giving feedback to teachers on their teaching because they feared this would have negative repercussions. A study by the Wellcome Trust (2010) asked pupils to imagine that they were primary teachers and to suggest how they should be assessed. They preferred to be given tests just after completing a topic rather than waiting for a longer period, as with end-of-year assessments.

Many schools use 'response buddies' or 'talking partners' to provide opportunities for pupils to feed back to each other on their work. It is important that they receive training on this and that ground rules are clearly understood and displayed as reminders. For instance, these might include:

» Telling partners the good things seen in their work.

» Listening to what they have to say.

» Making suggestions as clear as possible.

» Being fair and not talking about their work in a nasty way.

These kinds of comments appear in marking partner agreements that are popular in some schools. It is usual practice for partners to first point out something they like before suggesting an area to improve, but they should be directed to refer to the success criteria in doing so. Often a partner writes a comment in another child's book using a different coloured pencil and adds their initials. In some schools, teachers use short breaks known as check-ins, learning or pit stops during independent activities. Partners are asked to talk about how well they have met the success criteria for the lesson, to give reasons for their assessments and to provide examples. If well focused, these are sensible ideas because self-review and peer review are powerful means of retaining knowledge and clarifying understanding.

Why is it important, and what can you do?

Assessment for learning has become one of the dominant motifs in education over recent decades. However, despite initial optimism and government support, assessment for learning strategies have not been adopted widely enough in schools. Part of the problem remains that teachers continue to equate assessment with examinations and tests rather than better teaching (Stewart, 2012). Improving the quality of assessment is a frequent recommendation that features in school inspection reports. In cases where feedback is ineffective, it is too little, too late, too vague and too impersonal.

Within assessment for learning, feedback has been widely recognised as a key formative strategy that is likely to lead to an increase in standards (Black and Wiliam, 1998; Gibbs and Simpson, 2004). Decades of education research support the idea that by teaching less and providing more feedback, we can produce greater learning (see Bransford et al., 2000; Marzano et al., 2001; Hattie, 2009). However, feedback does not automatically lead to improvements in learning. Feedback can be significant but for the wrong reasons. Sweeping comments, sarcasm and ridicule can seriously demotivate learners and make things worse for them. At the most basic level, feedback needs to be clearly stated and it should be easy for learners to work out what they are being asked to do. If they have to reread teacher comments in books to make sense of what has been written, then this reflects poorly on the teacher. If they cannot understand oral feedback, again this raises questions about the quality of communication.

There is plenty of guidance available to teachers on how to improve particular feedback practices such as questioning (e.g. Pagliaro, 2011; Walsh and Satters, 2011; Pope, 2013). Wragg (2001) points out that the distinction between lower order questions (recalling facts) and higher order questions (going beyond facts) is rather crude. Factual recall can be a very demanding process – for example, recalling the formula of DNA – while an open-ended question, such as 'Why is the centre of London noisier than the local cemetery?', in theory, is a higher order one but is not as intellectually challenging.

It is also the case that teachers ask too many questions – at least several hundred a day. The problem with this is that not only do teachers take up more time than is necessary (thereby reducing the amount of time for pupils to talk), but teachers eventually answer some of these questions themselves. They work through 'answer pulling' routines, bringing pupils around to what they have in their heads. Teaching remains one of the few occupations where the answers to the vast majority of the questions asked are already known.

How teachers respond to pupils' answers is also important to building a climate of mutual respect and conveying the idea that feedback is a two-way process. Teachers need to be receptive to what pupils say, and they can show this in different ways:

1. By rephrasing the teacher's original question – e.g. 'Let me put it another way ...'
2. By seeking clarification – e.g. 'What do you mean when you say ...?'
3. By asking for examples – e.g. 'How would this work?'
4. By inviting the learner to rephrase things – e.g. 'Can you put it another way?'

Practitioners need to reflect on to whom they direct their questions, how often and when and how they respond to what pupils say. It is common for the same voices to be heard in classes when teachers ask questions. This is why some schools have introduced strategies to ensure that all pupils have the opportunity to answer a question at some point in the lesson, such as distributing a Q (question) card that individuals hold up.

While effective questioning is a critical teaching practice, there are times when it is inappropriate and alternatives should be considered. For instance, teachers might respond to learners through:

» Making statements – e.g. 'This is what we have said ...'
» Repeating what a child says – e.g. Child: 'It's a circle.' Teacher: 'It's a circle.' Child: 'No, it's a cuboid.'
» Highlighting different views – e.g. 'That's interesting. You think the Romans were cruel. Steve thinks they were brave.'
» Giving personal feelings – e.g. 'I'm a bit confused about this.'
» Offering non-verbal cues – e.g. nod of the head.
» Using fillers – e.g. 'uh-huh', 'mhmm'.
» Verbal and non-verbal expressions – e.g. 'Wow', smiling.
» Inviting others to talk – e.g. 'It is John's turn to say something now.'

Knowing how to respond to learners comes from understanding them as individuals and seeing the bigger picture. For instance, when a group discussion is flowing well and a shy individual begins to contribute, simply acknowledging this with a nod and a smile may be enough feedback rather than asking a supplementary question.

While most teachers recognise the importance of feedback, it remains challenging to implement efficiently and effectively with a class of thirty or so children. The following principles and practices can support teachers:

» Be systematic – keep a careful record of each child's progress.
» Use technology to save time – computer programmes that offer quizzes and other assessment exercises; record a podcast or video explaining a task; most schools have management information systems to track the progress of learners.
» Put the onus on learners to self-check and use reference materials such as dictionaries and encyclopaedias. Provide them with a different coloured pen when self-marking.
» Mark fewer pieces of work but focus on quality.

» Use statement banks – examples of common feedback phrases.
» Use marking codes.
» Set shorter assignments and tasks.
» Invite learners to submit their best work for marking.
» Consider using other adults in the school for 'special' feedback, depending on the piece of work (e.g. canteen assistants, governors, specialist coach, parent helpers, head teacher).
» Invite externals to feed back to pupils (e.g. librarians, curators, university school of education, local businesses).

According to the Sutton Trust and Education Endowment Foundation, effective feedback can add an extra eight months of learning gains in an academic year.[2] But if it were straightforward to introduce effective feedback then all schools would do so. The reality is that teachers need to rethink how they see feedback – not as a one-way street, but where learners themselves are trusted and taught to regularly give feedback on their own progress and that of others.

Conclusion

Effective feedback depends on mutually respectful relationships where learning occurs in a climate of trust, empathy and support, rather than fear and ridicule. Pupils need to feel at ease in the classroom, not worrying over whether they are doing the right thing. Teachers need to connect with children's experience of the world by sharing news, stories and anecdotes, listening with empathy to what they have to say and creating opportunities for them to demonstrate what they can do in different ways. In other words, schools need to provide broad, engaging and relevant learning. A relaxed but purposeful learning environment enables pupils to flourish.

Above all, being in tune with each learner means believing that everyone can improve with appropriate help and support, rather than seeing their ability as fixed. Pupils may not 'perform' well and succeed at a particular task because of all sorts of things going on in their lives – they

---

2 See https://educationendowmentfoundation.org.uk/toolkit/toolkit-a-z/.

may be tired from lack of sleep, hungry, dwelling on a recent argument with a friend or anxious about something at home. The task itself may not be particularly stimulating or accessible in terms of the level of language. More generally, factors within the environment (e.g. seating arrangements, noise, lighting, heating) may not be conducive to concentration. Put simply, if children are not in the right 'mood' for working then careless errors can be made. Effective teachers identify and address these barriers to learning through their meticulous planning and preparation *before* providing feedback. This might involve small adjustments, such as clearly labelling resources so that they are easily accessible or checking seating arrangements so that all can see a planned demonstration.

Summary

» Feedback is providing information about someone's performance and how this can be improved.

» High quality feedback is in tune with learners' needs, accurate, timely and specific.

» During the first half of the twentieth century, the American psychologists Edward Thorndike, Sidney Pressey and B. F. Skinner were pioneers in automated feedback.

» In more recent times, the value of constructive feedback has been highlighted by John Hattie and in the assessment for learning literature.

» One of the main implications arising from research for teachers is to provide more feedback during lessons.

Points for reflection and action

» Graham Nuthall (2007) suggests that teachers are unaware of between 70–80 per cent of what happens in a class. What are the implications here for giving accurate feedback?

» Watch the video called 'Austin's Butterfly' (available at https://www.youtube.com/watch?v=hqh1MRWZjms). What does Ron Berger's work reveal about the power of peer feedback? What are the implications for your own practice?

» The way you say things is very important. Learn this phrase: 'Mia, I think you could have presented this more neatly – do you agree?' Now try giving this feedback to a partner in the following manner:

- Whispering.
- Shouting.
- Slowly.
- Sharply.
- Spoken with a smile.
- Spoken with a frown.
- Spoken with a tear.
- In a monotone.
- In a carefree manner.

» Ask your partner how she feels after each alternative. Now try mixing up some of these with emphasis on certain words and discuss the effect.

Chapter 10

Reflective practice

Good teachers critically analyse their practice with a view to improving what they do

What is the big idea?

In his book *Winners*, Alastair Campbell, the former director of communications to Prime Minister Tony Blair, interviewed the most successful people in life. He found that many attributed their success to always striving to improve and moving beyond their comfort zone. Colm O'Connell, coach to Kenya's leading runners, told Campbell: 'The winner is the loser who evaluates himself correctly' (Campbell, 2015: 354). Those at the top of their profession, including teachers, are continually reflecting on their performance and impact on others. The skills of reflective practice are highly regarded in the world's most successful teacher education programmes such as those found in Singapore, Canada and Hong Kong (Schleisser, 2012). The big idea in this chapter is that reflective practice moves professionals on in their own learning by taking them out of 'autopilot' mode to a state where they are imagining and working towards a better world. This is achieved when practitioners question what they routinely do, focus on the consequences of their teaching, engage in professional dialogue with colleagues and consider how this and wider evidence can support improvement.

The term 'reflective practice' has dominated teacher education over recent decades, so much so that it has become something of a cliché. It is often used interchangeably with reflection, critical reflection, reflective thinking and reflexivity. The association of reflection with a mirror isn't helpful – a mirror reflects appearance in the here and now rather than hinting at what might be. It provides an image of what is directly in front of it. This is why Bolton (2014) suggests that looking 'through the mirror' is a more helpful metaphor, so that teachers can perceive a range of possible scenarios beyond what is immediately in front of them.

There are certainly many definitions of reflective practice, a term that is also popular in professions other than teaching, such as dentistry, medicine, law and social care. In nursing, for instance, reflective practice is simply defined as 'the examination of personal thoughts and actions' (Welsh Government, 2015: 2). Perhaps the simplest view of reflective practice is as asking searching questions about what teachers do, how they do things and whether improvements can be made. Moon (2004: 181) likens reflection to the imaginary instrument called a 'pensieve', which features in J. K. Rowling's *Harry Potter and the Goblet of Fire*: 'One simply siphons the excess thoughts from one's mind, pours them into the basin, and examines them at one's leisure. It becomes easier to spot patterns and links, you understand, when they are in this form' (Rowling, 2000: 518).

Reflective practice is more than mulling over what has happened during the day. Brookfield (1995: 3) describes reflective practice as 'hunting assumptions' where the values and beliefs that underpin actions are called into question. For instance, many newly qualified teachers are often advised 'Don't smile before Christmas', borne out of a concern that they will become too friendly with pupils and lose discipline. Reflective teachers recognise the need to maintain control but also see that humour has a key role to play in establishing a good rapport with pupils.

Reflective practice is not a technique but a way of looking at the world and recognising its complex make-up. This is particularly so when considering school life with all its variables. For some writers, critical reflection assumes a higher pitch in exploring professional issues, problems or dilemmas where there are no obvious answers. Sullivan et al. (2016) see reflection as something teachers must live, the key to understanding practice and central to action research.

There is no shortage of opportunities for reflection (see Table 10.1). Practitioners can reflect on their teaching methods, the curriculum, the progress of learners, professional relationships with others, the implementation of school policies and practices, the learning environment and learning experiences, as well as aspects of management and leadership. Above all, reflective practitioners should focus on how one's actions support the achievement of learners because, in reality, this is how the success (or otherwise) of teachers and schools are judged. What separates reflective practice from everyday thinking is its purpose and outcome. If it is successful, reflective practice changes perspectives or ways of working. It promotes new insight, ideas and understanding. As a result of the reflective process, it should be possible for a practitioner to say, 'I used to … (think, believe, say, do) but now I …'

Opportunity for reflection	Reflective practice
Thinking about a challenging experience such as teaching a poor lesson.	Discussing the lesson with a colleague, drawing up an action plan and monitoring the impact of any change.
Completing an evaluation of a training event such as a course or conference.	Using the evaluation to reflect on how you might apply new knowledge or skills in specific contexts.
Answering questions during a staff appraisal or review.	Reviewing the previous year, establishing objectives and success criteria for the year ahead.
Submitting lesson plans for review.	Responding to feedback comments to improve planning.
Surveying the views of parents/carers.	Using parental responses to strengthen communication between home and school.
Observing a colleague teach.	Noting strategies that could be adapted in your own practice.

Table 10.1. Opportunities for reflective practice.

Reflective practice can take different forms and operate at different levels. Moore (2004) identifies four types of reflective activity, following on from interviewing postgraduate trainee teachers: ritualistic reflection, pseudo-reflection, productive reflection and reflexivity.

Trainee teachers are familiar with completing lesson evaluations or learning journals and these activities are often taken as opportunities for reflection. Lesson evaluation pro formas can provide useful prompts to structure reflection, especially for beginning teachers. Most include questions along the lines of: were the learning objectives met? How do you know? What might you do differently next time? Some universities and schools also encourage practitioners to reflect on their feelings and zoom in on particular events. One of the challenges with using set lesson evaluation pro formas is that they can restrict thinking, so the inclusion of open-ended prompts is important. For some practitioners, the disciplined process of writing supports their deep thinking and provides a reference point for further reflection. But this is not the case for others who, for example, resent what they perceive as a loss of valuable time and question its value beyond the immediate lesson in hand.

More generally, there is a danger that reflections become superficial and the process ritualistic, based on compliance with course requirements to reflect (e.g. to write five lesson evaluations in a week answering set questions) rather than a genuine, open-ended dialogue to which no immediate action points or targets are agreed. This is often due to pressures placed on trainee or qualified teachers to complete paperwork and demonstrate the achievement of imposed standards or set assessment criteria. The worst scenario for those who genuinely see the value of reflective practice is for teachers to feel they have to 'tick boxes' to keep others off their backs in a culture that places a high value on competence and performativity. This then becomes self-defeating. One postgraduate student interviewed by Moore alluded to the difference between 'inking' and 'thinking' – being obsessed with what is written down on a piece of paper and what the ink says, in contrast to making the connection between 'what the ink says and what's up here, in your head' (Moore, 2004: 107). The challenge then is for practitioners to see that reflective practice can be liberating rather than limiting.

Moore (2004) also refers to 'pseudo-reflection' where there is a genuine intention to consider important issues but this does not lead to changes or improvement. The lack of action is often due to internal parameters set by the teacher who, for example, might not consider the full issue or topic. This might be because of a desire to avoid potentially controversial points that could lead to a reappraisal of practice, so the strategy is to downscale or recast such issues into more acceptable representations.

The higher levels of reflective practice are described as 'productive', 'authentic' or 'constructive' (Moore and Ash, 2002; Moore, 2004) where the practitioner is open to challenging existing views, beliefs and practices – and this leads to positive change. More often than not, this involves self-analysis and working closely with colleagues in undertaking some classroom research or enquiry.

Finally, reflexivity is a particular form of reflection that takes practitioners beyond the here and now to question their personal journeys (autobiographies) of how they got to where they are and how their values and beliefs shape their practice. The term is derived from the Latin meaning 'to turn back on oneself' – a mental contortion that means examining one's fundamental values, prejudices and beliefs. According to Bolton (2010: 14):

A reflexive-minded practitioner will ask ... why did this pass me by: where was my attention directed at that time? Reflexivity is: 'What are the mental, emotional and value structures which allowed me to lose attention and make that error?' This deep questioning is missed out if the practitioner merely undertakes reflection as practical problem-solving: what happened, why, what did I think and feel about it, how can I do it better next time?

Effective teachers often demonstrate reflexivity when faced with a change of circumstances. For example, this might involve being asked at short notice to teach older (or younger) pupils to cover for a colleague. Teachers have to wrestle with different pedagogical approaches and philosophies, forcing them to come to terms with their own values.

Who is behind it?

Since ancient times, philosophers have recognised the value of reflection as a means of questioning one's own assumptions. In 399 BC, the 70-year-old Socrates is said to have uttered the famous words, 'the unexamined life is not worth living', during his court trial – charged with not believing in the gods and corrupting the minds of young Athenians. For Socrates, what mattered was mental and moral well-being over and above materialism, and central to this was questioning one's values and beliefs.

But in the modern age, two American philosophers highlighted the importance of professionals engaging in reflective practice. John Dewey distinguished between the *routine* actions of teachers, where they base their decisions on custom, tradition and authority, and *reflective* action, where they question taken-for-granted knowledge. All practitioners and schools have their particular routines – demonstrated, for example, in the way children are expected to line up, respond to questions, their conduct during registration time or the manner by which classroom order is maintained. Routines are essential at home and at school. Clearly, schools need to be well run and orderly if children are to feel safe, secure and ready to learn. But while it is one thing to follow well-established routines, this does not mean that teachers should blindly carry out what others, often removed from the classroom, want them to do.

Dewey argued that reflective thinking is needed when teachers face doubts, problems or dilemmas. He defined reflection as 'a kind of thinking that consists in turning a subject over in the mind and giving it serious and consecutive considerations' (Dewey, 1933: 3). For Dewey (1944: 150), we reflect when we are emotionally unsettled over something that we don't fully understand, and we do so in order to re-establish our emotional balance. Whereas Dewey suggested that the cognitive response to an event that triggers reflection is one of surprise and perplexity, for many practitioners the emotions are more likely to be guilt, hope, fear, frustration, amusement and embarrassment (Tripp, 2012: xii). The key point is that emotions are very much part of reflective practice, which is not a purely cognitive exercise.

It was another American philosopher, Donald Schön (1930–1997), who is said to have coined the phrase 'reflective practitioner'. Schön's doctoral thesis was on Dewey's theory of enquiry and this provided the necessary stimulus to consider how knowledge acquired by professionals is, in practice, different from the kinds of knowing in academic textbooks, journals and scientific papers. When Schön's *The Reflective Practitioner: How Professionals Think in Action* appeared in 1983, it was widely acclaimed for exploring new territory. He described how practitioners reflect and acquire new knowledge. They reflect in action or, as Schön put it, 'on the hoof'. For teachers, this means making on-the-spot decisions during lessons – whether to ignore a minor disruption or not, how to respond if the Internet connection is lost, who to ask to demonstrate a teaching point and so forth. Those teachers who demonstrate reflection *in* action most effectively are not fazed by the unexpected and are able to discern the most appropriate action at the time. They may not respond in the same way if the situation is repeated because they take into account the context, such as the different needs of pupils, the time of day or likely consequence of actions. Schön also described reflection *on* action, when teachers review sessions afterwards and consider how they might do things differently, with a view to improving the quality of teaching, learning or the learning environment. This reflection can occur immediately or some time after the event and is not confined to a single experience. The reflective practitioner is likely to draw on wider knowledge gained from talking to colleagues, reading relevant literature and reflecting on personal experiences.

Reflection is a cyclical process that informs action (Figure 10.1). It is possible to reflect *before* action, when practitioners plan ahead to anticipate how lessons might develop and the kinds of challenges that could arise. In a sense, such reflection features in contingency planning and consideration of the question, 'What will I do if ...?' Reflection has to be purposeful and so reflection for action sets out what changes are to be made.

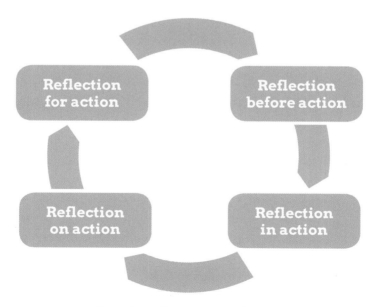

Figure 10.1. The cycle of reflection.

Paulo Freire (1921–1997), a Brazilian educator and philosopher, provided a different dimension to reflective practice. His most famous work, *Pedagogy of the Oppressed* (1970), is critical of what he called the 'banking' concept of education, in which students are viewed as empty accounts to be filled by the teacher. According to Freire, oppressed learners are subjected to a 'culture of silence' that suppresses their self-image. He witnessed at first hand the ignorance and poverty of peasants in rural Brazil. His father was a wealthy banker who lost his fortune in the Wall Street Crash of 1929, at which point the family moved to the countryside where Freire started to teach illiterate peasants. Through this he began to realise how the oppressed could and should have a voice. He questioned the traditional teacher–student relationship and its one-sidedness in terms of power, knowledge and freedom. In one session a peasant asks Freire (1970: 45), 'Why don't you explain the picture first? That way it'll take less time and won't give us a headache.' Freire (1970: 45) describes how even when his students generated lively discussions they would stop and apologise: 'Excuse us, we ought to keep quiet and let you talk. You are the one who knows, we don't know anything.'

Freire's key contribution was to highlight the concept of *praxis* – where theory (thought) and practice (action) unite to shape and change the world. This goes beyond action based on reflection to a commitment to transform human experience, to search for truth and to when educators take 'risky' decisions based on their own moral purpose. Freire was heavily influenced by Marxism and maintained that the oppressed needed not only to be free from poverty but also enjoy the freedom to create, question, challenge and explore. We can only experience true knowledge through restless, ongoing, critical enquiry with other people about their relations to the world. Reflective praxis is about challenging the status quo and empowering marginalised groups. It calls for practitioners to stand up and engage in debate over educational policies and initiatives that they envisage will be difficult to implement, educationally unsound, morally bereft or socially divisive. In a research context, this means building relationships based on trust. For teachers absorbed in praxis, the implication is that they make decisions informed by sound theory and enable learners to have a genuine voice in how and what they learn. This means empowering school councils and other forums so that learners discuss substantive issues, such as the quality of learning and teaching (Whitty and Wisby, 2007).

Freire's experience of teaching illiterate people in Latin America seems to belong to a very different world from modern advanced societies. However, there is the threat of a new 'culture of silence' emerging around young people and their technological experiences. Is technology empowering or disempowering, liberating or addictive and oppressive? It is not uncommon for millions of youngsters to be glued to their mobile devices and the subtle programming of minds that this brings. Paradoxically, however, the same technologies can democratise education so that teachers are no longer seen as unquestioned authorities and as knowing everything. In some schools, Freire's influence can be seen clearly – for example, teachers and learners at Rosendale Primary School, in London, have published a book together about learning in the school which is very much along the lines advocated by Freire (Atkins and Hopkins, 2012). Learners co-design 'generative' topics and follow lines of enquiry which lead to definite product outcomes – a poem, painting or model. These are presented to a range of audiences which evaluate them for impact and effectiveness. Ofsted has rated the school and the teaching as outstanding, praising the strong emphasis on learning in real-life situations (Ofsted, 2013b).

In terms of higher level critical reflection, an important figure in the twentieth century was Colonel John Flanagan (1906–1996), a psychologist in the US army. He introduced the Critical Incident Technique (CIT), which he described as:

A set of procedures for collecting direct observations of human behavior in such a way as to facilitate their potential usefulness in solving practical problems and developing broad psychological principles. The critical incident technique outlines procedures for collecting observed incidents having special significance and meeting systematically defined criteria. (Flanagan, 1954: 327)

The use of CIT grew out of studies on those training to be US pilots during the Second World War. Initially psychologists studied the specific reasons why pilot candidates were eliminated from flight training schools in 1941. Many of the reasons given by the elimination board members were of a general nature (e.g. 'unsuitable temperament', 'insufficient progress'), but a few cases described specific behaviours.

In a 1944 study of combat leadership, researchers asked serving pilots to describe incidents they observed that they thought were particularly helpful or a hindrance in completing their missions. Several thousand responses were categorised to produce a list of critical requirements of combat leadership (Flanagan, 1954). These studies sharpened the Air Force's selection and training procedures. At the end of the war, the psychologists established the American Institute for Research. Their studies highlighted the behaviours necessary across a range of occupations, from air traffic controllers to sales clerks and teachers. The data was gathered by means of the CIT and revolved around people telling stories about experiences they'd had. In particular, they were asked to retell one or several incidents that represented positive and/or negative aspects of the activity being studied.

Flanagan's legacy can be seen in the many textbooks recommending critical incidents as key points for reflection. Brookfield (1990: 84) defines critical incidents as 'vividly remembered events' which represent potential turning points in understanding. Obviously, teachers and other professionals can benefit from frameworks to support their reflection on critical incidents. One of the simplest models centres around three questions: What? So what? Now what? (Borton, 1970, Rolfe et al., 2001). When reviewing a particular incident, for instance, a teacher might ask:

» What was I trying to achieve (aims/learning objectives of the lesson)? What actions did I take? What was the response of the learners?

» So what does this tell me about my relationships in the class? So what was going through my mind as I acted? So what did I base my actions on?

» Now what do I need to do to improve my teaching or relationships? Now what broader issues need to be considered if this action is to be successful? Now what might be the consequences of this action?

However, there is also scope within reflective practice to think about more mundane daily actions. In fact, some writers argue that it is only by examining the easily forgettable moments that reflective practitioners really understand themselves (Sharkey, 2004).

Brookfield (1995) highlighted the importance of seeing one's own practices through four critical, interconnected lenses (Figure 10.2). The aim is to reach a more rounded understanding of practice by comparing

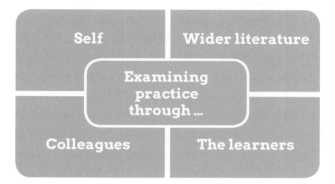

Figure 10.2. Brookfield's reflective lenses.

personal views of teaching episodes with those of learners, colleagues and theorists.

Over recent years, Andrew Pollard and his colleagues have contributed to our understanding of the characteristics of reflective practice (Pollard and Triggs, 1997; Pollard, 2014). Pollard and Tann (1993: 9–10) suggest that the reflective practitioner:

» Has an active concern with aims and consequences, as well as means and technical efficiency.
» Requires competence in methods of classroom enquiry (gathering data, analysis, evaluation) to support the development of teaching competence.
» Requires open-mindedness, responsibility and wholeheartedness.
» Is based on teacher judgement which is informed partly by self-reflection and partly by insights from educational disciplines.
» Is enhanced through collaboration and dialogue with colleagues.

Three key attributes of reflective practitioners, originally highlighted by John Dewey (1910), are open-mindedness, wholeheartedness and responsibility. Thinking teachers need to be open-minded to new ideas, wholehearted in seeking out fresh ways of doing things and responsible in acknowledging the consequences of what they do. Reflective practitioners do more than evaluate the technical aspects of lessons, such as the deployment of resources or teaching strategies. They probe beneath the surface to reveal underlying values and beliefs, acknowledging that human behaviour is complex and shaped by many forces.

In contrast, unreflective teachers are more accepting of what happens in school and education in general. They are less open-minded than reflective practitioners, less likely to explore alternatives and less inclined to carry out their own small-scale research. This does not mean that unreflective teachers do not think about their practice. Rather, it means that they are less receptive to seeing their practice through the eyes of others and opening this up for critical review. Pollard's notion of reflective teaching is closely aligned to classroom enquiry. Practitioners need to develop their research skills in locating evidence, interpreting data, drawing conclusions and reporting findings in order to inform their critical reflection. They are better placed to make sound judgement calls if they can refer to evidence.

Most models of reflective practice share common features. These include starting from a particular incident or experience, describing this in some detail, asking questions about 'why' and 'how', engaging with theory and planning for a better experience. The process involves both emotion and thought. It is cyclical in nature, rather than a linear process, with reflection going hand in hand with planning, teaching, management, assessment and evaluation. This is an important point because too often reflection is seen in linear terms as a post-lesson episode which is separate from the teaching experience.

Why is it important, and what can you do?

Reflective practice calls for time, self-motivation, emotional commitment and open-mindedness. It is potentially risky if the outcomes of personal reflections are shared with others who are less sympathetic to the process. Moreover, as one leading supporter of reflective practice acknowledges, for many professionals reflection is 'boring, a waste of time, too difficult, or too exposing' (Bolton, 2014: xviii). Despite these challenges, the value of reflective practice is widely recognised, particularly among teacher educators. Nonetheless, the fact that universities push reflective practice as a good idea should not be the driving force for teachers to become reflective. Rather, teachers need to be motivated by seeing the value of 'stepping outside' what they do and looking afresh at their practice. Larrivee (2000: 293) argues: 'Unless teachers develop the practice of reflection, they stay trapped in unexamined judgments, interpretations, assumptions, and expectations.'

Reflective practice not only benefits the individual practitioner, it also supports whole-school improvements (Day, 1999; Griffiths, 2000). Reflective practitioners are alert to institutional and broader cultural contexts within which they operate. Regular opportunities for teams to reflect are central to successful institutional self-evaluation (Menter et al., 2010). The *Teachers' Standards,* despite its emphasis on technical skills, acknowledges that 'appropriate self evaluation, reflection and professional development activity is critical to improving teachers' practice at all career stages' (DfE, 2011a: 7).

So what makes reflective practice worth the effort? It would be reassuring to say that being reflective automatically leads to better quality teaching and learning. Unfortunately there is no substantial research to suggest this is the case. We all know teachers who are not particularly reflective but are effective in the classroom. However, reflective practice done well:

» Increases self-awareness of teachers' strengths and areas for development.

» Empowers teachers to take control of their own professional development, setting targets and monitoring their progress against these.

» Introduces teachers to multiple perspectives and the value of uncertainty.

» Develops leadership skills by creating the habit of justifying decisions, drawing on reliable evidence and making connections.

Moreover, arguably reflective practice should not be judged through the narrow lens of teacher effectiveness. Rather, it should be judged in terms of whether it achieves what it sets out to achieve – namely, to contribute to the development of thoughtful teachers. Malderez and Wedell (2007) argue that what matters more than what teachers actually *do* is their understanding of *why* (where and when) they are doing it. Teachers can be effective in implementing what others direct them to do but lack the wherewithal to justify their actions. If teachers do things because they are expected to, they are likely to do so very differently from those who fully support the same thing. This is not an argument to justify subversion. Teachers have a professional duty to meet statutory requirements, but this should not be at odds with developing their own independent philosophy of teaching. Clearly, beginning teachers particularly value a certain degree of structure offered by the syllabus, lesson plans, published classroom materials and the national curriculum itself. But the capacity to reflect in, for and about practice can only enrich the professional development of teachers.

How to develop reflective skills

While there are many books and websites championing reflective practice, relatively few describe how teachers can improve their reflective skills. As with any skills, deliberate everyday practice is the key to developing the capacity to reflect well. Researchers in the United States have estimated that it takes between twenty and thirty hours of training for experienced teachers to view events objectively, with the same number of hours again needed to practise the skills of reflection (Wildman and Niles, 1987). More recently, Kaufman (2013) suggests that it takes twenty hours to learn anything sufficiently well – not to reach the level of expertise but to perform well enough for your own purposes. The key factors that make for effective reflection are support, time and space. Support is needed from leaders and administrators, not only in terms of creating a collaborative and open environment, but also in helping teachers come to terms with the potentially uncomfortable outcomes of their honest reflections.

Typically, teachers' reflective skills progress through several stages, steps or levels, depending on the model. This involves progressing from describing to analysing events; from focusing on the microclimate of the classroom to the broader educational landscape; from asking 'what' to 'why' and 'what if' questions; from accepting to challenging the context for learning; and from considering personal views to engaging with theories and expert viewpoints. McGregor and Cartwright (2011) offer a useful model showing the movement from routine responses to events (levels 1 and 2) to more reflective, sophisticated analysis of practice (Table 10.2).

Level	Reflective level
1st	Being able to identify and describe a critical incident or happening. The *what* of a situation.
2nd	Being able to explain *why* you did it the way you did or *why* the critical incident arose.
3rd	Being able to recognize that there were *different ways* to act in the critical happening or incident.
4th	Being able to devise a way of *finding out* whether one approach was better than another leading up to that kind of critical incident.
5th	Comparing evidence to decide *which* approach worked best, to avoid an incident arising again, and *why*.

Table 10.2. Progression in reflective practice.

Source: McGregor and Cartwright (2011: 236).

Steps 1 and 2 are straightforward descriptions of what happened and why, while the third step provides only hypothetical answers. It is only at the fourth and fifth steps that practitioners begin to explore whether changes in practice are worthwhile. At these higher levels of reflection, practitioners are engaging in metacognition by thinking through what they did, what they might change and how this could be evaluated. But they are also considering the reflective process itself – for instance, how often they take time out to reflect, the extent to which they value reflective practice and the techniques they use to document their reflections.

There are various means of recording and supporting reflective practice (see Table 10.3). The choice very much depends on whether there are plans to share outcomes with others and the time and resources available.

More structured approaches are useful for systematically collecting data but these are more time consuming than informal discussions. The most common technique, popularised in teacher training courses, is the use of reflective journals or diaries. Supporters claim that journal writing is empowering, therapeutic and nurturing (see Moon, 2001). For some people, the act of writing is liberating and helps them to come to terms with whatever is troubling them. It also sharpens thinking processes in terms of how to express thoughts. For others, reflective writing is not something they find easy – they may feel anxious about recording personal musings, fearing who might read and act on these. They may lack confidence in the autobiographical style of writing or feel uncertain over what to write and how much they should record. Dye (2011) advises trainee teachers to adopt an SOS approach to writing by focusing on *self, others* and the *situation*.

There are also particular ethical tensions relating to journals, such as respecting the privacy of the writer but also establishing clear boundaries

Strategy	Notes
Reflective journals or diaries	Record incidents, ideas and reflections gained from different sources such as observations and training courses.
Session observation	Agree a focus (e.g. questioning skills) to observe a colleague or for her/him to observe you.
Feedback	Part of professional dialogue, and often following a lesson observation, feedback can take various forms (e.g. formal, informal, general, specific, directive, open-ended).
Video stimulated reflective dialogue	Video-record a lesson, or part of a lesson, and focus on particular behaviours. Review with an experienced colleague.
E-learning tools	Technologies such as online forums, blogs, e-portfolios (webfolios) and virtual learning environments can all support learning and reflection.
Graphic organisers	Visual tools such as mind maps, diagrams and charts can aid recall and understanding.
Professional discussions	Conversations with a colleague or mentor about an aspect of practice or professional development goal.
Problem-based learning	Real-life scenarios used as a basis to develop critical thinking needed for effective reflective practice.
Learner voice	Set aside time for learners to complete evaluations or talk to them about their learning and use these to inform reflections.

Table 10.3. Strategies to support reflective practice.

over what can and cannot be said. For example, journal writers need to avoid naming individuals or writing in such a way that third parties can easily identify them. The format of journals can vary: some are structured with question prompts, exercises and headings to follow; others are unstructured and free flowing; and many are semi-structured, with stage-specific prompts. The design and format much depends on the purpose for which the journal is kept. Moon (2001) provides suggestions on how journals can be used productively and starting points for writing, such as writing a list of 'things I am good at' or 'things I would like to change in the way I …' Another technique is called stepping stones, where practitioners take a topic and list their first memory of it in terms of a word or short phrase, then a second, third and so on until the present day. This creates a chronological list of eight or so items. This can be undertaken as a group word association exercise where individuals share memories, which are then used as a basis for group reflection. Moon suggests that these stepping stone lists will differ considerably from one day to the next.

The use of technologies to record and stimulate reflections has grown in popularity. Teachers can create their own podcasts (audio stories) or download those produced by others and use these as a stimulus for reflection. For example, in 2015, BBC Radio 4 ran a series called *The Educators* on great educationalists whose ideas are shaping education today.[1] These included John Hattie, Salman Khan, Jo Boaler and Sugata Mitra.

Blogs or online diaries can be written within a closed and trusted environment (such as a university or school virtual learning environment) or for the general public. For many trainee teachers, opportunities to collaborate online provides immediate access to much valued emotional support during the ups and downs of training. But blogging and the sharing of e-portfolios can also contribute to teachers' thinking about professional issues and dilemmas.

The most controversial and fastest growing form of reflection is the use of social networking. Trainee and experienced teachers use applications such as Facebook, Twitter and Bebo to offer advice, share ideas and engage in discussion. Trainees typically use social networking to discuss school placements and classroom ideas. However, the extent to which these e-learning tools support deep reflection is under researched. What

---

1 See http://www.bbc.co.uk/programmes/b04dwbkt.

is clear is that teachers are increasingly using digital technologies to access the latest information on education, check out professional development opportunities and follow the kernels of wisdom disseminated by the likes of Ewan McIntosh (http://edu.blogs.com).

These positive applications are counterbalanced by concerns over the unethical use of social network sites which surface from time to time. While most complaints involve teachers starting inappropriate relationships with students, in some instances teachers have found themselves in trouble for being critical of colleagues or other members of the school community. The growing importance of such issues is reflected in the guidance issued by trade unions to its members and ever expanding school policies on everything from information technology to acceptable use and now social media policies.

Lesson observations are a potentially rich source for reflection. Most schools have systems in place to enable teachers to observe each other's practice. Sometimes this extends to observing teachers in other schools. Where such observations have a clear focus they can prove a useful stimulus for reflection. While any shared discussion should be conducted respectfully, if it is to contribute to changes or improvements in practice then it should not become too cosy or self-congratulatory. It requires an open-minded, receptive spirit demonstrated by both observed and observer, sharing the common goal of analysing practice with a view to extending knowledge and understanding the agreed focal points.

The use of video-stimulated reflective dialogue is one way of honing reflection skills. Teachers review video-recorded extracts of their sessions with an experienced coach who skilfully moves the discussion on from initial superficial description (e.g. their appearance on screen) to more perceptive analysis of teaching (e.g. the quality of interaction with learners). The Japanese lesson study model – where triads of teachers come together to plan, teach, review and reflect on a lesson in detail – has gained popularity in recent years. The focus is very much on scrutinising three case studies of pupils' work, rather than the actions of teachers.

Frequency and quality of reflection

Reflective practice supports evaluation, classroom enquiry and profess-ional dialogue. The prompts suggested in Table 10.4 invite practitioners to *quantify* what they do. The exercise can also be completed in small teams. Some writers argue that reflection has more meaning when it is undertaken as a shared activity rather than in isolation. Reflective practice should not be seen as a one-off or occasional experience but integrated through day-to-day practice.

One of the challenges with reflective practice is whether (and if so, how) it should be assessed. Given that reflective practice is a highly personal experience, it seems incongruous to talk in terms of external assessment. But what kind of evidence would indicate low or high quality reflection? How do teachers know whether they are getting better at reflecting? Malderez and Wedell (2007: 151) suggest four criteria to judge the quality of reflection:

1. The ability to notice.
2. The ability to learn from what teachers notice.
3. The ability to explain why they do what they do.
4. The impact of such reflection on actual teaching.

The ability to notice calls for close attention to detail; not only what learners and teachers say and do but also their body language and movement – for instance, the frequency of out-of-seat behaviour demonstrated by a learner or the direction of a teacher's questioning. Reflective observers do not jump to conclusions. If they see three children yawning they do not assume that this is an indicator that the lesson is boring. It may simply be due to lack of sleep. If they see many hands shoot up in response to a teacher's question (e.g. 'What is 8 x 7?'), this may not necessarily indicate understanding but could indicate enthusiasm.

The use of assessment criteria for reflection raises further questions – for example, how is 'impact' measured, and who does the measuring? Malderez and Wedell (2007) value teachers' own assessment and encourage them to document their progress through reflective diaries, supplemented by session observations and post-lesson discussions. They are also mindful of the challenges of observations, pointing out that much of this still assesses a teacher's performance in a narrow range of technical skills rather than other goals of teacher education, such as reflective practice.

Prompt		Scale				
		Never	Rarely	Sometimes	Often	Always
Lesson evaluations						
1a	How often do I evaluate my lessons?					
1b	In my evaluations how often do I think about 'why' and 'so what' as well as what happened?					
1c	How often do I modify my lessons as a result of reflection?					
Listening to the view of others						
2a	How often do I talk to a colleague about learning and teaching?					
2b	How often do I apply wise suggestions to improve my practice?					
2c	How often do I 'look inside' the school for inspiration?					
2d	How often do I listen and act upon the views of others (e.g. learners, teaching assistants) when reflecting on how to improve lessons?					
2e	How often do our team/staff meetings include discussions about how to improve the quality of learning and teaching?					

Prompt		Scale				
		Never	Rarely	Sometimes	Often	Always
Engaging with research						
3a	How often do I read relevant research literature?					
3b	How often do I compare different sources of evidence when deciding what actions to take?					
3c	How often do I undertake action research as a result of reflecting upon learning and teaching?					
Professional development						
4a	How often do I evaluate my professional development activities, such as attending courses?					
4b	How often do I incorporate ideas from professional development activities into my practice?					

Table 10.4. Prompts for quantifying reflective practice.

Conclusion

Critics claim that reflective practice is little more than thinking about what you do and point out that there is little direct evidence that reflection improves teaching. But practice does – or, at least, deliberate practice that has a clear focus on improvement and where teachers reflect and act on feedback. The phrase 'reflective practice' has become so ubiquitous that the link between the two is sometimes underplayed. There is also a danger of seeing reflection as a luxury that busy teachers can ill afford. The reality is that the most effective teachers are continually mulling over what they do and making fine-tune adjustments to their pedagogy in the light of experience, discussion and research.

Universities have not always helped the profession by making reflection a higher plane abstract concept and one that is assumed to be good for those entering teaching. Teachers need time and effort to reflect well but they also need to be convinced that this is an important thing to do. Furthermore, they need practical suggestions on how to improve their reflective skills. One way forward is to draw close links between the theoretical basis of reflection (i.e. models and frameworks) and the top priorities facing teachers and school leaders. So, for example, schools are expected to evaluate their performance regularly and draw up improvement or development plans, including priorities, timescales and measurable success criteria. There are opportunities here for individuals to reflect on their own contribution to whole-school priorities.

Summary

» Reflective practice is defined in different ways but in schools it essentially means asking searching questions about what teachers do. It involves carefully describing and analysing decisions to see whether improvements can be made.

» Reflexivity goes beyond practical problem solving to question the values and beliefs that underpin actions.

» John Dewey and Donald Schön were among the educators who popularised reflective practice, while Paulo Freire argued that reflection should transform human experience.

» There are many ways to record reflective thinking including the use of journals and technologies.

» Teachers can improve their reflective skills by moving from describing what happened to comparing experiences to decide which is the best way forward.

Points for reflection and action

» Metaphors are useful ways to examine one's own values and beliefs about teaching. As you reflect on what teaching means to you, do you liken it to (a) gardening, (b) rock climbing, (c) policing, (d) building, (e) deep-sea diving, or do you have another metaphor?

» Use the prompts in Table 10.1 and Figure 10.3 to review the times and ideas for quality reflection in the busy week.

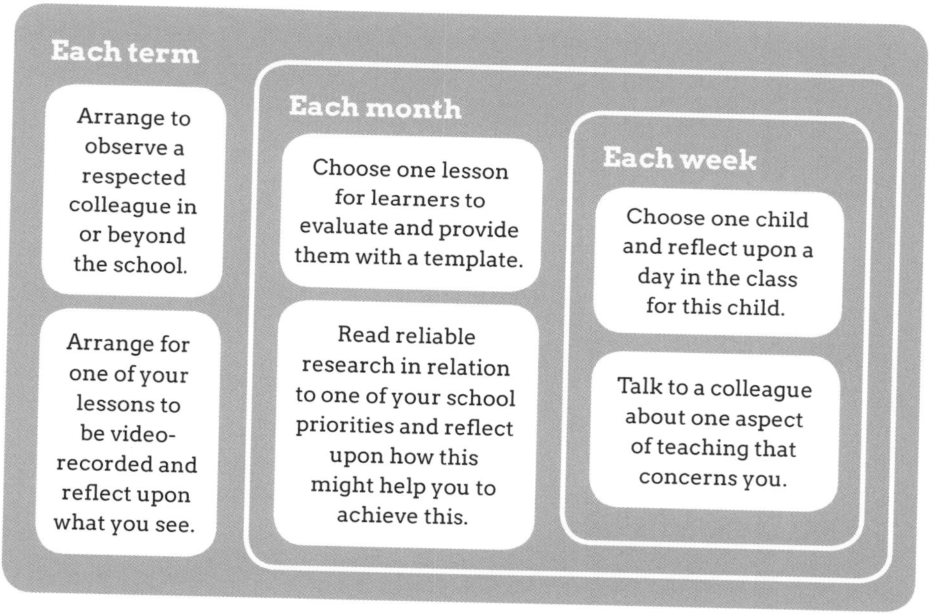

Each term

Arrange to observe a respected colleague in or beyond the school.

Arrange for one of your lessons to be video-recorded and reflect upon what you see.

Each month

Choose one lesson for learners to evaluate and provide them with a template.

Read reliable research in relation to one of your school priorities and reflect upon how this might help you to achieve this.

Each week

Choose one child and reflect upon a day in the class for this child.

Talk to a colleague about one aspect of teaching that concerns you.

Figure 10.3. Prompts to consider opportunities for regular reflective practice.

Chapter 11

Research

Research has a central role to play in the professional development of teachers

What is the big idea?

Former Education Secretary Estelle Morris regards the effective use of data and other research evidence as the next big idea in education, on a par with the introduction of technologies. She points out that teachers need less ideology and more firm evidence on which to base their practice (Morris, 2014). There are promising signs – for instance, the growth in grassroots research through organisations such as ResearchED, which brings together teachers who want to improve the links between classroom practice and research.[1] The big idea in this chapter is that research should inform what schools do and that the use of evidence should feature strongly in the teaching profession.

Research is one of those overused words that can easily lose its meaning. It originates from the Latin word *circare* (meaning 'to go around, to wander'), so the underlying metaphor is that research is an intellectual 'walking around' or exploration. Re-search conveys the idea of going around again but without a clear destination in mind. In the broadest sense of the word, research is about gathering information in order to advance knowledge. In education, there are many activities that fall under the umbrella term of research. These include investigating

---

1 See www.workingoutwhatworks.com.

proposed changes to the curriculum, the impact of interventions, surveying the views of stakeholders on one or more issues, systematic literature reviews, longitudinal studies tracking the experience of learners (e.g. the Millennium Cohort Study) and small-scale classroom projects. Perhaps the best-known definition of education research was provided by Lawrence Stenhouse (1975: 142), who described the process as 'systematic enquiry made public'. It is systematic in the disciplined manner by which information is gathered against clear research questions or hypotheses. The enquiry can draw on a range of techniques, such as observations, surveys and interviews, but their choice needs to be justified. In order for any observations to be made 'public', information needs to be recorded in an accessible format that allows for straightforward analysis and interpretation.

Those carrying out such research vary in their backgrounds. Most researchers come from academic or professional backgrounds employed by universities, charities or research centres, such as the NFER. But there are also many practitioners who undertake their own classroom-based or action research. So research is not something that is only done *for* practitioners. Action research also enables teachers to explore small-scale issues affecting their own setting with a view to improving their practice. Building on from the previous chapter, action research is a form of self-reflective enquiry where classroom evidence is collected and analysed. Teachers reflect on new emerging knowledge and adjust their practice in light of the findings. Hence, research has a key role to play in teachers' professional development.

The big idea in this chapter is not that every teacher should be actively engaged in their own classroom research. This is simply impractical given the workload pressures on many teachers. However, if research is so important to teachers' professional development, then it makes sense for every teacher to be at least equipped with the necessary skills to undertake research as and when appropriate. BERA (2014: 12) point out that the goal should be for every teacher to be 'research informed and research inquisitive'.

However, not everyone supports the idea of teachers becoming researchers. One of the world's most influential educationalists, John Hattie, is clear on the matter: teachers should leave research to academics and concentrate on evaluating the impact of what they do. Hattie is dismissive of action research, pointing out that there is no hard evidence that it improves the quality of teaching (see Stewart, 2015). Hattie's argument is that research is often about causality and how well something has been implemented, rather than the impact that he sees as the most important driver for teachers.

The key issue here is how research is defined and perceived. Some writers distinguish between research with a lower case 'r' to denote small-scale classroom-based enquiry and large-scale research with a capital 'R'. The former does not require detailed knowledge of research techniques, large sample sizes or published outcomes. Rather it focuses on two very simple questions:

1. What is troubling or interesting me about what is happening in my class or school?
2. What can I/we do about it?

The first question is effectively a professional interest, hunch or itch that needs attention. This may stem from reflecting on one's own teaching practice, wider whole-school issues identified in the school development plan or something read in the education media. Perhaps the school is keen to develop peer-to-peer teaching and wants to know whether making arrangements for Year 6 pupils to mentor younger readers improves the reading skills of both groups. In an after-school club, a teacher may puzzle over whether there is any mileage in getting young footballers to devise their own training programme. A Year 9 history teacher might have heard from a science colleague about the value of concept cartoons and wonder whether using such visuals would help develop his learners' understanding of historical interpretations. An early years teacher keen to develop links with parents might ask, 'If I give parents some games and puzzles to borrow, will this improve children's confidence in mathematics and strengthen parental engagement?'

The second question puts teachers in the driving seat to explore their research interests, either on their own or with colleagues. There are many examples of teachers who have undertaken modest classroom research and who testify to the positive outcomes for learners. For example, a Year 1 teacher eager to breakthrough with her reluctant writers decided to enlist them as co-researchers in a project to find out if where they wrote made any different to how they wrote. The strategy was devised to get children to think about the process of writing and how different locations influence how we write (cited by Claxton et al., 2011: 90). They were invited to take part in the experiment and encouraged over the term to write anywhere – in the dark, lying on their backs, in the staffroom, when it was raining, in a nearby estate, on a coach and so on. She reported a remarkable increase in writing confidence (from 20 per cent to 62 per cent as judged by the old level 1c in the national curriculum).

There is plenty of support for the notion of teachers as researchers. The British Educational Research Association's report, *Research and the Teaching Profession* (BERA, 2014), makes a strong case for schools to become research-rich environments and for teachers to become 'research literate', if the UK is to develop self-improving educational systems. Research literate is defined as the extent to which someone is familiar with a range of research methods, the latest research findings and the implications for practitioners. The report states: 'To be research literate is to "get" research – to understand why it is important and what might be learnt from it, and to maintain a sense of critical appreciation and healthy scepticism throughout' (BERA, 2014: 40).

The BERA report argues that research empowers teachers and school leaders to better understand how to increase their impact in the classroom and beyond. Research builds capacity within the system so that more teachers can self-evaluate and self-improve. The report is unequivocal on what teachers need to do: 'To be at their most effective, teachers and teacher educators need to engage with research and enquiry – this means keeping up to date with the latest developments in their academic subject or subjects and with developments in the discipline of education' (BERA, 2014: 6).

According to the NFER, there are four main barriers to schools engaging in research:

1. **Lack of time** – making evidence-informed practice a more significant priority.
2. **Lack of capacity** – getting a shared understanding of what is meant by engaging in evidence-informed practice.
3. **Lack of access** – finding rigorous and relevant research and support for action research.

4. **Lack of relevance** – the need for clear, practical and subject-specific research that has a direct and measurable impact on teaching and learning. (Judkins et al., 2014)

The NFER did not find that a lack of funding was a major barrier. Most teachers want to know what works in their specific context, rather than what works in general. They want jargon-free information and clear messages about how research can make a difference to their everyday practice. For busy practitioners, research may seem something of a luxury that they cannot afford. However, action research enables teachers to pursue topics they are passionate about and in the process sharpen their thinking. One head teacher of a secondary school in Chelmsford gives examples of the research culture he is trying to create (Sherrington, 2013). This includes the theatre studies department using video to improve self and peer assessment and moving towards 'cloud-based exercise books' where students can upload and critique recorded footage of their performances.

Who is behind it?

Since the seventeenth century, the use of experiments in the natural sciences (biology, chemistry, physics) had been recognised as the key to advances in scientific knowledge and understanding. Experiments were admired because they provided the necessary controls and measures to identify cause-and-effect relationships. By the late nineteenth and early twentieth century, just as atoms and molecules were subject to predictable laws, so interest gathered in the question of whether patterns in children's behaviour could be detected. John Dewey, chair of the department of philosophy at the University of Chicago from 1896 to 1904, set up an experimental Laboratory School. Dewey reassured parents that the school would not experiment with children, but for children. He wanted to see whether his progressive theories worked so, for example, children learned to read and write in the context of real-life experiences such as cooking – deciphering cookbooks, writing up their favourite recipes, counting eggs and measuring ingredients. He also wanted learners to explore contemporary debates, working as a democratic community of problem solvers. Unfortunately, Dewey never published evidence on the effects of his Laboratory School experiment on children.

In the same year that Dewey's school closed, the psychologist Edward Thorndike wrote *An Introduction to the Theory of Mental and Social Measurements* (1904). Thorndike's contribution was to signal the importance of statistical data that could be measured and analysed. Dewey rejected the application of deterministic concepts of the physical sciences in the classroom – that is, children should not be reduced to objects, inert atoms to be studied with a resulting loss of individuality. Thorndike, on the other hand, wanted to examine the process of learning and believed that teachers could be supported through the collection of data. Both Dewey and Thorndike were pioneers in the science of teaching, albeit from different perspectives.

In the United States, the use of statistical analysis was spurred on by the desire to identify effective teaching behaviours using systematic observation techniques. Ned Flanders (1970) designed a coding system called Flanders Interaction Analysis Categories (FIAC) to measure variations in the level of control exercised by teachers over classroom incidents. The system described rather than evaluated teacher behaviour by coding, at three-second intervals, interactions between teachers and pupils using ten categories (e.g. praise, asking a question, giving directions, student talk, silence). Flanders used the system between 1954 and 1970 to study teaching styles. He found that students taught by 'indirect teachers' (i.e. those who used encouragement, acknowledged feelings and built on children's ideas) made greater learning gains and were more independent than those taught by direct methods (e.g. lecturing and giving directions). Detractors point out that Flanders' system does not show why or in what context teacher–pupil interactions occur, undervalues student talk, ignores non-verbal gestures and is very time consuming to administer.

Other coding systems were developed but the dominance of quantitative methods came under attack during the 1960s. Critics argued that not enough attention was being given to the complexity of classroom behaviour and that the use of arbitrary time sampling, a feature of systematic observation, overlooked natural patterns of interaction in the class. Alternative approaches to educational research that focused on understanding the context through case studies and life histories started to gain support. The outcome has been described as 'paradigm wars' between quantitative and qualitative researchers (Punch and Oancea, 2014). In more recent times, there have been steps to bring together these traditions into 'mixed methods research'.

Social scientist Kurt Lewin (1890–1947) is usually credited with the idea of teachers undertaking their own classroom-based research (Lewin, 1946). He believed that teachers could improve their practice through a process of collaborative enquiry. The cyclical nature of action research has been described in various ways. Stringer (2013) conceives this as a 'look, think and act' spiral process. The first stage involves building the picture by establishing the purpose and focus, the second requires interpreting and explaining situations, leading to the final phase of resolving problems.

Action research ran into criticisms in the 1980s because the combined role of teacher and researcher meant that many teachers lacked the research skills to undertake enquiries and communicate findings to an academic community that became sceptical of its value. Its fortunes picked up again in the 1990s following the contribution of Donald Schön in the associated field of reflective practice. The cycle of stepping back, reflecting, collecting information, observing and so on is empowering and gives teachers a sense of professional autonomy. The dilemma over split roles is sometimes addressed by involving two individuals, one to undertake the action and the other doing the research. Some writers (e.g. Stringer, 2013) use this to distinguish between practitioner and action research – the former directly involves the teacher in the enquiry, while the latter brings others into play.

Practitioner research continues to attract criticism in terms of potential bias and subjectivity, vested interests in the results and the difficulty of reaching any reputable generalisations on the basis of a small-scale enquiry. However, many of the criticisms equally apply to other research approaches – all researchers carry 'baggage' as there is no such thing as a position-free project. Even those who argue for the objectivity of quantitative-led research cannot deny that researchers (and those who sponsor them) have their own values. The message for any researcher is to plan carefully, ensure informed consent of participants is obtained and acknowledge that insider knowledge brings understanding but also challenges.

Today, action research still has a sizeable following around the world. In the UK, writers such as Bill Lucas have lent strong support for grassroots practitioner research on the grounds that it can lead to improvements in teaching and learning (Lucas et al., 2013). It also offers opportunities to work in partnership with other schools and universities. Supporters do not claim that action research is the answer to teachers' problems, but it can stimulate thinking on practical ideas that have 'worked' for at least one other teacher – to be played around with and adapted accordingly.

During the 1980s and 1990s, the notion of evidence-based practice in education gained momentum. This grew out of pressures to make the educational system (i.e. schools, colleges, universities) more accountable not only to government but also to parents, employers and other stakeholders. It was influenced by evidence-based practice in medicine. In 1996, David Hargreaves delivered a milestone lecture for the Teacher Training Agency in which he contrasted how research was being used in the teaching and medical professions. He argued that education research offered poor value for money in terms of improving the quality of education in schools. Unlike doctors, teachers had not benefited much from research. One of the reasons, argued Hargreaves, was that education research was almost entirely conducted by academics, not school practitioners. Moreover, very few published findings were read, let alone acted upon, by practitioners. Teachers relied largely on personal preference and trial-and-error experience to improve their teaching rather than research evidence. On the other hand, practising doctors actively contributed to research, providing an evidence-based medical profession.

Although much educational research has been perceived as irrelevant and inaccessible, since Hargreaves' lecture there have been a number of important longitudinal studies. The Teaching and Learning Research Programme (TLRP, 2000–2012) was the largest research programme in the UK and worked across all phases, from preschool settings to work-based learning. Around 700 researchers worked on 100 projects. Their findings are available on the TLRP website and culminated in support materials for schools, including the drawing up of ten principles for effective pedagogy. Hargreaves was criticised for over-playing comparisons with medicine (Edwards, 1996; Norris, 1996). However, he opened up an important debate over the role of research in education: what constitutes reliable evidence? What are the most effective teaching strategies? Can these be applied universally? Should research conducted by practitioners be held in the same regard as 'academic' research? (Burton and Bartlett, 2005).

In 2013, the Westminster government recognised the need to provide professionals with robust evidence when it set up a network of What Works Centres to guide social policy. In education, the responsibility lies with the Sutton Trust and the Education Endowment Foundation. The widely cited Toolkit (Higgins et al., 2013) presents evidence for a range of interventions (e.g. homework, ability grouping, digital technology, physical environment), summarising their average impact on attainment, the strength of the evidence supporting them and their cost. The authors update the Toolkit to reflect new evidence – so, for example, cost estimates for digital technology (previously information and computer technologies) have been reduced to moderate, based on the prevalence of cheaper laptops and tablet PCs in schools.

It is important to carefully reflect upon these types of findings. One of the problems with the 'what works' philosophy is that the things highlighted as effective practice do not, unfortunately, seamlessly transfer to other contexts. The 'average' impact may not reflect the experience in a particular school. This is because schools are unique institutions with their own mix of personalities, social contexts and cultural needs. Moreover, as Cassen and McNally (2015) point out, the language of what works is contested. There is a danger with checklist resources that the research context is not fully consulted and the findings are then applied indiscriminately.

The use of meta-analyses in educational research has gained in popularity over recent years. These represent a quantitative synthesis of findings from previous studies and aim to provide a cumulative knowledge base. When the term 'meta-analysis' was first used, it referred to a philosophy rather than a statistical technique (Glass et al., 1981). Glass argued that literature reviews should be as systematic as first-hand research and the results of individual studies should be discussed in the context of distributions of findings. Since then, meta-analysis has become a widely accepted research tool, cutting across various disciplines.

Professor John Hattie's research based on 800 meta-analyses of more than 50,000 studies has become widely known (Hattie, 2009). His Visible Learning materials rank different influences on student achievement ('effect sizes'), as reported in studies around the world. Hattie found that the average effect size of all the interventions he studied was 0.40. Therefore, he used this as a 'hinge point' (average effect) to judge the relative success of interventions and to discover what has the greatest influence on student learning. An effect size of 1.0 is typically associated with advancing learners' achievement by one year or a leap of two grades in GCSE (e.g. from grade C to A); an effect size of 0.5 is equivalent to a leap of one grade at GCSE. Among the leading interventions are self-report grades (1.44), Piagetian programmes (1.28), feedback (0.73) and metacognitive strategies (0.69). Hattie's ranking, which is updated regularly on his website (http://visible-learning.org) to take into account new studies, is useful as a discussion point among leaders and teachers for reviewing and evaluating their own practices, but its conclusions should be regarded with caution. The danger is applying the headline findings without much thought; at a recent Visible Learning conference, a head teacher confidently proclaimed that her school, which was following the Visible Learning programme, disregarded any interventions below 0.4. Critics suggest that, at least in some areas, Hattie may be talking through his hat in reducing the complexities of classroom life to decimal points. For example, to suggest that reducing classroom size makes little difference (0.2) to student learning is to underestimate the importance of freeing teachers to do things differently (Snook et al., 2009).

But this is to miss Hattie's key argument. Reducing class size *does* make a positive difference, but the evidence indicates that teachers do not significantly change their practice when moving from teaching whole classes to teaching small groups. Teaching quality varies not because of the size of the class but because of the strategies used. Hattie's contribution goes beyond providing a list of things that work well – everything has an impact on children's learning. The key question is its relative value. Hattie uncovers the story underlying the data and summarises this by arguing that schools need to 'know thy impact' – in other words, become evaluators of their performance.

Why is it important, and what can you do?

Research has a central role in the professional development of teachers around the world (Schleicher, 2014; Tabberer, 2013). The world's leading systems of continuing professional development include clear pathways for teachers to learn from and develop their research. In Singapore, for example, all teachers gain a secure grounding in school-based enquiry or research methods. When schools draw on research evidence in their decision making, this adds credibility to what they do and say. Decisions based on solid research are more likely to be taken seriously and acted on than those based on a personal whim or fad. BERA (2013) sets out the case for why education research matters, citing examples in many areas, from disability to early years policy and practice. My view is that one of the strongest arguments for using and participating in educational research is that it helps teachers to sort out myths from realities and identify the kinds of practices that are most likely to make a difference to raising standards of achievement in school. In short, teacher learning is a necessary condition for pupils' learning (James, 2005).

Clearly it takes time and effort to nurture a research culture. At each stage of the research process, teachers need to be motivated and have the time to plan research, collect data, analyse findings, reflect on and share results. Leaders need to be fully behind teachers in providing the necessary space and resources so that research is not seen as 'another thing to do'. They can be supportive in forging strategic partnerships with teacher education providers and research centres so that teachers are guided in developing research skills. Forming a research team enables teachers to share responsibilities such as completing background reading.

For practitioners interested in research but with limited time, it is natural to feel overwhelmed before one begins. Where does one start? Much will depend on the nature and scale of the research, the prior experience of the researcher and the expertise within the research team (if working with others). If pursuing action research, it's useful to gain a sense of what has been previously researched on the topic. Although action research is unique by its very nature, other practitioners or professional researchers may have undertaken similar enquiries.

How does a practitioner know which research to trust? The PARC acronym provides some straightforward points to consider – the extent to which research findings are presentable, accurate, reasonable and credible (Figure 11.1).

Whether material appears on a website, in a professional journal or at a conference, it's worth considering a few questions: how well is it presented? How convincing are the arguments? Do they stack up? Are full references provided? What do you know about the author's credentials?

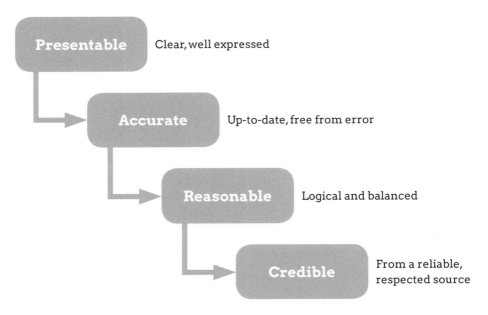

Figure 11.1. PARC prompts to review the quality of research.

These are not always straightforward questions to answer and it is not uncommon for well-respected professional researchers to be quizzed over both their presentation and content. For instance, take the subject of digital technologies in the early years. John Siraj-Blatchford is a strong advocate of young children using ICT. Yet House (2012: 105) claims that Siraj-Blatchford's article for *Nursery World* (2010) is littered with 'a litany of unsubstantiated assertion and uncritical lip-service' paid to so-called 'scientific research'. Ultimately, judging the quality of educational research comes down to whether it is accepted as valid, reliable and authoritative, particularly by knowledgeable peers in the field.

There is no substitute for understanding research than actually doing it. It is beyond the scope of this chapter to discuss in detail how to undertake research in an ethical and productive manner. There is no shortage of guides available. While there are many models to consider, Figure 11.2 offers a simple format to begin based around four key questions. There are many sources that teachers can use to inform their research. These include 'grey literature' – materials emanating from government, academia, business and industry in print and electronic formats. The school will provide key sources for research, both in terms of data on pupil attainment and documentary evidence such as pupils' books and policies. Interviews and observations also provide important first-hand sources for researchers.

Research is an ethical business. At every stage of the process, the guiding principle is to avoid harm and, if possible, to produce some gain for participants and the wider research community. This means carefully planning the methods of collecting and storing data, checking and rechecking the accuracy of findings and acting in a sensitive manner throughout the research process. Researchers can run into difficulties if they ignore fundamental ethical principles, such as gaining voluntary informed consent from participants and respecting confidentiality and anonymity. But research is rarely a straightforward black-and-white process and potentially controversial issues can arise at any time. In a democratic society researchers are entitled to ask questions and investigate challenging topics, but they should do so in ways that respect the dignity and privacy of fellow humans. Researchers need to think about why and how they want to use their research, the ownership of data and what will happen as a result of the research. The standard advice for researchers is provided by the British Educational Research Association in its *Ethical Guidance for Educational Researchers* (BERA, 2011), which is free to download from its website (www.bera.ac.uk).

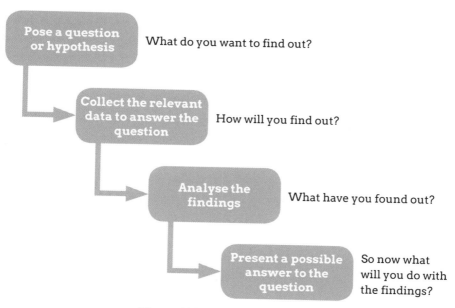

Figure 11.2. A simple format for research.

It is often the first step in the research process that is the most daunting. Formulating clearly expressed research questions that are realistic to pursue in the time available is a challenge for experienced researchers. One of the common pitfalls is being too broad and ambitious. The following question stems can help:

» What is the relationship between ...? (seeks to explain)
» If I do X will Y happen? (explores relationships)
» What happens if ...? (seeks to experiment)
» What and how? (seeks to describe)
» Why? (seeks to explain or critique)
» How can we understand ...? (seeks to interpret or understand)

Once research questions are clear, the methods to capture the data need to be agreed on. Quantitative (numerical) data is usually acquired by using tools such as surveys and questionnaires, while qualitative (mainly words) data is often gained through interviews or observations. Many research projects use a combination of approaches and the lines are frequently blurred. Sometimes researchers adopt very creative methods to gather data, such as counting nose prints left on museum exhibit glass and then estimating visitors' ages by measuring the height from ground level (cited by Bailey, 1994). Or analysing online discussions, such as parental views of head lice (the National Health Service website estimates that one in three primary children experience this) on Mumsnet Talk, to see what this reveals about parental responsibility and how the advice compares to official guidance in the medical literature. These novel approaches raise questions about how we find out about life: why are parents happy to discuss head lice in a discussion forum but unlikely to broadcast this at the school gate?

Once the data is captured it needs to be analysed. If the researcher wants to find out how the school is performing – for instance, in the teaching of reading or science – then it is sensible to review data such as test scores over a period of at least three years to establish a pattern or trend. This is more reliable than drawing conclusions on the basis of a year group's performance. Having said this, for individual learners the data may be very revealing, so teachers and leaders should not lose sight of the individual behind the data. It can be an informative exercise to track the performance of a learner or group throughout the year to see what the data suggests about how well they are doing. This becomes more powerful when these learners are interviewed to tap into their learning experiences and feelings – something that quantitative data cannot provide. Unless research leads to change then it has very little value for schools. Hence, some thought needs to be given to how research is shared within and beyond the school, what actions are needed in terms of revising policies and practices and whether the research was worth the effort.

Identifying good practice, analysing why this is the case and doing more of it is very much the basis of an approach called appreciative inquiry. Cooperrider and Srivastva (1987), who came up with the idea, wanted to use positive experiences as a stimulus for change within an organisation. Their model is based on four stages:

1. **Discovering** – finding out the best and most positive experiences participants had in their organisation.
2. **Dreaming** – thinking creatively about the future.
3. **Designing** – devising plans for the future which reflect participants' views of good practice and visions. This phase involves producing provocative propositions which are statements about what the participants want to achieve.
4. **Delivering** – the energy moves towards action planning and working out what will need to happen to realise the provocative propositions.

Appreciative inquiry (AI) is an alternative to the problem-solving approach that usually underpins action research (see Shuayb et al., 2009). AI does require knowledge of leading figures in the respective fields and so professional networking is very much part of the approach.

There is a wide range of organisations that provide research relevant to education. In the UK, among the most established is the National Foundation for Educational Research (NFER), formed in 1946 to fund research on educational provision (www.nfer.ac.uk). It is now the largest independent provider of education research. The Centre for the Use of Research and Evidence in Education (CUREE) is an internationally recognised centre of expertise in the field. The resources section of its website offers examples of research projects in schools, as well as 'research tasters' based around questions such as, 'How can we guide group discussion effectively?' (www.curee.co.uk). The Education Resources Information Center (ERIC), based in the United States, provides a gateway into education research journals (http://eric.ed.gov).

The UK has a number of world-leading university departments and centres that specialise in education research, including Cambridge, Glasgow, Durham and Southampton. University College London's Institute of Education (IOE) was ranked the world's leading centre for education in 2014 and currently around a quarter of the education research carried out by UK universities emanates from here. These universities have sought to make research accessible to practitioners through conferences, videos and briefings – the IOE, for example, has over a hundred research briefings on its website (www.ioe.ac.uk/research/96163.html). The IOE also holds a copy of every book published on education in the UK and hosts key research findings, such as those associated with the Evidence for Policy and Practice Information and Co-ordinating Centre (EPPI-Centre).

There are many resources available to support teachers and others to engage in research. The National Teacher Research Panel (NTRP), set up in 1999, offers a teacher perspective on research. Its members are practising teachers and tutors who advise on how to promote teaching as an evidence-based profession. Its website includes examples of practitioner research summaries on topics such as, 'What do you mean I should think for myself?' and 'Making the strange familiar: emphasising the role of mathematics across the curriculum' (www.ntrp. org.uk). The NFER has also produced mini 'how to' research guides to support teachers in undertaking their own research on topics including planning, using techniques such as focus groups and writing up findings (www.nfer.ac.uk/schools/research-in-schools/how-to-guides.cfm). The Mapping Educational Specialist knowHow initiative summarises research on pedagogy from around the world and allows teachers to contribute to the knowledge base – for instance, by submitting evidence on topics such as assessment, digital books and visual literacy (www.meshguides.org).

Conclusion

Mention of the word research can be off-putting for many teachers who equate it immediately with further academic study and spending a lot of time reading about theory. However, a different way to look at research is to think about improving school life and the experiences of both learners and teachers. Often, schools invest precious time and money in bringing in resources or interventions in the hope that they will improve educational outcomes, particularly for those who need to catch up, without knowing whether they work or what alternatives are available. This is why research summaries produced by the likes of the Sutton Trust–Education Endowment Foundation are important for schools. These 'what works' resources should be used as reference points for staff discussion rather than as prescriptions.

Research at school level and between schools offers leaders and teachers opportunities to learn from each other and enhance their professional status. Well-conceived action research is the most effective form of professional development. It invites practitioners to examine their own practice and to ask challenging questions about how pupils learn. Those who doubt the value of educational research might ponder over what education would be like if no research was undertaken. How would we know what teachers, learners, parents and others think, for instance, about government policies relating to the curriculum and assessment? How confident would policy-makers be in their decision making? How would the educational system develop? Above all, how would we know what needs to improve and why?

Summary

» Educational research is about systematically exploring issues in education and making the findings public.
» Effective research is presentable, accurate, reasonable and credible.
» Both quantitative and qualitative research have value and offer insight into education.
» The social scientist Kurt Lewin is credited with introducing the notion of action research.
» All research should be underpinned by ethical considerations – BERA provide a code to follow.
» There is a wide range of organisations and resources to support teachers in their research.

» Over recent years there has been an emphasis on evidence-informed practice, with developments of 'what works well' centres such as the Sutton Trust–Education Endowment Foundation.

Points for reflection and action

» Visit the MESH guides website and explore topics and resources that interest you: www.meshguides.org.

» Contribute to a forum or event run by a research group such as ResearchED: www.workingoutwhatworks.com.

» Good research is often controversial; if it were not, then we would not learn much. But what are the boundaries for educational researchers? Is covert observation for research purposes ever justified in educational settings?

Chapter 12

Professional leadership

Effective school leadership operates at all levels and is about shared vision, support and securing improvement

What is the big idea?

The final big idea in this book is that, in an increasingly complex and unpredictable world of education, everyone in a school has a contribution to make to leadership. It is based on the premise that we all have leadership potential. Although there are different models of leadership, the thrust of this chapter supports what is called distributed leadership. Distributed leadership is essentially a model that moves away from an all-powerful iconic figurehead to multiple leaders (teachers, support staff and the learners themselves) with shared responsibilities. Most writers recognise that leadership is about getting people on board to solve common problems and working towards a shared vision (Brighouse, 2001; Lambert, 2003; Zaccaro et al., 2004).

But, according to Bolman and Deal (1991: 408), we have come to 'focus too much on the actors and too little on the stage on which they play their parts'. A survey of leadership in 2007 found that most heads spent their time in areas of accountability, improvement planning, managing teachers and implementing new initiatives (PricewaterhouseCoopers, 2007). The survey discovered that, in an ideal world, head teachers would prefer to delegate the management of buildings, budgets, staff development and special educational needs (SEN) to other staff.

There is emerging evidence that distributed leadership is more effective in motivating teachers and student achievement than a focused (single person) leadership (Leithwood et al., 2006a). It seems that there is no loss of power or influence on the part of head teachers when responsibilities are transferred to others. Advocates argue that the traditional top-down model of leadership is no longer fit for purpose in the twenty-first century (Harris, 2014). The exact patterns of distributed leadership vary from one school to the next but the most effective ones are those that are clearly coordinated and have well-defined roles.

However, distributed leadership goes beyond role-based functions expressed in job descriptions. It focuses on building a network of relationships – interactions more than actions (Harris and Spillane, 2008) – within and beyond the school. Its popularity reflects the belief that the effective leadership of a modern school, whatever its size, is too complex for single-person leadership. Schools are required to work closely with multiple agencies and other schools in professional networks. Leaders are expected to be proficient in the collection and analysis of student data. There are further expectations that schools should play a key role in bringing communities together. Then there are curriculum reforms and initiatives to interpret, implement and evaluate. These demands often pull senior leaders out of school on a regular basis. This necessitates the sharing of leadership decisions and puts the emphasis on 'collective intelligence' (Brown and Lauder, 2001) rather than individual thinking.

The multifaceted aspects of leading a school are indicated by Ofsted's criteria for assessing the quality of leadership (Ofsted, 2015). To be considered outstanding, leadership needs to demonstrate a broad range of competencies, from how well specific grants are used (e.g. the pupil premium to support disadvantaged learners) to the effectiveness of safeguarding, from the extent to which staff are motivated, respected and effective to how well the school engages parents. While the customary references to values, ambition and high expectations remain, it is clear that judgements on school leadership reflect current political concerns – for instance, the extent to which the school promotes British values such as democracy. Clearly, leadership calls for a raft of skills and qualities that are unlikely to be present in one individual.

The model of distributed leadership is a sustainable one. The idea is that senior leaders build capacity so that when they leave or are absent, the school or college continues to flourish. In practice, however, the extent to which distributed leadership is adopted in schools is unclear. A review of the school leadership landscape (Earley et al., 2012) points out that the typical structure for leadership teams in primary schools remains one head and one deputy. In secondary schools, there is more variety but typically senior leadership teams comprise one head, one or two deputies and three or four assistants. The review does not go into detail about leadership styles or the distribution of decision making, but it notes that because of the increasing complexity of school leadership, developing internal school capacity and effective partnerships is essential if schools are to navigate their way around the changing policy landscape and pressures from bodies such as Ofsted.

While the quality of senior leadership in schools is reported to have improved considerably since the 1990s (PricewaterhouseCoopers, 2007), there are concerns that in some cases pressurised heads are taking things out on staff – media reports suggest that 'Headteachers are just big bullies' (*The Telegraph*, 2015). Some teachers find particular leadership styles oppressive and unsupportive, leaving them demoralised. Recent reports present a gloomy picture of teacher well-being with unnecessary workload top of teacher concerns (Precey, 2015). In Wales, one survey indicates that nearly half of the 450 teachers surveyed thought about quitting because of stress (Jones, 2015). Stress is not confined to urban schools. In the Highlands of Scotland there is a similar picture where the number of teachers signed off on sick leave has quadrupled in two years, while a nationwide survey found that only a third of Scottish teachers would recommend teaching to others (Findlay, 2015).

Clearly, the role of the head is fundamental to the success or otherwise of the school. According to Dame Sally Coates, who has forty years' experience in education, the head is the key – 'a source of stability, direction and reassurance in what can be a volatile environment' (Coates, 2015: 237). She likens the head to a shock absorber and advocates her own 'headstrong' (assertive) model of leadership. She says this is not a top-down approach because leaders at all levels in a school need to be assertive and the test of effective leadership is how the school runs in the absence of the leader. Central to her transformation of Burlington Danes Academy in south London, which she took over when it was in rapid decline, was meticulous planning. Coates started by taking some of the staff to see an effective school (her old one): 'I wanted them to hear the patter of footsteps on calm corridors, to see smiling teachers enjoying their craft … to quash the defeatism that they had come to accept' (Coates, 2015: 19).

Effective leaders do not tolerate excuses for underachievement, such as blaming parents or the community within which children are raised. They have high expectations for all learners, which they reinforce, and take decisive action in securing their strategic vision. What does high expectations look like? Coates (2015) cites examples such as having a focus on learning and not behaviour, ensuring that books are free from graffiti, marking work at least every two weeks with clear guidance on how learners can improve and developing higher order thinking skills through questioning. It means building confidence and self-belief among those students who may think of themselves as failures to raise their aspirations to achieve.

Understandably, there are leaders who succumb to inspection pressures, illustrated by the response of one head teacher to Sir John Jones (2015), who when asked about his school replied: 'We are good with outstanding features.' Mick Waters (2013: 328) reckons there is 'a lot less laughter and a lot less fun' in schools these days and it is difficult for heads to keep sunny side up.

What we do know is that the most effective senior leaders in both school and non-school contexts demonstrate similar qualities and practices. Leithwood et al. (2006a) identify four sets of core skills around building vision and setting direction, understanding and developing people, redesigning the organisation, and managing the teaching and learning programme.

Shared vision

Building vision involves establishing a shared purpose and working towards common goals. This does not happen overnight – commentators suggest it can take between five to seven years (Smith, 2011). However, particularly in the context of schools with significant weaknesses, leaders need to inject a sense of urgency and establish clear short-term priorities if the school is to begin to turn around. Later, once the school has made progress in meeting these priorities, much more staff involvement is necessary in setting the school's strategic direction. Such ownership is vital to sustain improvement. Understanding and developing people involves providing professional development and individual support through, for example, mentoring and modelling appropriate values. Redesigning the organisation requires investment so that the school environment is conducive to optimal teaching and learning. Action is taken to build professional networks with other schools, establish close links with parents and form strategic partnerships within the community. Finally, managing the teaching and learning programme is about monitoring what goes on in school – that is, 'buffering staff against distractions from their work' (Leithwood et al., 2006a: 7).

Senior leaders need to set the right priorities for their learners. This process should involve whole-school discussions and may entail resolving differences over 'what ought to be' – one of the functions of principal leaders is to build schools around shared values. The late Stephen Covey, an internationally respected authority on leadership, highlighted the importance of 'principle-centred leadership' and making the right choices (Covey, 1999; 2004). The quality of leadership, he says, comes down to an essential choice over how to maintain power through 'coercion, utility or legitimacy' (Covey, 1999: 104). Principle-centred leaders avoid instilling fear among others and do not over-react to their mistakes. In the short term, they may focus on practical issues, such as accumulating information and resources and simplifying policies and procedures. Over the longer term, they may seek to cultivate expertise among staff and create a climate where reasons are shared while maintaining commitment to goals.

In deciding on the right priorities for a school, leaders should have regular auditing systems in place. These should, as a minimum, reveal learners' standards of literacy and numeracy, digital competence, the achievement of particular groups of learners, standards of behaviour, provision for social well-being and opportunities to access a broad and balanced curriculum. Many schools use inspection frameworks as prompts to review their performance. Broadly speaking, these cover academic standards; matters of care, support and guidance; the quality of teaching and learning; the curriculum; and leadership and management issues. Evaluation processes should enable senior leaders and colleagues to check progress regularly – for example, by analysing 'live' data from literacy and numeracy tests – so that further support can be provided if necessary.

Hattie (2012) is at pains to point out that regularly evaluating the impact of what leaders and teachers do is critical to the school's success.

What really matters is that any vision statements mean something in practice. So, a school that claims to value twenty-first-century learning and bans the use of mobile phones, or talks up the importance of equality of opportunity but has a high rate of exclusions, has some serious thinking to do. It is one thing to have 'Inspiring Minds' emblazoned on the school uniform or in the school foyer, but this means little if much of the teaching is dreary. It can be a sobering exercise to ask individuals in a leadership team, including governors, what they think matters most in a school and what it should stand for.

As Jim Collins, author of *Good to Great* (2001), put it, getting the right people on the bus is the first human resources challenge in any organisation. The main priority for school leaders is to develop a high quality teaching staff. For educational leaders, one of the major challenges is how to support and encourage colleagues while at the same time retain a clear focus on objectives, which may mean travelling at an unfavourable pace and/or direction. In short, head teachers in conjunction with governors are sometimes faced with the unenviable task of dismissing incompetent staff, despite instigating a programme of support. Particularly in these circumstances, leaders need to be socially and emotionally intelligent. However, tackling underperformance is not something that senior leaders should duck or procrastinate over. The impact on learners' progress and achievement from being taught by a poor teacher is well documented. Sally Coates (2015), who turned around a 'failing' school, recalled that in her challenging conversations she tried to be direct, open, frank and honest. She avoided judging the person but described their behaviour and performance based on the evidence. Performance management should not necessarily be seen in negative, deficit terms. It can result in relieving pressures on other staff and introduce much needed whole-school training and development.

Unfortunately, there are a few teachers who do not want to further their professional development and have disengaged from the process. Sir John Jones (2015) describes cynical teachers in the staffroom as those who have retired but who have not told their heads. This presents a significant challenge for senior leaders, especially if there are no competency issues in terms of the quality of teaching. Even when there are serious questions about the performance of teachers, some leaders play 'pass the parcel' and seek out ways to move them on to other schools – one estimate is that only one in five incompetent teachers are sacked (Collins, 2011). A NFER study of the most successful schools found that leaders and managers hold teachers to account but in a supportive way. They are clear about the balance between support and challenge, expressed by one head as follows: 'we try to light the fire within, not the fire below' (Taylor, 2005: 5).

Simon Sinek (2009) suggests that there are two ways to influence human behaviour: manipulation or inspiration. One of the most common manipulation techniques is to instil fear among others. In business terms, the simple idea is that if you do not buy a product or service then something bad could happen to you or you would be worse off without them. In education, fear is widely used to control behaviour – many children and young people are fearful of the consequences of not getting things right or not following the rules. Studies of inspirational or transformational school leaders report that they prioritise developing a common mission, building teams and working towards ambitious goals. They try to develop the school's capacity to work together to overcome challenges. Interestingly, one extensive piece of meta-research, covering twenty-two studies and nearly 3,000 principals, found that transformational leaders were not as successful as 'instructional leaders', who focused on the quality and impact of everyone in school on student learning (see Hattie, 2012).

The importance of leaders showing flexibility and tailoring their approaches to the context was one of the key findings from the most extensive research on contemporary leadership in recent times. The Effective Leadership and Pupil Outcomes Project (Day et al., 2009) focused on schools that were identified to have significantly raised pupil attainment levels over a relatively short three-year period (2003–2005). In subsequent years, many of these schools continued to maintain or improve their results. The most effective heads used a combination of strategies 'layered' within and across the schools' developmental phases. In the early phase, heads tended to prioritise improving the physical environment of the school in order to create more positive, supportive conditions for teaching and learning. They also established clear expectations and processes regarding behaviour, restructured the senior leadership team and implemented performance management and training opportunities for all staff. In the middle phase, heads focused on analysing data on pupils' progress and achievement to inform decision making. In the final phase, they concentrated on enriching the curriculum and further distributing leadership duties. Heads working in schools in more challenging contexts focused first on policies and practices for good behaviour, and then on improvements to the physical environment and the quality of teaching and learning.

Who is behind it?

For most of the nineteenth and twentieth centuries, the leadership of organisations (including schools) was based on a hierarchical, linear and mechanical model inspired by the heroes of industry, commerce, politics and war. The likes of Wellington, Churchill and other 'great men' provided the charisma to inspire others. Most leaders operated on the principle of 'expect and inspect'. Employees, including teachers, followed predetermined standards and routines against which their performance was measured and assessed. Compliance was the order of the day. The study of educational leadership is a relatively new field. By the 1980s, the relevance of the hierarchical model of leadership was being called into question as the business of schooling became more complex. The 1988 Education Reform Act gave schools more powers in allocating resources, which meant increased responsibilities in managing people and finances. As a result, the professional role of senior leaders came into sharper focus.

Theories of leadership consistently explore the importance of how leaders relate to others, as well as how they accomplish tasks. In terms of situational theory, Hersey and Blanchard (1982) suggest that as leaders increase in their own maturity, they move through four stages: telling, selling, participating and delegating (see Table 12.1).

Stages 1 and 2 focus on completing the task, while stages 3 and 4 are more concerned with developing independence and responsibility. The key point to take from situational theory is that the style to be deployed depends on the context and the maturity of the followers. There are times when individuals will be seeking clear direction, when they feel genuinely exasperated and do not know how to proceed. In this context, a 'telling'

Stage	Description
1. Telling	Leaders tell people what to do, when, where and how to do it.
2. Selling	Leaders provide information and direction, but there is more two-way communication and attempts to 'sell' the message to get other people on board.
3. Participating	Leaders focus more on the relationship and less on direction. They work with the team and share decision-making responsibilities.
4. Delegating	Leaders take on a monitoring role and pass on responsibility to others.

Table 12.1. Situational leadership styles.

style makes sense. Individuals are told the objectives, steps, resources and tools necessary to achieve these. At other times, followers may have a partial sense of what to do but need the confidence and guidance to carry this through. They may need to be persuaded of the task's value and their contribution therein. Occasionally followers fully understand what needs to be done and why, drawing on their previous experience and even offering their own input on how this can be achieved more effectively or efficiently. Here, the leader focuses on the task outcomes and allows space for the followers to contribute. Finally, a delegating style is based on contexts where the followers complete the task independently and the role of the leader is to monitor progress. Situational leadership theory applies in both directions, so followers can also express their views on whether they want more or less independence and guidance.

The theory of distributed leadership originated in the late 1980s amidst the increased workload pressures associated with the Local Management of Schools (LMS) (see Gronn, 2003). This led to a loosening of roles, the widening of senior leadership teams and the development of middle leaders. More recent workforce reforms have also contributed to the further distribution of leadership responsibilities. Distributed leadership is now a widely endorsed practice, although Lumby (2013) points out that there are persistent structural barriers to overcome. She is referring in particular to the limited opportunities for women and those from ethnic minority backgrounds. Her stark conclusion is that the effect of distributed leadership theory is to maintain the power status quo.

There are many individual researchers who have contributed to our understanding of school leadership (e.g. Reynolds, 1992; Hopkins et al., 1994; Hargreaves, 2005). Among the most significant is the Canadian-based Michael Fullan, who has been chronicling educational change and improvement since the 1970s. In *The New Meaning of Educational Change* (2015) he identifies assumptions about change that should and should not be made. For instance, he advises leaders to assume that conflict and disagreement are both inevitable and necessary for successful change. Fullan's advice is that complex changes in education may require top-down or external initiation, but they can only be sustained through shared decision making and control. Leaders need to strike a balance in their approach to change. He calls this the 'too tight–too loose dilemma' (Fullan, 2008: 12). Too much freedom can lead to a vague sense of direction, while clearly defined structures can be too constraining and generate resistance. The way forward, according to Fullan, involves leaders working on peer relationships, interaction and learning in relation to a common purpose, such as improving literacy. Creating a culture of collaboration within and beyond schools takes time. In one secondary school, the head gave everyone a £50 voucher to spend on improving the school based on the school development plan. It was an immediate success in building affinity for the school and pride in its environment – six cleaners bought a water feature for an open area of the school, designated as a peace garden, while lunchtime supervisors bought goalposts (Smith, 2011).

Debates have increasingly centred on measuring the impact of educational leadership rather than describing its characteristics. There is now widespread agreement over what good leadership looks like but less consensus over how to build leadership capacity. Most leadership development focuses on what Chris Argyris (1923–2013) called 'single loop' learning (adjustments to techniques), rather than 'double loop' learning (changes to underlying assumptions on which teaching, learning and leadership are based) (Argyris, 1976). Viviane Robinson's meta-analysis of twenty-six studies on the impact of school leadership showed that the more leadership is focused on teaching and learning and the professional development of teachers, the greater its impact (Robinson, 2007). The single most important factor, according to Robinson, is when leaders participate with teachers in professional learning. This can occur formally (e.g. through staff meetings) or informally (e.g. discussions about specific teaching problems).

In the UK, the major organisation that has contributed to leadership development is the National College for Teaching and Leadership (NCTL). It was established in 2000 as the National College for School Leadership as a non-departmental public body and through various name changes merged with the Teaching Agency in 2013 to become the National College for Teaching and Leadership – an executive agency sponsored by the Department for Education. Its primary purpose is to improve leadership in schools and colleges through professional development, such as its National Professional Qualification for Headship (NPQH) and the Future Leaders fast-track programme. It also advises the government on school leadership issues. Since 2006, the NCTL has identified National Leaders of Education and National Support Schools to provide support for schools in the most challenging contexts. Since 2012, the NCTL has also designated National Leaders of Governance – outstanding governors charged with supporting any aspect of school governance. It also undertakes research into new models of leadership, such as executive heads, co-headships and leading trusts and chains.

In the 1990s, Sam Stringfield called for the development of what he called 'high reliability schools' where leaders monitored carefully the effectiveness of critical factors within the system and took immediate action to contain any negative effects that occurred. The idea was adapted from high-risk occupations such as traffic controllers and nuclear plant operators where mistakes and errors have significant consequences. The distinctive characteristic of high reliability organisations is not the absence of errors but the ability to contain the effects. The leaders anticipate high risks and put in place strategies to minimise the likelihood of these happening. For the general public, their reliability is high because they are trusted not to make significant mistakes and to immediately resolve any that do occur. Extending the idea to schools, leaders are able to exercise control over the most significant factors that affect how well learners achieve, such as the quality of feedback and teacher–learner relationships. Stringfield and his two co-researching professors have found that secondary schools which have applied the principles of high reliability organisations have seen strong gains in pupils' achievement (Stringfield et al., 2008). But schools are not the same as air-traffic control towers. Whereas schools deal largely with the unpredictability of human interactions, the latter are concerned with physical processes.

Along similar lines, numerous writers have suggested that schools are best analysed in terms of 'systems thinking' (Davies and West-Burnham, 2003; Barnard, 2013). Leaders are encouraged to see the school in terms of connected inputs, throughputs and outputs. This business model suggests that understanding the school is about examining relationships between certain inputs (e.g. teaching strategies) and desired outcomes (e.g. higher exam passes). The relationships between the people who work and learn in school – both informal (e.g. friendships, climate, culture) and formal (e.g. management duties, hierarchies) – is the key driver to improve schools. Banathy (1991) described the characteristics of systems thinking to include transforming the way information is processed. Rather than seeing schooling as a 'one-to-many' orientation (e.g. the teacher distributing information to many students, the single leader 'dictating' the direction for staff), systems thinking promotes 'many-to-one' orientation where learners can access many different sources (e.g. books, websites, multimedia, speakers, materials, equipment) beyond the teacher.

Proponents of systems thinking, such as the US-based Waters Foundation (www.watersfoundation.org), argue that it enables leaders to make sense of complexity and manage the process of change. It also equips learners with the tools necessary to improve the quality of their thinking. For instance, the Waters Foundation provides visual tools to develop the inferential skills necessary to make sense of stories, historical events or mathematical formulae. In these contexts, the system equates to the inherent structures of the subject content rather than the school itself. Essentially, systems thinking encourages leaders, teachers and learners to explore how the parts relate to the whole (of whatever system is being explored) and how an action in one part in the system can affect the entire thing. For Barnard (2013) the problem with schools is not their performance but their linear organisation. Schools would function better, he argues, if they focused less on separating things out and more on making connections.

Why is it important, and what can you do?

The importance of effective leadership is widely recognised as the second key driver in raising standards in school, close behind the quality of teaching (Marzano et al., 2005). We know a great deal about effective school leadership, even though much of the literature actually describes what commentators think leaders should know, do or value in order to be effective (Leithwood et al., 2006b). While good leadership can be driven by an inspirational figure, all the evidence suggests that this is not enough – heads need the support of teaching assistants, teachers, middle leaders and governors if schools are to flourish (see Figure 12.1). Above all, leaders need to identify the most successful practice in their schools and share it. There is a strong argument to suggest that if senior leaders can work with colleagues to develop consistently good teaching, then this is 'outstanding' – given that in a typical school, the majority of teachers will teach well, a few will be cutting-edge and a few underperforming.

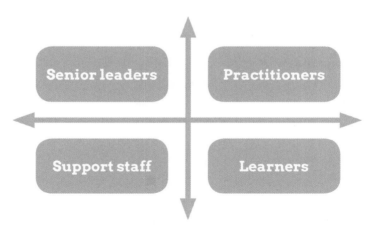

Figure 12.1. Feedback in a learning organisation needs to operate across roles.

Senior leaders

Senior leadership extends beyond the individual head teacher to include assistant or deputy heads and school governors. Much of the literature on senior leadership agrees that developing a whole-school commitment to learning (both of children and adults) is the key to success. Peter Senge is a world-renowned expert on management and organisational learning. He coined the phrase 'the learning organization', defined as an organisation that is open to new ideas and 'continually expanding its capacity to create its future' (Senge, 2006: 14). This notion of creating a culture of learning among staff is important in sustaining effective leadership in a school. The role of 'top leaders' (i.e. principals or head teachers) is to cultivate leadership skills in others and thereby create a community of leaders who can take the school forward after they have left. In many schools, there are Leaders of Learning reflecting this shift from an authority-centred to a learning-centred establishment (Coe et al., 2014). Hattie (2012: 175) argues that 'learning leaders' can truly make the difference when they zoom in on student and adult learning by asking questions such as, 'Do students acquire essential knowledge and skills?', 'How do we know?' and 'How can we use that evidence of student learning to improve instruction?' Notice that the key questions are not 'What is taught?' or 'How was it taught?'

Even when 'super heads' are parachuted into failing schools to turn them around, some of these fail because there are no effective middle managers to back them up (Taylor, 2005). On the other hand, successful schools have strong middle leaders and managers (phase leaders in primaries or departmental heads in secondary schools) who seek to develop a love of learning, or 'scholarship' to use a term that has come back into fashion. This focus on learning is often reflected in job titles – learning directors, leaders of learning and so forth.

Middle leaders

Middle leaders often take responsibility for whole-school curriculum planning, model good teaching, interpret assessment data and show initiative in tackling issues. They can prove valuable assets in supporting senior leaders in their everyday conversations with colleagues. On the other hand, they can ebb away at confidence in the school direction by distancing themselves from senior leaders with comments such as, 'They have told me to tell you …', 'This wouldn't have been my decision but …' and 'Don't shoot the messenger.' Leaders in the most successful organisations air their differences in private and agree collective responsibility. The development of cliques can be damaging to securing whole-school objectives.

One of the ways in which middle leaders can prove a real asset to senior leaders is running meetings efficiently and productively. The circulation of agendas a week or so ahead of meetings enables colleagues to at least have the chance to gather their thoughts on the topics to be discussed. While administrative matters need to be discussed, meetings should include opportunities to discuss the core business of schools – teaching and learning. Middle leaders can make a valuable contribution in chairing brisk, lively discussions and recording clear action points with designated leads and timescales. Weekly briefing meetings for phase or departmental teams contribute to effective communication, especially if they include support staff and trainee teachers. These are useful opportunities for managers to gain feedback from colleagues. Middle leaders also play an important part in the writing of school policies and handbooks. These are often best expressed in concise formats using bullet points and diagrams to communicate the main messages. Schemes of work need to include key elements such as objectives, teaching methods and assessment strategies. They should also be reviewed in the light of curriculum changes.

Leaders also need to keep a close eye on professional development activities to ensure that these match priorities at both the individual and whole-school level. Increasingly, professional development is adopting more diverse formats, including online materials and school-to-school networks. For leaders, what matters most is the impact professional development has on the quality of teaching and learning. It is standard procedure for teachers to complete evaluations of training events but it is rare for schools to follow up on whether such training actually changes classroom practice. The use of 'learning walks', scrutiny of learners' books, critical reflective discussions and lesson observations are examples of how managers can engage with colleagues on the question of impact.

Teachers as leaders

Leadership also comes from the classroom. Effective teachers model leadership skills in the way they approach the three core functions of planning, teaching and assessment in lessons. By providing learners with opportunities to have a say in what, how and sometimes where they learn, teachers are modelling leadership skills such as decision making, management of resources and planning. They are creating the conditions in which learners become increasingly confident in the control of their learning. By providing regular opportunities for learners to review their own work and that of their peers, teacher leadership demonstrates the principles of co-agency and trust. The *Huffington Post* asked the world's leading educational bloggers to suggest ways in which teachers could demonstrate leadership (Rubin, 2015). They offered a variety of suggestions including sharing teaching practices with others via social networking, consulting students for input on lessons and assignments, and 'trying something new that you are not good at, and being silly and funny'.

Although teaching is the main responsibility of classroom teachers, it has been acknowledged for some time that they are well placed to extend their influence beyond the classroom and contribute to whole-school decisions about instruction and the curriculum (Livingston, 1992). The dual role of teacher and leader can present tensions and so calls for well-defined roles. All teachers are expected to model learning in their classes and participate in continuing professional development, thereby contributing to school improvement. Merideth (2007) argues that all teachers should be leaders and puts forward a REACH model to support their development. This describes the kind of behaviour expected of teachers as leaders:

» **Risk taking** – teachers who seek challenges and create new processes.
» **Effectiveness** – teachers who model best practice, professional growth and heart.
» **Autonomy** – teachers who display initiative, independent thought and responsibility.
» **Collegiality** – teachers who promote community and interactive communication skills.
» **Honour** – teachers who demonstrate integrity, honesty and professional ethics.

Support staff

In recent years, the number of teaching assistants (TAs) has mushroomed in schools. In 1992 there were 72,320 teachers and educational support assistants in the UK. By 2014 this had increased to 491,669 – an increase of 580 per cent (ESRC, 2016: 55). Their contribution in supporting teachers and learners has been subject to considerable discussion following the research published by the likes of the Sutton Trust–Education Endowment Foundation and John Hattie (2015). Generally, TAs are directed to work with less able pupils and those with special educational needs. The Deployment and Impact of Support Staff (DISS) project found that pupils who received the most support from TAs made less progress over the year compared with similar pupils who received little or no TA support (Blatchford et al., 2012). This is partly because the presence of TAs can have unintended consequences – reducing, for example, the overall amount of interaction that these pupils have with their teacher, their peers and the mainstream curriculum.

How should leaders react to such findings? While there are undoubtedly many highly trained and effective TAs, they face a number of organisational challenges over which they have little or no control that mitigate against their effectiveness (Webster et al., 2013). Teachers (as leaders) and assistants need to be clear over their respective roles. Discussion can revolve around how best to deploy the expertise of both teachers and their assistants – for example, TAs might take on a 'roving' role around the classroom, monitoring work and behaviour and providing support as and when necessary. At the same time, teachers can sit alongside focused groups for a sustained period of time. Or the room could be divided into 'zones' with each adult leading groups in their zone. Research reinforces good common sense in pointing out that teams are effective when there are clearly shared goals and regular opportunities for TAs to reflect on these (Vincent et al., 2005). It also highlights the importance of giving TAs a say in classroom management and the planning of sessions, so that a teacher's status and power are not seen as barriers to TAs demonstrating leadership skills themselves.

Conclusion

So what of the future of professional leadership in schools and colleges? One trend is a move towards collective or distributed rather than individual leadership. This has implications in terms of developing a democratic environment where the views of all are considered. Given recent austerity measures, it also seems that teachers will be expected to take greater responsibility for their own professional development, working with colleagues and within and beyond schools as part of professional networks, rather than looking to external consultants. Finally, much greater focus is needed on using digital technologies and other innovations to drive leadership development (Petrie, 2011). In the UK, the use of IRIS Connect is an example of how some schools are using video technology to enhance teachers' professional development through coaching, reflection and feedback on video-recorded lessons. This technology enables leaders to provide remote in-ear coaching with leaders listening in on the on-the-spot work of teachers, along the lines of referees in rugby internationals. Although these are early days, this is potentially opening up new insights into how teachers make decisions and reflect in action, although the extent to which their behaviour is modified as a result of using the technology is less certain.

One of the challenges for leaders is developing a culture in which lesson observations (remote or first hand) are welcomed by staff as a means of professional development, rather than resisted and perceived as a threat. Staff should be reassured that inspectors in both England and Wales focus on collective whole-school judgements about teaching and have moved away from individual teacher judgements. Lesson observations, although still significant, are only one form of evidence; the analysis of data, reviewing learners' books and talking to them can provide a clearer picture of learners' progress and achievement. To develop a climate that values observations, it is important that teachers and their assistants, rather than only senior leaders, carry these out. Governors, who are ultimately responsible for the school, also have a role to play in observing lessons and understanding what is happening on the ground. As Gardner (1995: 22) notes, leadership is 'a process that occurs within the minds of individuals who live in a culture'.

Summary

» Leadership involves setting a clear strategic direction, establishing shared values and vision and building a sense of community.
» All those working in educational contexts can demonstrate leadership.

» There are different leadership styles but it is difficult to say which is the most effective in creating a climate for learning and raising standards.
» Many leadership ideas in education originated in business.
» The National College for Teaching and Leadership is an important source of support for leaders.
» The ultimate goal for leaders is to promote deep learning.

Points for reflection and action

» It has been said that taking a school from poor to good is about tightening up, but the journey from good to outstanding is about letting go. How do you think digital technologies might assist you in such a journey?
» Think about your school motto or vision statement. Can you give three examples of how you have demonstrated this in the last week?
» The National College for Teaching and Leadership has a suite of online modules for leadership development. These cover topics such as building teams, coaching, partnership working, starting a new role, leading teams and working with parents and the community. Browse these at www.nationalcollege.org.uk and find resources that suit your needs.

Conclusion

The teaching profession is saturated with ideas. Unfortunately, some of these are half-baked or fundamentally flawed. Take the field of neuroscience and education. Della Sala and Anderson (2012) highlight some of the craziest ideas, such as the London borough council which in 2008 reportedly paid £90,000 of its hard-earned education budget to provide foot massages for unruly pupils. They critique many other examples, including suggestions that chewing gum should be encouraged in class because it aids memory and attention or, at the very least, reduces stress – think of the gum-chewing Alex Ferguson, the ex-Manchester United football manager, prowling the touchline during tense games. But teachers simply do not have the time or expertise to challenge or explore further what are often presented as credible ideas based on sound research. This is why the likes of the Sutton Trust are so important in providing teachers with an accurate lens from which to view research and draw out the implications for their practice. More generally, academics in education have a responsibility to ensure that research findings and their implications are made clear.

In writing this book, I wanted to provide teachers with a reliable overview of a dozen key ideas which lie at the core of educational practice. It began by raising philosophical issues concerning the role of schools, the purpose of education and the nature of learning. It is easy to lose sight of these fundamentals when there is so much emphasis on capturing 'what works well' in the classroom. However, taking time to reflect upon personal beliefs and values can actually sharpen one's practice. This is why I have included points for reflection throughout the book. Hopefully, these will stimulate discussion and debate on a range of topics. If the teaching profession is to retain credibility, it needs professionals who can argue their corner in a rigorous way. This means demonstrating reflectivity by asking probing questions and challenging established practices. Teaching should not be reduced to coaching by script.

When describing the ideas in this book, I was invariably drawn back to the question of what education is for and the intellectual traditions that have shaped our educational systems. In discussions with students over the years, it has always concerned me how very few are able to go beyond the names of Piaget, Dewey or Montessori. The history of educational ideas may not be particularly popular in university courses, but without a frame of reference teachers will struggle to participate fully in informed debates. As the 'Who is behind it?' sections show, many ideas we take for granted have been around for a long time. The essential debates around childhood, education and schools have not changed a great deal since ancient times. Obviously, education in the twenty-first century has brought a unique set of challenges – the rise of digital technologies being an obvious example. Nonetheless, the goals of education have basically revolved around transmitting selected knowledge and skills and cultivating desired values (as discussed in Chapters 3, 4 and 5). While the relative importance of these elements of learning has long been debated, they all clearly have a place in a broad and balanced curriculum.

Schools seek to achieve good academic outcomes. However, judging the success of a school should go beyond how well learners perform in examinations. It should include how well the school cares for and guides its learners. Ultimately, this depends on the quality of relationships and interaction between leaders, teachers and learners. This was the basic message in Chapter 6 – namely, that educators need to work to a moral purpose that sets high expectations for all learners based on a genuine conviction that schools can transform lives. This is particularly important for children from the poorest families and neighbourhoods. Politicians of different persuasions acknowledge that we have one of the most inequitable educational systems in the developed world (Gove, 2011; Reay, 2012). Having a moral purpose means refusing to accept that this is inevitable and doing something positive to make education more equitable. Of course, schools cannot do this alone. They need to work closely alongside parents and the wider community, local authorities and health and social services.

As Chapter 7 noted, skilled teachers draw on a range of approaches, including direct instruction, to achieve their educational goals. These goals are expressed in different ways and in varying degrees of specificity. A review of educational aims and values in six countries (to 2006) found that some (e.g. England, Scotland and Sweden) focused on raising pupils' attainment, especially promoting pupils' literacy and numeracy skills, whereas others (e.g. Germany and the Netherlands) emphasised the more holistic development of the child – the social, emotional and cognitive (Shuayb and O'Donnell, 2008). Ultimately, the extent to which educational goals are achieved at school level depends largely on the quality of teachers and leaders. Good teachers who have strong subject knowledge and who can effectively communicate this to learners are vital. Leaders who support and challenge teachers to perform well and who care about learners also make a significant difference to the prospects of children and young people.

Unfortunately, teacher morale in the UK is very low – excessive tests, paperwork and accountability and unnecessary workload and pupils' disruptive behaviour are among the reasons typically cited. In recent times there have been regular stories in the education press about teachers and leaders quitting or threatening to leave the profession (e.g. Boffey, 2015). There is also a shortage of high quality leaders in schools, with recruitment firms paid substantial sums to headhunt potential leaders (Selvarajah, 2015). There are implications here about improving the status, employment conditions and self-image of teachers. Teachers need more (but not complete) professional autonomy in making decisions about the curriculum (as described in Chapter 8). They need effective and sustained professional development so their knowledge is at the cutting edge. Accountability, often seen as a dirty word, should be recast so that schools increasingly take responsibility to evaluate what they do and how well they perform against agreed benchmarks. This largely underpins the ideas in Chapter 12 about professional leadership.

While I would argue that knowing, understanding and engaging with the ideas presented in this book is necessary for teachers, particularly those new to the profession, this is not sufficient if we are to see improvements in the quality of schooling. What is needed is a commitment to quality and equity – quality in the sense of promoting a richness and depth of learning experiences and equity in terms of addressing the impact of disadvantage in education. Schools who take the UNCRC seriously already demonstrate such a commitment. In practical terms, Table 13.1 summarises some of the major implications for practitioners who want to take forward the thinking presented in this book.

Chapter	Idea	Major implications
1	**Education** – education goes beyond the school gates and is a lifelong experience	Make strong and sustained links with parents and the wider community
2	**Childhood** – children need time and space to explore, enjoy learning and develop as children rather than miniature adults	Personalise learning and create an environment where children want to ask questions, find things out and take risks
3	**Knowledge** – knowledge is the foundation for learning	Find out what children already know about topics before teaching and ensure that lessons build on this prior knowledge
4	**Skills** – learners need to develop a broad range of skills in real-life, relevant contexts	Draw on children's personal and local experiences and topical events to engage their interest, but take them beyond the familiar
5	**Dispositions** – effective learning depends on cultivating positive dispositions	Model the kinds of qualities and attitudes that you want children to develop, such as persistence, curiosity and hard work
6	**Ethics** – teachers' conduct should be guided by a moral purpose	Whatever you say or do, try to consider whether this is in the best interests of learners and weigh up the likely consequences of decisions for them, you and the wider profession

Chapter	Idea	Major implications
7	**Instruction** – direct instruction is a tried-and-tested means of effective teaching	Provide clear structure in lessons, including shared learning objectives, explanation of key teaching points and appropriate use of demonstration and summaries
8	**Curriculum** – the curriculum is all the learning and assessment activities in school, both planned and unintentional, that contribute to agreed educational goals	Agree as a team what you want learners to achieve. Then regularly review how the curriculum is supporting this, drawing on learners' views
9	**Feedback** – providing personalised, accurate, specific and timely feedback is one of the keys to improving learning	Teach less and give more high quality feedback before, during and after lessons
10	**Reflective practice** – good teachers critically analyse their practice with a view to improving what they do	Regularly ask probing questions about the why and how of teaching
11	**Research** – research has a central role to play in the professional development of teachers	Look on research as having the potential to improve the quality of school life and as something that you can engage with without adding too much to your workload
12	**Professional leadership** – effective school leadership operates at all levels and is about shared vision, support and securing improvement	Foster leadership skills in the classroom but look beyond to see what contribution you can make in the school and within professional networks

Table 13.1. Key ideas and implications for practitioners.

It could be argued that in a world of too many choices, the ideas that stick are those that stand out. In his 2003 TED Talk, the entrepreneur Seth Godin points out that if you are driving down a country road and you see a cow then that's no big deal. But if it is purple then you will take notice. In time, if all cows become purple then the novelty wears off. In education, there is no shortage of purple cows but the danger is that novel ideas soon become outdated. In this book, I have played safe by choosing twelve ideas, most of which have proved distinctive in their longevity and transferability, being at the core of sound educational practice. The multi-talented American composer, writer and artist John Cage, the son of an inventor, once said that he couldn't understand why people are frightened of new ideas when he was frightened of the old ones. Some teachers might be fearful of some of the old ideas presented in this book. They may not subscribe to the notion of direct instruction or basing lessons on core knowledge. Others may frown on giving learners space in lessons to take risks, ask questions and follow their own enquiries.

One of the book's central arguments has been to move away from polarised debates and to strike a balance between different teaching approaches. This means knowing what is appropriate in any given context and supporting teachers in making wise decisions. Think about children using computers. Many show remarkable ingenuity and risk in exploring complex games or programmes. They are not fearful of trying things out. Of course, they invariably get immediate feedback that tells them how they are doing. But at other times the environment does not provide this. Teachers need to take the lead by transmitting knowledge and getting learners to think about the key concepts in their lessons. On occasion, simply telling children, rather than letting them discover things, can be the most efficient and effective use of resources.

Another of the book's themes has been the need for teachers to practise and then adapt ideas. This has been prompted through each chapter's points for reflection and action. We know that effective and committed teachers practise skills that they want to improve. Generations of teachers have received advice on how to improve their teaching skills. Consider the following:

» Get to know the *name* of every child in your class as soon as possible.
» *The voice.* Talk slowly and clearly. Make your voice pleasant and vary its tones. Avoid slang and slovenly speech.

» *The eyes*. Use your eyes well. Let every child feel that he or she comes within your ken. If you are talking to or dealing with one child, do not let the others feel that they are free to play.

» When preparing the lesson beforehand, consider carefully the capabilities of the class.

» Think out the aim of the lesson carefully for yourself and let your preparation be guided by this.

» Do not attempt to recover the attention of the class by shouting or clapping your hands, or hitting the desk with a ruler. A pause in your teaching or a question directed to the offender will probably be more effective.

» If your question fails to get any response, do not supply the answer yourself, but try again by wording your question differently.

» Always try and form a contact between the topic of the lesson and the experience of the children. Make full use of local colour.

» Bear in mind that there is often a tendency for the teacher to do too much of the work himself. Encourage the children to talk, of course in a disciplined way, and do not always rest content with very short answers, no matter how correct.

» Interest yourself in the playground activities of the children.

» Avoid general threats such as, 'The next boy who speaks will be ...'

» Your own attitude will be reflected in the class. Don't slouch. Keep your hands out of your pockets. Be neat in appearance and gentlemanly in your bearing. Show that you are keen to work and thus preserve an atmosphere of work in the classroom. (cited in Grigg, 1998: 268–270)

This advice was provided in 1930, although it is worth reflecting upon its continued relevance. Do you notice references to what we might call personalised learning? What about drawing on pupils' prior knowledge and experience? Is the guidance on instructional techniques valid today? Teachers then were expected to apply this advice and were observed by tutors teaching classes of children both in university and in school – the key point being that students practised before taking full charge of a class. Sometimes they practised among themselves until they perfected their techniques.

There is a danger that the importance of teaching *practice* is overlooked in an era of observation, judgements, measurement and accountability.

Doug Lemov and his colleagues (2012) make the point that heart surgeons practise a specific, complex technique known as suturing by dissecting oranges. They break down this technique step by step. They need to get it right. Lemov has filmed the practice of excellent teachers in some of the most disadvantaged school communities in the United States. He wanted to capture what they did and so he watched around 10,000 hours of video footage over a decade of research. This work culminated in *Teach Like a Champion* (2015), in which Lemov recounts sixty-two techniques demonstrated by those excellent teachers. There are similarities between their approaches (e.g. maintaining a strong voice, asking targeted questions and being very visible) and the historic guidance given above. There are also many differences. One of the key findings is that great teachers vary considerably in their style – some were quiet, others animated; some kept to the basics, while others veered away from the set curriculum. Yet, what emerged was the capacity of these teachers to adapt new ideas to their own contexts as well as common practices that proved effective across the board. If *Big Ideas in Education* prompts you to try out some fresh (or even old) ideas, re-examine your thinking and practice, then it will achieve its purpose.

Bibliography

Ackerman, D. S. and Gross, B. L. (2010) 'Instructor Feedback: How Much Do Students Really Want?', *Journal of Marketing Education* 32 (August): 172–181.

Adams, R. (2015) 'School League Tables Raise Pupils' Stress But Fail to Reduce Attainment Gaps', *The Guardian* (4 April).

Adey, P., Dillon, J. and Adey, J. (2012) *Bad Education: Debunking Myths in Education*. Maidenhead: Open University Press.

Alexander, R. (ed.) (2010) *Children, Their World, Their Education: Final Report and Recommendations of the Cambridge Primary Review*. Abingdon: Routledge.

Alexander, W. R. (1972) 'Community Involvement in Curriculum', *Educational Leadership* (May): 655–657. Available at: http://www.ascd.org/ASCD/pdf/journals/ed_lead/el_197205_alexander.pdf.

Allen, K. (2013) 'Half of Recent UK Graduates Stuck in Non-Graduate Jobs, Says ONS', *The Guardian* (19 November).

American Association of Colleges of Teacher Education (2010) *21st Century Knowledge and Skills in Educator Preparation*. New York: Pearson.

Anderson, L. W. and Krathwohl, D. R. (eds.) (2001) *A Taxonomy for Learning, Teaching, and Assessing: A Revision of Bloom's Taxonomy of Educational Objectives*. New York: Longman.

Apple, M. (2013) *Can Education Change Society?* New York: Routledge.

Argyris, C. (1976) *Increasing Leadership Effectiveness*. New York: Wiley.

Aristotle (2003) *The Nicomachean Ethics*, ed. H. Tredennick, tr. J. A. K. Thomson. New York: Penguin.

Arthur, J. (2003) *Education with Character: The Moral Economy of Schooling*. Abingdon: Routledge.

Arthur, J., Kristjansson, K., Walker, D., Sanderse, W. and Jones, C. (2015) *Character Education in UK Schools: Research Report*. Birmingham: University of Birmingham.

Assessment Reform Group (2002) *Assessment for Learning: 10 Principles*. Available at: http://www.aaia.org.uk/content/uploads/2010/06/Assessment-for-Learning-10-principles.pdf.

Association of School and College Leaders (ASCL) (2014) *Response to the Carter Review of Initial Teacher Training: Response of the Association of School and College Leaders*. Available at: http://www.ascl.org.uk/news-and-views/news_news-detail.response-to-the-carter-review-of-initial-teacher-training.html.

Atkins, K. and Hopkin, N. (2012) *How We Learn What We Learn*, 2nd edn. London: Rosendale School. Available at: https://issuu.com/rosendale/docs/how_we_learn.

Austin, H. (2015) 'Bradford Stabbing: 14-Year-Old Boy Arrested After Teacher Attacked During Science Lesson', *The Independent* (11 June).

Baars, S., Bernardes, E., Elwick, A., Malortie, A., McAleavy, T., McInerney, L., Menzies, L. and Riggall, A. (2014) *Lessons from London Schools: Investigating the Success*. Cambridge: CfBT.

Baer, D. (2014) '3 Public Speaking Tips From the Most Popular TED Talk Ever', *Business Insider* (22 August). Available at: http://www.businessinsider.com/ted-talk-how-schools-kill-creativity-2014-8?IR=T.

Bailey, K. (1994) *Methods of Social Research*. New York: Free Press.

Bailey, R. (2011) *Letting Children Be Children: Report of an Independent Review of the Commercialisation and Sexualisation of Childhood*. London: DfE.

Ball, S. (2008) *The Education Debate: Policy and Politics in the Twenty-First Century*. Bristol: Policy Press.

Banathy, B. H. (1991) *Systems Design of Education: A Journey to Create the Future*. Englewood Cliffs, NJ: Educational Technology Publications.

Baptist Union of Great Britain, the Methodist Church, the Church of Scotland and the United Reformed Church (2013) *The Lies We Tell Ourselves: Ending Comfortable Myths About Poverty*. London: Methodist Church in Britain.

Barber, M. (2009) *Impossible and Necessary: Are You Ready for This?* London: Nesta.

Barber, M., Whelan, F. and Clark, M. (2010) *Capturing the Leadership Premium: How the World's Top School Systems are Building Leadership Capacity for the Future*. London: McKinsey & Company.

Barnard, P. (2013) *The Systems Thinking School: Redesigning Schools from the Inside-Out*. Lanham, MD: Rowman & Littlefield.

Baron-Cohen, S. (2011) *Zero Degrees of Empathy: A New Theory of Human Cruelty and Kindness*. London: Allen Lane.

Bartlett, J. and Miller, C. (2011) *Truths, Lies and the Internet*. London: Demos.

BBC (1996) *Reputations: Albert Speer: The Nazi Who Said Sorry* [video], *BBC Two* (2 May).

BBC (2006) 'Pupils "Must Learn About Nappies"', *BBC News* (1 August). Available at: http://news.bbc.co.uk/1/hi/education/5223768.stm.

BBC (2008) 'Rose Denounces Impact of Testing', *BBC News* (20 October). Available at: http://news.bbc.co.uk/1/hi/education/7680895.stm.

BBC (2013) 'Self-Portraits and Social Media: The Rise of the "Selfie"',
    BBC News (12 June). Available at: http://www.bbc.co.uk/news/
    magazine-22511650.

Beare, H., Caldwell, B. J. and Millikan, R. H. (1989) *Creating an Excellent
    School: Some New Management Techniques*. London: Routledge.

Beare, H., Caldwell, B. and Millikan, R. H. (1993) 'Leadership', in M. Preedy
    (ed.), *Managing the Effective School*. London: Paul Chapman, pp. 141–162.

Becta (2010) *The Impact of Technology on Children's Attainment in English: A
    Review of the Literature*. Coventry: Becta.

Bennett, T. (2012) 'School Councils: Shut Up, We're Listening', *The Guardian*
    (12 March).

Berliner, D. C. (1996) 'Educational Psychology Meets the Christian Right:
    Differing Views of Children, Schooling, Teaching, and Learning', *Teachers
    College Record* 98(3): 381–417.

Bernstein, B. (1970) 'Education Cannot Compensate for Society', *New Society*
    15(387): 344–347.

Biggs, J. and Collis, K. (1982) *Evaluating the Quality of Learning: The SOLO
    Taxonomy*. New York: Academic Press.

Black, P. and Wiliam, D. (1998) *Inside the Black Box: Raising Standards Through
    Classroom Assessment*. London: King's College.

Blatchford, P., Webster, R. and Russell, A. (2012) 'Challenging the Role and
    Deployment of Teaching Assistants in Mainstream Schools: The Impact
    on Schools. Final Report on Findings from the Effective Deployment of
    Teaching Assistants (eDTA) Project'. Available at: http://maximisingtas.
    co.uk/assets/content/edtareport-2.pdf.

Bloom, B. S. (1971) 'Mastery Learning', in J. H. Block (ed.), *Mastery Learning:
    Theory and Practice*. New York: Holt, Rinehart and Winston, pp. 47–63.

Bloom, B. S., Engelhart, M. D., Furst, E. J., Hill, W. H. and Krathwohl,
    D. R. (1956) *Taxonomy of Educational Objectives: The Classification of
    Educational Goals. Handbook I: Cognitive Domain*. New York: David
    McKay.

Boaler, J. (2009) *The Elephant in the Classroom: Helping Children Learn and
    Love Maths*. London: Souvenir Press.

Bobbitt, F. (1918) *The Curriculum*. Boston, MA: Houghton Mifflin.

Boffey, D. (2015) 'Half of All Teachers in England Threaten to Quit as Morale
    Crashes', *The Observer* (4 October).

Bolman, L. G. and Deal, T. E. (1991) *Reframing Organizations: Artistry, Choice
    and Leadership*. San Francisco, CA: Jossey-Bass.

Bolton, G. (2014) *Reflective Practice: Writing and Professional Development*, 4th
    edn. London: Sage.

Borton, T. (1970) *Read, Touch, and Teach: Student Concerns and Process
    Education*. New York: McGraw Hill.

Bourdieu, P. (1991) *Language and Symbolic Power*, tr. G. Raymond and M. Adamson. Cambridge: Polity Press.

Bower, G. H. (1972) 'Mental Imagery in Associative Learning', in L. W. Gregg (ed.), *Cognition in Learning and Memory*. New York: Wiley, pp. 51–88.

Bowlby, J. (1944) 'Forty-Four Juvenile Thieves: Their Characters and Home Life', *International Journal of Psychoanalysis* 25: 107–128.

Bransford, J., Brown, A. L. and Cocking (eds.) (2000) *How People Learn: Brain, Mind, Experience, and School*. Washington, DC: National Academy Press.

Brighouse, T. (2001) 'Doomed to Succeed: The Eldorado of School Leadership', *Leading Edge* 5(2): 65–76.

British Educational Research Association (BERA) (2011) *Ethical Guidance for Educational Researchers*. London: BERA.

British Educational Research Association (BERA) (2013) *Why Educational Research Matters: A Briefing to Inform Future Funding Decisions*. London: BERA.

British Educational Research Association (BERA) (2014) *Research and the Teaching Profession*. London: BERA.

Brookfield, S. (1990) 'Using Critical Incidents to Explore Learners' Assumptions', in J. Mezirow (ed.), *Fostering Critical Reflection in Adulthood*. San Francisco, CA: Jossey-Bass, pp. 177–193.

Brookfield, S. (1995) *Becoming a Critically Reflective Teacher*. San Francisco, CA: Jossey-Bass.

Brown, M. (2012) 'Traditional Versus Progressive Education', in P. Adey and J. Dillon (eds.), *Bad Education*. Maidenhead: Open University Press, pp. 95–109.

Brown, P. and Lauder, H. (2001) *Capitalism and Social Progress: The Future of Society in a Global Economy*. New York: Palgrave.

Brumberg, J. (1997) *The Body Project: An Intimate History of American Girls*. New York: Random House.

Bullough, R. V. (2011) 'Ethical and Moral Matters in Teaching and Teacher Education', *Teaching and Teacher Education* 27: 21–28.

Burgess, T. (2002) *The Devil's Dictionary of Education*. London: Continuum.

Burkard, T. (2004) *After the Literacy Hour*. London: Centre for Policy Studies.

Burns, J. (2015) 'Extra Screen Time "Hits GCSE Grades"', *BBC News* (4 September). Available at: http://www.bbc.co.uk/news/education-34139196.

Burton, D. and Bartlett, S. (2005) *Practitioner Research for Teachers*. London: Paul Chapman.

Buzan, T. (2003) *Mind Maps for Kids: An Introduction*. London: Thorsons.

Cadwalladr, C. (2015) 'The "Granny Cloud": The Network of Volunteers Helping Poorer Children Learn', *The Guardian* (2 August).

Campbell, A. (2015) *Winners: And How They Succeed*. London: Hutchinson.

Campbell, E. (2003) *The Ethical Teacher*. Maidenhead: Open University Press.

Carline, B. (2008) *What Pupils Really Think About Their Schools*. London: Continuum.

Carpenter, H., Papps, I., Bragg, J., Dyson, A., Harris, D., Kerr, K., Todd, L. and Laing, K. (2013) *Evaluation of Pupil Premium Research Report*. Centre for Equity in Education, University of Manchester and Newcastle University.

Carr, W. and Kemmis, S. (1986) *Becoming Critical: Education, Knowledge and Action Research*. Lewes: Falmer.

Carswell, D. (2013) 'We Do Not Need a National Curriculum: Schools Should Be Free to Opt Out', *The Telegraph* (9 July).

Carter, A. (2015) *Carter Review of Initial Teacher Training (ITT)*. London: DfE.

Cassen, R. and McNally, S. (2015) *Making a Difference in Education: What the Evidence Says*. Abingdon: Routledge.

Cattaneo, M. A., Oggenfuss, C. and Wolter, S. C. (2016) 'The More, the Better? The Impact of Instructional Time On Student Performance', Working Paper 115. University of Zurich, Institute for Strategy and Business Economics. Available at: http://repec.business.uzh.ch/RePEc/iso/leadinghouse/0115_lhwpaper.pdf.

Children's Society (2015) *The Good Childhood Report 2015*. London: Children's Society.

Christodoulou, D. (2014) *Seven Myths about Education*. Abingdon: Routledge.

Cicchetti, D. and Rogosch, F. A. (2009) 'Adaptive Coping Under Conditions of Extreme Stress: Multilevel Influences on the Determinants of Resilience in Maltreated Children', *New Directions for Child and Adolescent Development* 124: 47–59.

Clark, L. (2009) 'Teachers Moan That New Code of Conduct Will Stop Them Getting Drunk at Weekends', *Daily Mail* (4 September).

Clarke, S. (2003) *Enriching Feedback in the Primary Classroom*. London: Hodder Education.

Claxton, G. (2002) *Building Learning Power: Helping Young People Become Better Learners*. Bristol: TLO Ltd.

Claxton, G. (2008) *What's the Point of Schools? Rediscovering the Heart of Education*. Oxford: OneWorld.

Claxton, G., Chambers, M., Powell, G. and Lucas, W. (2011) *The Learning Powered School: Pioneering 21st Century Education*. Bristol: TLO Ltd.

Claxton, G. and Lucas, B. (2015) *Educating Ruby: What Our Children Really Need to Learn*. Carmarthen: Crown House Publishing.

Clay, D. and Thomas, A. (2014) *Review of Military Ethos Alternative Provision Projects: Research Report*. London: DfE.

Coates, S. (2015) *Head Strong: 11 Lessons of School Leadership*. Melton: Woodbridge.

Coe, R., Aloisi, C., Higgins, S. and Major, L. E. (2014) *What Makes Great Teaching? Review of the Underpinning Research*. London: Sutton Trust.

Available at: http://www.suttontrust.com/wp-content/uploads/2014/10/What-Makes-Great-Teaching-REPORT.pdf.

Coffield, F., Moseley, D., Hall, E. and Ecclestone, K. (2004) *Learning Styles: A Systematic and Critical Review*. London: Learning and Skills Development Agency.

Collins, J. (2001) *Good to Great: Why Some Companies Make the Leap ... And Others Don't*. New York: HarperCollins.

Collins, N. (2011) 'One in Five "Incompetent" Teachers Sacked', *The Telegraph* (25 December).

Comin, D. and Hobijn, B. (2008) 'An Exploration of Technology Diffusion'. Available at: http://www.hbs.edu/faculty/Publication%20Files/08-093.pdf.

Confederation of British Industry (CBI) (2013) *Changing the Pace: CBI/Pearson Education and Skill Survey 2013*. London: CBI/Pearson.

Confederation of British Industry (CBI) (2014) *Gateway to Growth: CBI/Pearson Education and Skill Survey 2014*. London: CBI/Pearson.

Cook, J. (1992) 'Negotiating the Curriculum: Programming for Learning', in G. Boomer, N. Lester, C. Onore and J. Cook (eds.), *Negotiating the Curriculum: Educating for the 21st Century*. London: Falmer Press, pp. 15–31.

Cooperrider, D. L. and Srivastva, S. (1987) 'Appreciative Inquiry in Organizational Life', in R. W. Woodman and W. A. Pasmore (eds.), *Research in Organizational Change and Development, Vol. 1*. Stamford, CT: JAI Press, pp. 129–169.

Costa, A. and Kallick, B. (2008) *Learning and Leading with Habits of Mind: 16 Characteristics of Success*. Alexandria, CA: ASCD.

Costa, A. and Kallick, B. (2014) *Dispositions: Reframing Teaching and Learning*. Thousand Oaks, CA: Corwin.

Coughlan, S. (2015) 'Schools Put on Front Line Against Extremism', *BBC News* (19 June). Available at: http://www.bbc.co.uk/news/education-33166420.

Covey, S. R. (1999) *Principle-Centred Leadership*. London: Simon & Schuster.

Covey, S. R. (2004) *The 7 Habits of Highly Effective People*. New York: Franklin Covey.

Csikszentmihalyi, M. (2002) *Flow: The Psychology of Happiness*. London: Random House.

Cunningham, P. (2012) *Politics and the Primary Teacher*. London: Routledge.

Dartnell, L. (2015) *The Knowledge: How to Rebuild Our World After an Apocalypse*. London: Vintage.

Darwin, C. (1871) *The Descent of Man, and Selection in Relation to Sex*. London: John Murray.

Davies, J. B. and West-Burnham, J. (eds.) (2003) *Handbook of Educational Leadership and Management*. London: Pearson.

Day, C. (1999) 'Researching Teaching Through Reflective Practice' in J. Loughran (ed.), *Researching Teaching: Methodologies and Practices for Understanding Pedagogy*. London: Falmer Press, pp. 215–232.

Day, C., Sammons, P., Hopkins, D., Harris, A., Leithwood, K., Gu, Q., Brown, E., Ahtaridou, E. and Kington, A. (2009) *The Impact of School Leadership on Pupil Outcomes*. London: DCSF.

De Bono, E. (2004) *How to Have a Beautiful Mind*. London: Random House.

De Lange, J. (2005) *Measuring Mathematical Literacy in Encyclopaedia of Social Measurement*. Amsterdam: Elsevier-Reed.

Deakin Crick, R. and Goldspink, C. (2014) 'Learner Dispositions, Self-Theories and Student Engagement', *British Journal of Educational Studies*: 1–17.

Della Sala, S. and Anderson, M. (2012) *Neuroscience in Education: The Good, the Bad and the Ugly*. Oxford: Oxford University Press.

Department for Business, Innovation and Skills (DBIS) (2012) *The 2011 Skills for Life Survey: A Survey of Literacy, Numeracy and ICT Levels in England*. London: DBIS.

Department for Children, Schools and Families (DCSF) (2005) *Extended Schools: Building on Experience*. Nottingham: DCSF.

Department for Children, Schools and Families (DCSF) (2007a) *Diversity & Citizenship: A Curriculum Review*. Nottingham: DCSF.

Department for Children, Schools and Families (DCSF) (2007b) *The Children's Plan: Building Brighter Futures*. Nottingham: DCSF.

Department for Children, Schools and Families (DCSF) (2008a) *The Impact of Parental Involvement on Children's Education*. Nottingham: DCSF.

Department for Children, Schools and Families (DCSF) (2008b) *21st Century Schools: A World-Class Education for Every Child*. Nottingham: DCSF.

Department for Children, Schools and Families (DCSF) (2008c) *Learning Together To Be Safe*. Nottingham: DCSF.

Department for Children, Schools and Families (DCSF) (2008d) *The Assessment for Learning Strategy*. Nottingham: DCSF.

Department for Children, Schools and Families (DCSF) (2009a) *The Impact of the Commercial World on Children's Wellbeing: Report of an Independent Assessment*. Nottingham: DCSF.

Department for Children, Schools and Families (DCSF) (2009b) *Improving Subject Pedagogy Through Lesson Study: Handbook for Leading Teachers in Mathematics and English*. Nottingham: DCSF.

Department for Children, Schools and Families (DCSF) (2009c) *Independent Review of the Primary Curriculum: Final Report* [Rose Review]. Nottingham: DCSF.

Department for Children, Schools and Families (DCSF) (2009d) *Personalised Learning: A Practical Guide*. Nottingham: DCSF.

Department for Children, Schools and Families (DCSF) (2010) *A Guide to Enterprise Education*. Nottingham: DCSF.

Department for Education (DfE) (2010) *The Importance of Teaching: The Schools White Paper 2010*. London: DfE.

Department for Education (DfE) (2011a) *Teachers' Standards*. London: DfE.

Department for Education (DfE) (2011b) *The National Strategies 1997–2011*. London: DfE.

Department for Education (DfE) (2011c) *Framework for the National Curriculum. A Report by the Expert Panel for the National Curriculum Review*. London: DfE.

Department for Education (DfE) (2012) *Statutory Framework for the Early Years Foundation Stage* (EYFS). London: DfE.

Department for Education (DfE) (2013) *Permanent and Fixed Period Exclusions from Schools in England: 2011 to 2012 Academic Year*. London: DfE.

Department for Education (DfE) (2014) *Keeping Children Safe in Education: Statutory Guidance for Schools and Colleges*. London: DfE.

Department of Education and Science (DES) (1985) *The Curriculum from 5 to 16*. Curriculum Matters No. 2. London: DES.

Department for Education and Skills (DfES) (2003) *Every Child Matters*. Norwich: TSO.

Department for Education and Skills (DfES) (2005) *Excellence and Enjoyment: Social and Emotional Aspects of Learning: Guidance*. Nottingham: DfES.

Department for Education and Skills (DfES) (2007) *Social and Emotional Aspects of Learning (SEAL): Guidance Booklet*. Nottingham: DfES.

Dewey, J. (1910) *How We Think*. New York: D.C. Heath & Co.

Dewey, J. (1933) *How We Think: A Restatement of the Relation of Reflective Thinking to the Education Process*. Chicago, IL: Henry Regnery.

Dewey, J. (1938) *Experience and Education*. New York: Kappa Delta Pi.

Dewey, J. (1944) *Democracy and Education*. New York: Free Press.

Didau, D. (2015) *What If Everything You Knew About Education Was Wrong?* Carmarthen: Crown House Publishing.

Donaldson, G. (2015) *Successful Futures: Independent Review of Curriculum and Assessment Arrangements in Wales*. Cardiff: Welsh Government.

Donnelly, L. (2015) 'All Children Should Receive Weekly "Happiness" Lessons from the Age of Five', *The Telegraph* (14 February).

Doughty, E. (2015) 'New Research Finds That Life Begins at 60', *The Telegraph* (19 November).

Dunn, E. W., Aknin, L. B. and Norton, M. I. (2008) 'Spending Money on Others Promotes Happiness', *Science* 319(5870): 1687–1688.

Dweck, C. (2006) *Mindset: The New Psychology of Success*. New York: Random House.

Dye, V. (2011) 'Reflection, Reflection, Reflection. I'm Thinking All The Time,

Why Do I Need a Theory or Model of Reflection?', in D. McGregor and L. Cartwright (eds.), *Developing Reflective Practice: A Guide for Beginning Teachers*. Maidenhead: Open University Press, pp. 217–234.

Earley, P., Higham, R., Allen, R., Allen, T., Howson, J., Nelson, R., Rawar, S., Lynch, S., Morton, L., Mehta, P. and Sims, D. (2012) *Review of the School Leadership Landscape*. Nottingham: National College for School Leadership.

Early Education (2011) *Code of Ethics*. London: Early Education.

Economic and Social Research Council (ESRC) (2016) *Britain in 2016*. Swindon: ESRC.

Economist Intelligence Unit (2015) *The Learning Curve*. London: Pearson.

Education Select Committee (2015) 'Purpose and Quality of Education in England Inquiry Launched' (30 November). Available at: http://www. parliament.uk/business/committees/committees-a-z/commons-select/ education-committee/news-parliament-2015/purpose-quality-education-evidence-15-16/.

Edwards, T. (1996) 'The Research Base of Effective Teacher Education', *Research Intelligence* 57: 7–12.

Egan, D. (2012) *Communities, Families and Schools Together: A Route to Reducing the Impact of Poverty on Educational Achievement in Schools Across Wales*. London: Save the Children.

Ehrich, L. C., Kimber, M., Millwater, J. and Cranston, N. (2011) 'Ethical Dilemmas: A Model to Understand Teacher Practice', *Teachers and Teaching: Theory and Practice* 17(2): 173–185.

Einstein, A. (1954) *Ideas and Opinions*. New York: Random House.

Eisner, E. W. (2000) 'Benjamin Bloom, 1913–99', *Prospects: The Quarterly Review of Comparative Education* XXX(3): 387–395.

Elkind, D. (2006) *The Hurried Child: Growing Up Too Fast Too Soon*, 25th anniversary edn. Cambridge, MA: Da Capo Press.

Elliott, R. and Leonard, C. (2004) 'Peer Pressure and Poverty: Exploring Fashion Brands and Consumption Symbolism Among Children of the British Poor', *Journal of Consumer Behaviour* 3(4): 347–359.

Engelmann, S. and Carnine, D. (1982) *Theory of Instruction: Principles and Applications*. New York: Irvington.

Ennis, R. H. (1996) 'Critical Thinking Dispositions: Their Nature and Accessibility', *Informal Logic* 18(2&3): 165–182.

Ericsson, K. A., Krampe, R. T. and Tesch-Romer, C. (1993) 'The Role of Deliberate Practice in the Acquisition of Expert Performance', *Psychological Review* 100(3): 363–406.

Erricker, J. (2000) 'Moral Education in Relationships to Community', in C. Erricker and J. Erricker (eds.), *Reconstructing Religious, Spiritual and Moral Education*. London: Routledge, pp. 81–106.

Espinoza, J. (2015a) 'Faith Schools "Damaged By British Values Curriculum"', Says MP', *The Telegraph* (12 March).

Espinoza, J. (2015b) 'Vince Cable: Fight Against Extremism Will Lead to "Bland" Society', *The Telegraph* (27 October).

Everett, F. (2016) 'Will a Longer School Day Really Make Our Children Smarter?' *The Telegraph* (18 March).

Facer, K. (2011) *Learning Futures: Education, Technology and Social Change*. London: Routledge.

Fenton, B. (2006) 'Junk Culture "Is Poisoning Our Children"', *The Telegraph* (12 September).

Fenton, S. (2015) 'Children Don't Need to Learn Times Tables Because They Can Look Them Up On Their Phones, Says NUT Leader', *The Guardian* (4 January).

Findlay, S. (2015) 'Highland Teacher Stress Figures Are the Tip of the Iceberg', *Inverness Courier* (3 October).

Finnigan, M. (2011) *They Did You Can: How to Achieve Whatever You Want in Life with the Help of Your Sporting Heroes*. Carmarthen: Independent Thinking Press.

Fisher, R. (2001) 'Philosophy in Primary Schools: Fostering Thinking Skills and Literacy', *Reading* (July): 67–73.

Fisher, R. (2005) *Teaching Children to Think*. Cheltenham: Nelson Thornes.

Flanagan, F. M. (2006) *The Greatest Educators Ever*. London: Continuum.

Flanagan, J. C. (1954) 'The Critical Incident Technique', *Psychological Bulletin* 51(4): 327–358.

Flanders, N. (1970) *Analyzing Teaching Behaviour*. Reading, MA: Addison-Wesley.

Flavell, J. H. (1976) 'Metacognitive Aspects of Problem Solving', in L. B. Resnick (ed.), *The Nature of Intelligence*. Hillsdale, NJ: Lawrence Erlbaum Associates, pp. 231–236.

Flutter, J. and Rudduck, J. (2004) *Consulting Pupils: What's In It for Schools?* London: RoutledgeFalmer.

Flynn McCarthy, L. (2014) 'What Babies Learn in the Womb', *Parenting*. Available at: http://www.parenting.com/article/what-babies-learn-in-the-womb.

Forsyth, J. (2014) 'Michael Gove's Moral Mission', *The Spectator* (7 June).

Fox, T. (2016) 'Four-Year-Old Who Mispronounced "Cucumber" As "Cooker Bomb" Faced Terror Warnings, Family Say', *The Independent* (12 March).

Freire, P. (1970) *Pedagogy of the Oppressed*. New York: Seabury.

Fullan, M. (2008) *The Six Secrets of Change: What the Best Leaders Do to Help Their Organizations Survive and Thrive*. San Francisco, CA: Jossey-Bass.

Fullan, M. (2015) *The New Meaning of Educational Change*, 5th edn. New York: Teachers College Press.

Furedi, F. (2009) *Wasted: Why Education Isn't Working*. London: Continuum.

Furnham, A. (2010) 'Adrian Furnham: The Happy Results of a Sunny Disposition', *Sunday Times* (20 June).

Gagné, R. (1985) *The Conditions of Learning and the Theory of Instruction*, 4th edn. New York: Holt, Rinehart, and Winston.

Gallo, C. (2014) *Talk Like Ted: The 9 Public-Speaking Secrets of the World's Top Minds*. London: Macmillan.

Galton, M., Simon, B. and Croll, P. (1980) *Inside the Primary Classroom*. London: Routledge & Kegan Paul.

Gardner, H. (1995) *Leading Minds: An Anatomy of Leadership*. New York: Basic Books.

Garner, R. (2009) 'Schools Urged to Teach Good Parenting Skills', *The Independent* (2 February).

Garner, R. (2012) 'The Oldest Master: Student Who Left School at 14 Gets His Third Degree at 90', *The Independent* (4 May).

Garner, R. (2014a) 'Gove's Revolution: Pupils Return to Traditional Subjects in Huge Numbers', *The Independent* (27 January).

Garner, R. (2014b) 'Tests-and-Targets Culture Lowers Pupils' Self-Esteem, Claims Report', *The Independent* (12 April).

Gayle, D. (2016) 'Children in England Near Bottom in International Happiness Table', *The Guardian* (16 February).

Geake, J. (2008) 'Neurological Myths in Education', *Educational Researcher* 50(2): 123–134.

General Teaching Council for Scotland (2012) *Code of Professionalism and Conduct*. Edinburgh: General Teaching Council for Scotland.

General Teaching Council for Wales (2009) *Code of Professional Conduct and Practice for Registered Teachers*. Cardiff: General Teaching Council for Wales.

Gersten, R., Taylor, M. J., Keys, T. D., Rolfhus, E. and Newman-Gonchar, R. (2014) *Summary of Research on the Effectiveness of Math Professional Development Approaches*. Washington, DC: US Department of Education.

Gerver, R. (2010) *Creating Tomorrow's Schools Today*. London: Continuum.

Gesell, A. (1940) *The First Five Years of Life: A Guide to the Study of the Preschool Child*. New York: Harper.

Giardiello, P. (2013) *Pioneers in Early Childhood Education: The Roots and Legacies of Rachel and Margaret McMillan, Maria Montessori and Susan Isaacs*. Abingdon: Routledge.

Gibbs, G. and Simpson, C. (2004) 'Conditions Under Which Assessment Supports Students' Learning', *Learning and Teaching in Higher Education* 1: 3–31.

Glass, G. V., McGaw, B. and Smith, M. L. (1981) *Meta-Analysis in Social Research*. Beverly Hills, CA: SAGE.

Godin, S. (2003) 'How to Get Your Ideas to Spread' [video], *TED*. Available at: https://www.ted.com/talks/seth_godin_on_sliced_bread?language=en.

Goldacre, B. (2009) *Bad Science*. London: Harper Perennial.

Goleman, D. (1995) *Emotional Intelligence: Why It Can Matter More Than IQ*. London: Bloomsbury.

Goodall, O. (2007) 'War and Peace with Young Children', in H. Claire and C. Holden (eds.), *The Challenge of Teaching Controversial Issues*. Stoke on Trent: Trentham Books, pp. 27–39.

Goodlad, J. (1979) *Curriculum Inquiry: The Study of Curriculum Practice*. New York: McGraw-Hill.

Gove, M. (2011) 'Michael Gove on the Moral Purpose of School Reform'. Speech to the National College for School Leadership, Birmingham, 16 June.

Griffiths, V. (2000) 'The Reflective Dimension in Teacher Education', *International Journal of Educational Research* 33: 539–555.

Grigg, R. (1998) *History of Trinity College Carmarthen*. Carmarthen: University of Wales Press.

Grigg, R. (2015) *Becoming An Outstanding Primary Teacher*, 2nd edn. Abingdon: Routledge.

Grigg, R. and Hughes, S. (2012) *Teaching Primary Humanities*. Harlow: Pearson.

Grigg, R. and Lewis, H. (2016) *An A–Z of Learning Outside the Classroom*. London: Bloomsbury.

Gronn, P. (2003) *The New Work of Educational Leaders*. London: Paul Chapman.

Gunter, M., Estes, T. and Mintz, S. (2007) *Instruction: A Models Approach*. New York: Pearson.

Gurney-Read, J. (2015) 'Lord Baker: Vital Practical Skills Missing from Schools', *The Telegraph* (26 February).

Guskey, T. R. (2001) 'Benjamin S. Bloom's Contributions to Curriculum, Instruction and School Learning'. Paper presented at the Annual Meeting of the American Educational Research Association, Seattle, Washington, 10–14 April.

Habermas, J. (1991) *The Theory of Communicative Action: Reason and the Rationalization of Society*. Oxford: Polity Press.

Hadow, H. (1931) *The Primary School* [Hadow Report]. London: HMSO.

Hagger, H., Burn, K., Mutton, T. and Brindley, S. (2008) 'Practice Makes Perfect? Learning to Learn as a Teacher', *Oxford Review of Education* 34(2): 159–178.

Haidt, J. (2001) 'The Emotional Dog and its Rational Tail: A Social Intuitionist Approach to Moral Judgment', *Psychological Review* 108(4): 814–834.

Hall, K. and Øzerk, K. (2008) *Primary Curriculum and Assessment: England and Other Countries*. Cambridge: University of Cambridge.

Halpern, D. (2005) *Social Capital*. Cambridge: Polity Press.

Halstead, J. M. (2011) 'Is Moral Education Working? Extracts from the Diary of a Twenty-First Century Moral Educator', *Journal of Moral Education* 40(3): 339–347.

Hampson, M., Patton, A. and Shanks, L. (2012) *10 Ideas for 21st Century Education*. London: Innovation Unit.

Hanover, T. (2011) 'Outsourcing Education: The Rise of Virtual Schools', *World Socialist* (1 September). Available at: https://www.wsws.org/en/articles/2011/09/virt-s01.html.

Hansford, B. C., Ehrich, L. C. and Tennent, L. (2004) 'Formal Mentoring Programmes in Education and Other Professions: A Review of the Literature', *Education Administration Quarterly* 40(4): 518–540.

Hanushek, E. and Woessmann, L. (2010) *Education and Economic Growth: Economics of Education*. Amsterdam: Elsevier.

Hargreaves, A. (ed.) (2005) *Extending Educational Change: International Handbook of Educational Change*. Dordrecht: Springer.

Hargreaves, A. and Fullan, M. (1998) *What's Worth Fighting for in Education?* Buckingham: Open University Press.

Hargreaves, D. H. (1996) 'Teaching As a Research-Based Profession: Possibilities and Prospects' (Teacher Training Agency Annual Lecture). London: Teacher Training Agency.

Hargreaves, L., Cunningham, M., Everton, T., Hansen, A., Hopper, B., McIntyre, D., Maddock, M., Mukherjee, J., Pell, T., Rouse, M., Turner, P. and Wilson, L. (2008) *The Status of Teachers and the Teaching Profession: Views from Inside and Outside the Profession*. London: DfES.

Harland, J., Moor, H., Lord, P., Kinder, K., Kaur, S. and Johnson, F. (2003) *Talking 4: The Pupil Voice on the Key Stage 4 Curriculum. Key Stage 4 Phase Short Report* (Report 4 of the Northern Ireland Curriculum Cohort Study). Belfast: Council for the Curriculum Examinations and Assessment.

Harris, A. (2014) *Distributed Leadership Matters: Perspectives, Practicalities, and Potential*. London: SAGE.

Harris, A. and Chapman, C. (2002) *Effective Leadership in Schools Facing Challenging Circumstances*. Nottingham: National College for School Leadership.

Harris, A. and Spillane, J. (2008) 'Distributed Leadership Through the Looking Glass', *Management in Education* 22(1): 31–34.

Harrison, A. (2010) 'Gove's Top Degree Plan for Teachers Criticised', *BBC News* (17 September). Available at: http://www.bbc.co.uk/news/education-11330193.

Hattie, J. (2009) *Visible Learning: A Synthesis of Over 800 Meta-Analyses Relating to Achievement*. Abingdon: Routledge.

Hattie, J. (2012) *Visible Learning for Teachers*. Abingdon: Routledge.

Hattie, J. (2013) 'Understanding Learning: Lessons for Learning, Teaching and Research'. Available at: http://research.acer.edu.au/cgi/viewcontent.cgi?article=1207&context=research_conference.

Hattie, J. (2015) *What Doesn't Work in Education: The Politics of Distraction*. London: Pearson.

Hattie, J. and Timperley, H. (2007) 'The Power of Feedback', *Review of Educational Research* 77(1): 81–112.

Hattie, J. and Yates, G. (2014a) 'Using Feedback to Promote Learning', in V. A. Benassi, C. E. Overson and C. M. Hakala (eds.), *Applying the Science of Learning in Education: Infusing Psychological Science into the Curriculum*. Washington, DC: American Psychological Association, pp. 45–58.

Hattie, J. and Yates, G. (2014b) *Visible Learning and the Science of How We Learn*. Abingdon: Routledge.

Hauser, M. (2006) *Moral Minds: How Nature Designed Our Universal Sense of Right and Wrong*. London: Little, Brown.

Haydon, G. (2011) 'The Moral Agenda of Citizenship Education', in D. Lawton, J. Cairns and R. Gardner (eds.), *Education for Citizenship*. London: Continuum, pp. 136–147.

Hayes, T. J. (1999) 'Traditional Education vs. Direct Instruction: What's the Difference between These Teaching Methods?' *Education Reporter* 156. Available at: http://www.eagleforum.org/educate/1999/jan99/focus.html.

Henley, D. (2009) 'Blurred Boundaries for Teachers', *The Guardian* (23 September).

Heppell, S. (2006) 'Personalised Learning: A Discussion On How Imaginative Use of ICT Can Raise Standards Through Tailoring Education to Individual Students'. Available at: http://image.guardian.co.uk/sys-files/Guardian/documents/2006/01/10/apple_white_paper_personalised_learning.pdf.

Hersey, P. and Blanchard, K. H. (1982) *Management of Organization Behavior: Utilizing Human Resources*. Englewood Cliffs, NJ: Prentice Hall.

Heydenberk, W. R. and Heydenberk, R. (2015) 'Why Well-Educated Westerners are Joining the Islamic State', *Washington Post* (25 March).

Higgins, S., Katsipataki, M., Kokotsaki, D., Coleman, R., Major, L. E. and Coe, R. (2013) *The Sutton Trust–Education Endowment Foundation Teaching and Learning Toolkit*. London: Education Endowment Foundation.

Hilbert, M. and López, P. (2011) 'The World's Technological Capacity to Store, Communicate, and Compute Information', *Science* 332(6025): 60–65.

Hill, C. (2008) *Collaboration and Speaking and Listening in the Primary Classroom*. National Teacher Research Panel. Available at: http://www.ntrp.org.uk/sites/all/documents/Colin%20Hill_FINAL.pdf.

Hill, L., Stremmel, A. and Fu, F. (2005) *Teaching As Inquiry: Rethinking Curriculum in Early Childhood Education*. Boston, MA: Pearson.

Hill, R. (2012) *Teach First: Ten Years of Impact*. London: Teach First.

Hines, B. (1968) *A Kestrel for a Knave*. London: Penguin.

Hirsch, D. (2007) *The Knowledge Deficit: Closing the Shocking Education Gap for American Children*. New York: Houghton Mifflin.

Hirst, P. H. (1975) *Knowledge and the Curriculum*. London: Routledge.

Historical Association (2007) *T.E.A.C.H. Teaching Emotional and Controversial History 3–19*. London: Historical Association.

HM Government (2011) *Prevent Strategy*. Norwich: TSO.

HM Government (2015) *Channel Duty Guidance: Protecting Vulnerable People from Being Drawn Into Terrorism. Statutory Guidance for Channel Panel Members and Partners of Local Panels*. London: Home Office.

HMI (1978) *Primary Education in England. A Survey by HM Inspectors of Schools*. London: HMSO.

HMI (1980) *A View of the Curriculum*. Matters for Discussion No. 11. London: HMSO.

Hodges, D. (2014) 'All Faith-Based Schools Are Trojan Horse Schools. Let's Ban Every Single One of Them', *The Telegraph* (10 June).

Hoffman, S. (2015) *Championing Children's Rights in Times of Austerity: Local and Regional Authorities' Responsibilities*. Available at: https://cronfa.swan.ac.uk/Record/cronfa23351.

Holder, M. D. (2012) *Happiness in Children: Measurement, Correlates and Enhancement of Positive Subjective Well-Being*. Kelowna, BC: University of British Columbia.

Holt, J. (1964) *How Children Fail*. New York: Pitman Press.

Holt, J. (1981) *The John Holt Manual on Homeschooling*. Boston, MA: Da Capo Press.

Holt, J. (2004 [1976]) *Instead of Education: Ways to Help People Do Things Better*. Boulder, CO: Sentient Publications.

Hopkins, D. (2007) *Every School a Great School*. Buckingham: Open University Press.

Hopkins, D. (2013) *Exploring the Myths of School Reform*. Buckingham: Open University Press.

Hopkins, D., Ainscow, M. and West, D. (1994) *School Improvement in an Era of Change*. London: Continuum.

Horowitz, A. (2014) 'I Always Defended Michael Gove. Then I Met Him', *The Spectator* (15 March).

House, R. (2012) 'The Inappropriateness of ICT in Early Childhood', in S. Suggate and E. Reese (eds.), *Contemporary Debates in Childhood, Education and Development*. London: Routledge, pp. 105–120.

Hoyle, E. (1969) *The Role of the Teacher*. London: Routledge & Kegan Paul.

Hurley, C. (ed.) (2002) *Could Do Better*. London: Pocket Books.

Husbands, C. and Pearce, J. (2012) *What Makes Great Pedagogy? Nine Claims from Research*. Nottingham: National College for School Leadership.

Hyerle, D. (2008) *Visual Tools for Transforming Information Into Knowledge*. Thousand Oaks, CA: Corwin.

Ingvarson, L. C. and Hattie, J. (eds.) (2008) *Assessing Teachers for Professional Certification: The First Decade of the National Board for Professional Teaching Standards. Vol. 11: Advances in Program Evaluation*. Amsterdam: Elsevier Press.

Irons, A. (2008) *Enhancing Learning Through Formative Assessment and Feedback*. Abingdon: Routledge.

Jackson, P. (1968) *A Life in Classrooms*. New York: Holt, Rinehart and Winston.

James, M. (2005) 'Teacher Learning for Pupil Learning', in *Teaching Texts, Learning-Centred Leadership II*. Nottingham: National College for School Leadership, pp. 127–138.

Jamison, J. (2001) 'Secondary School Pupils' Views of Health Education within PSHE', *Topic* 25 (spring), item 4.

Jay, T. (2009) 'Do Offensive Words Harm People?' *Psychology, Public Policy, and Law* 15(2): 81–101.

Jeffreys, B. (2015) 'Rising Numbers of Pupils Home Educated', *BBC News* (21 December). Available at: http://www.bbc.co.uk/news/education-35133119.

Johnson, M. (2007) *Subject to Change: New Thinking on the Curriculum*. London: Association of Teachers and Lecturers.

Johnson, R. (1976) 'Really Useful Knowledge: Radical Education and Working-Class Culture, 1790–1848', in J. Clarke, C. Critcher and R. Johnson (eds.), *Working-Class Culture: Studies in History and Theory*. London: Hutchinson, pp. 75–112.

Johnson, S. (2011) *Where Good Ideas Come From: The Seven Patterns of Innovation*. London: Penguin.

Johnston, I. (2014) 'Scotland the Best Educated Country in Europe, Claims ONS Report', *The Independent* (6 June).

Jones, A. (2014) 'School Tests Causing Pupil Stress, Teachers' Survey Finds', *BBC News* (29 October). Available at: http://www.bbc.co.uk/news/uk-wales-29810114.

Jones, A. (2015) 'Nearly Half of Teachers "Think of Quitting" – NUT Cymru', *BBC News* (17 September). Available at: http://www.bbc.co.uk/news/uk-wales-34144933.

Jones, J. (2015) Keynote Address: In-Service Training Day, Canons Primary School, Bedworth, 2 November.

Jones, R. S. (2013) 'Education Reform in Korea', OECD Economics Department Working Paper No. 1067. Paris: OECD. Available at: http://dx.doi.org/10.1787/5k43nxs1t9vh-en.

Judd, T. (2010) 'As One Teacher is Cleared of Pupil Assault, Another Tells of Her Life Sentence', *The Independent* (19 May).

Judkins, M., Stacey, O., McCrone, T. and Inniss, M. (2014) *Teachers' Use of Research Evidence: A Case Study of United Learning Schools*. Slough: NFER.

Kagan, S. and Kagan, M. (1994) 'The Structural Approach: Six Keys to Cooperative Learning', in S. Sharan (ed.), *Handbook of Cooperative Learning Methods*. London: Greenwood Press, pp. 115–133.

Kame'enui, E. J., Carnine, D. W., Dixon, R. C., Simmon, D. C. and Coyne, M. D. (2002) *Effective Teaching Strategies That Accommodate Diverse Learners*. Upper Saddle River, NJ: Merrill Prentice Hall.

Kassam, K. S., Koslov, K. and Mendes, W. B. (2009) 'Decisions Under Distress Stress Profiles Influence Anchoring and Adjustment', *Psychological Science* 20(11): 1394–1399.

Katz, L. G. (1988) 'What Should Young Children Be Doing?', *American Educator: The Professional Journal of the American Federation of Teachers* (summer): 29–45.

Katz, L. G. (1993) *Dispositions as Educational Goals*. Urbana, IL: ERIC Digest. Available at: http://files.eric.ed.gov/fulltext/ED363454.pdf.

Katz, L. G. and Chard, S. C. (2000) *Engaging Children's Minds: The Project Approach*. Stamford, CT: Ablex Publishing.

Kaufman, J. (2013) *The First 20 Hours: How to Learn Anything … Fast*. London: Penguin.

Kendrick, K. (2014) 'Bear Grylls: "Schools Should Teach Children Survival Skills"', *Huffington Post* (14 August). Available at: http://www.huffingtonpost.co.uk/2014/08/14/bear-grylls-schools-should-teach-children-survival-skills_n_7328552.html.

Kennedy, M. (2013) 'Van Gogh Sunflowers To Be Reunited in National Gallery Exhibition', *The Guardian* (28 October).

Kidd, D. (2014) *Teaching: Notes from the Frontline*. Carmarthen: Independent Thinking Press.

Killen, M. and Smetana, J. G. (eds.) (2014) *Handbook of Moral Development*. New York: Psychology Press.

Ko, J. and Sammons, P. (2013) *Effective Teaching: A Review of Research and Evidence*. Reading: CfBT.

Kohlberg, L. (1976) 'Moral Stages and Moralization: The Cognitive ± Developmental Approach', in T. Lickona (ed.), *Moral Development and Behavior: Theory, Research and Social Issues*. New York: Holt, Rinehart & Winston, pp. 31–53.

Kohlberg, L. (1984) *The Psychology of Moral Development: The Nature and Validity of Moral Stages (Essays on Moral Development, Vol. 2)*. New York: Harper & Row.

Kohn, A. (2004) 'Feel-Bad Education', *Education Week* 24(3): 44–45.

Kohn, A. (2015) 'The Perils of "Growth Mindset" Education: Why We're
	Trying to Fix Our Kids When We Should Be Fixing the System', *Salon* (16
	August).
Koppel, G. (2014) 'Why Is Oxbridge Taking Fewer State School Students?' *The
	Guardian* (27 May).
Kounin, J. (1970) *Discipline and Group Management in Classrooms*. New York:
	Holt, Rinehart and Winston.
Labaree, D. (1999) 'The Chronic Failure of Curriculum Reform', *Education
	Week* 18: 42–44.
Lambert, L. (2003) 'Shifting Conceptions of Leadership: Towards a
	Redefinition of Leadership for the Twenty-First Century', in B. Davies
	and J. West-Burnham (eds.), *Handbook of Educational Leadership and
	Management*. London: Pearson, pp. 5–15.
Lambros, A. (2004) *Problem-Based Learning in Middle and High School
	Classrooms*. Thousand Oaks, CA: Corwin Press.
Lancy, D. (2008) *The Anthropology of Childhood*. Cambridge: Cambridge
	University Press.
Larrivee, B. (2000) 'Transforming Teaching Practice: Becoming the Critically
	Reflective Teacher', *Reflective Practice: International and Multidisciplinary
	Perspectives* 1(3): 293–307.
Larson, R. W. (2000) 'Toward a Psychology of Positive Youth Development',
	American Psychologist 55(1): 170–183.
Lavy, V. (2015) 'Do Differences in Schools' Instruction Time Explain
	International Achievement Gaps? Evidence from Developed and
	Developing Countries', *Economic Journal* 125: 397–424.
Lawes, S., Ledda, M., McGovern, C., Patterson, S., Perks, D. and Standish, A.
	(2007) *The Corruption of the Curriculum*. London: Civitas.
Layard, R., Dunn, J. and the Panel of the Good Childhood Inquiry (2009)
	A Good Childhood: Searching for Values in a Competitive Age. London:
	Penguin.
Ledda, M. (2007) 'English As a Dialect', in S. Lawes, M. Ledda, C. McGovern,
	S. Patterson, D. Perks and A. Standish, *The Corruption of the Curriculum*.
	London: Civitas, pp. 11–27.
Ledda, M. (2010) 'Knowledge Must Come First, Then Teaching', *The Telegraph*
	(19 January).
Lee, J. (2013) 'No. 1 Position in Google Gets 33% of Search Traffic [Study]',
	Search Engine Watch (20 June). Available at: http://searchenginewatch.
	com/sew/study/2276184/no-1-position-in-google-gets-33-of-search-traffic-
	study.
Leithwood, K., Day, C., Sammons, P., Harris, A. and Hopkins, D. (2006a)
	Seven Strong Claims About Successful School Leadership. Nottingham:
	National College for School Leadership.

Leithwood, K., Day, C., Sammons, P., Harris, A. and Hopkins, D. (2006b) *Successful School Leadership What It Is and How It Influences Pupil Learning*. Nottingham: National College for School Leadership.

Lemov, D. (2015) *Teach Like a Champion*. San Francisco, CA: Jossey-Bass.

Lemov, D., Woolway, E. and Yezzi, K. (2012) *Practice Perfect: 42 Rules for Getting Better at Getting Better*. San Francisco, CA: Jossey-Bass.

Lewin, K. (1946) 'Action Research and Minority Issues', *Journal of Social Sciences* 2: 34–46.

Little, T. (2015) *An Intelligent Person's Guide to Education*. London: Bloomsbury.

Livingston, C. (1992) 'Introduction: Teacher Leadership for Restructured Schools', in C. Livingston (ed.), *Teachers as Leaders: Evolving Roles*. Washington, DC: National Education Association, pp. 9–17.

Lockwood, A. L. (1997) *Character Education: Controversy and Consensus*. Thousand Oaks, CA: Corwin Press.

Lord, P. and Jones, M. (2006) *Pupils' Experiences and Perspectives of the National Curriculum and Assessment*. Slough: NFER.

Losada, M. and Heaphy, E. (2004) 'The Role of Positivity and Connectivity in the Performance of Business Teams: A Nonlinear Dynamics Model', *American Behavioral Scientist* 47(6): 740–765.

Louv, R. (2005) *Last Child in the Woods: Saving Our Children from Nature-Deficit Disorder*. London: Atlantic Books.

Lucas, B. and Claxton, G. (2011) *New Kinds of Smart*. Maidenhead: Open University Press.

Lucas, B., Claxton, G. and Spencer, E. (2013) *Expansive Education: Teaching Learners for the Real World*. Maidenhead: Open University Press.

Lumby, J. (2013) 'Distributed Leadership: The Uses and Abuses of Power', *Educational Management Administration & Leadership* 41(5): 581–597.

Lyons, N. (1990) 'Dilemmas of Knowing: Ethical and Epistemological Dimensions of Teachers' Work and Development', *Harvard Educational Review* 60(2): 159–180.

MacBeath, J., Frost, D. and Peddar, D. (2008) *The Influence and Participation of Children and Young People in their Learning (IPiL) Project*. London: General Teaching Council for England.

Malderez, A. and Wedell, M. (2007) *Teaching Teachers: Processes and Practices*. London: Continuum.

Mansell, W. (2008) 'Research Reveals Teaching's Holy Grail', *TES* (21 November).

Marsh, S. (2015) 'Five Top Reasons People Become Teachers – and Why They Quit', *The Guardian* (27 January).

Marzano, R. J., Pickering, D. J. and Pollock, J. E. (2001) *Classroom Instruction That Works*. Alexandria, VA: ASCD.

Marzano, R. J., Waters, T. and McNulty, B. A. (2005) *School Leadership That Works: From Research to Results.* Alexandria, VA: ASCD.

Maslovaty, N. (2000) 'Teachers' Choice of Teaching Strategies for Dealing with Socio-Moral Dilemmas in the Elementary School', *Journal of Moral Education* 29(4): 429–444.

Mathias, P. (2009) *How Do School Leaders Successfully Lead Learning?* Nottingham: National College for School Leadership.

Mazur, E. (1997) 'Peer Instruction: Getting Students to Think in Class', in E. F. Redish and J. F. Rigden (eds.), *The Changing Role of Physics Departments in Modern Universities.* Proceedings of the International Conference on Physics Undergraduate Education. Woodbury, NY: American Institute of Physics, pp. 981–988.

McCulloch, J. (2011) *Subject to Change: Should Primary Schools Structure Learning Around Subjects or Themes?* Harlow: Pearson.

McGregor, D. and Cartwright, L. (2011) 'Taking the Longer Term View: How Reflective Practice Can Sustain Continuing Professional Development', in D. McGregor and L. Cartwright (eds.), *Developing Reflective Practice: A Guide for Beginning Teachers.* Maidenhead: Open University Press, pp. 235–250.

McKinsey & Company (2007) *How the World's Best-Performing School Systems Come Out On Top.* Available at: http://mckinseyonsociety.com/how-the-worlds-best-performing-schools-come-out-on-top/.

McLeod, S. and Lehmann, C. (eds.) (2012) *What School Leaders Need to Know About Digital Technologies and Social Media.* San Francisco, CA: Jossey-Bass.

McNair, A. (1944) *Teachers and Youth Leaders* [McNair Report]. London: HMSO.

Meier, D. (1995) *The Power of Their Ideas: Lessons for America from a Small School in Harlem.* New York: Beacon Press.

Menter, I., Hulme, M., Elliot, D. and Lewin, J. (2010) *Literature Review on Teacher Education in the 21st Century.* Edinburgh: Scottish Government.

Merideth, E. M. (2007) *Leadership Strategies for Teachers.* Thousand Oaks, CA: Corwin Press.

Merrick, R. (2014) 'Academies and Free Schools Blamed for Rise in Teenage Pregnancies', *Northern Echo* (22 October).

Mezirow, J. (1990) *Fostering Critical Reflection in Adulthood: A Guide to Transformative and Emancipatory Learning.* San Francisco, CA: Jossey-Bass.

Miller, G. A. (1956) 'The Magical Number Seven, Plus or Minus Two: Some Limits On Our Capacity for Processing Information', *Psychological Review* 63: 81–97.

Miller, R., Shapiro, H. and Hilding-Hamann, K. E. (2008) *School's Over: Learning Spaces in Europe in 2020. An Imagining Exercise on the Future of*

Learning. Luxembourg: Office for the Official Publications of the European Communities.

Mitra, S. (2010) 'The Child-Driven Education', *TED* (September). Available at: http://www.ted.com/talks/sugata_mitra_the_child_driven_education/transcript?language=en.

Mitra, S. (2013) 'Advent of Google Means We Must Rethink Our Approach to Education', *The Guardian* (15 June).

Mitra, S. and Crawley, E. (2014) 'Effectiveness of Self-Organised Learning by Children: Gateshead Experiments', *Journal of Education and Human Development* 3(3): 79–88.

Moon, J. (2001) 'Learning Through Reflection', in F. Banks and A. Shelton Mayes (eds.), *Early Professional Development for Teachers*. Maidenhead: Open University Press, pp. 364–378.

Moon, J. (2004) *A Handbook of Reflective and Experiential Learning: Theory and Practice*. London: Routledge.

Moon, J. (2005) *We Seek It Here. A New Perspective on the Elusive Activity of Critical Thinking: A Theoretical and Practical Approach*. London: Higher Education Academy. Available at: https://www.heacademy.ac.uk/sites/default/files/2041_0.pdf.

Moore, A. (2004) *The Good Teacher: Dominant Discourses in Teaching and Teacher Education*. London: RoutledgeFalmer.

Moore, A. and Ash, A. (2002) 'Reflective Practice in Beginning Teachers: Helps, Hindrances and the Role of the Critical Other'. Paper presented at the Annual Conference of the British Educational Research Association, University of Exeter, 12–14 September. Available at: http://www.leeds.ac.uk/educol/documents/00002531.htm.

Moore, S. (2011) 'Yes, Our Children Are Growing Up Too Soon. But Blame Capitalism, Not Sex', *The Guardian* (11 June).

More, C. (1980) *Skill and the English Working Class, 1870–1914*. London: Croom Helm.

Morris, E. (2014) 'Teaching Needs Less Ideology, and More Evidence', *The Guardian* (25 November).

Morse, B. (2012) 'Why Critical Thinking Is Overlooked By Schools and Shunned By Students', *The Guardian* (Teacher Network Teacher's Blog) (12 September). Available at: http://www.theguardian.com/teacher-network/2012/sep/12/critical-thinking-overlooked-in-secondary-education.

Mourshed, M. (2010) *How the World's Most Improved School Systems Keep Getting Better*. London: McKinsey & Company.

Muijs, D. and Reynolds, D. (2011) *Effective Teaching: Evidence and Practice*. London: SAGE.

Mulholland, H. (2012) 'Millions Paid Out to Teachers for Classroom Assaults and Accidents', *The Guardian* (5 April).

Music, G. (2014a) *The Good Life: Wellbeing and the New Science of Altruism, Selfishness and Immorality*. Abingdon: Routledge.

Music, G. (2014b) 'Raising Driven Yet Amoral Children?' *The Telegraph* (1 June).

National Association of Schoolmasters Union of Women Teachers (NASUWT) (2011) *Phonics Screening Check: Survey Results*. Birmingham: NASUWT.

National Curriculum Council (1993) 'Spiritual and Moral Development: A Discussion Paper'. York: NCC.

Neelands, J., Belfiore, E., Firth, C., Hart, N., Perrin, L., Brock, S., Holdaway, D. and Woddis, J. (2015) *Enriching Britain: Culture, Creativity and Growth*. Warwick: University of Warwick.

Nietzsche, F. (1990 [1889]) *Twilight of the Idols* and *The Anti-Christ*, tr. R. J. Hollingdale. London: Penguin.

Noddings, N. (1992) *The Challenge to Care in Schools: An Alternative Approach to Education*. New York: Teachers College Press.

Norris, N. (1996) 'Professor Hargreaves, the TTA and Evidence-based Practice', *Research Intelligence* 57: 2–4.

Northern Ireland Audit Office (2013) *Improving Literacy and Numeracy Achievement in Schools*. Belfast: Northern Ireland Audit Office.

Nunes, T., Schliemann, A. D. and Carraher, D. W. (1993) *Mathematics in the Streets and in Schools*. Cambridge: Cambridge University Press.

Nussbaum, M. (2011) *Creating Capabilities: The Human Development Approach*. Cambridge, MA: Harvard University Press.

Nuthall, G. (2007) *The Hidden Lives of Learners*. Wellington: NZER Press.

Ofqual (2015) *Improving Functional Skills Qualifications*. London: Ofqual.

Ofsted (2009a) *Twelve Outstanding Secondary Schools: Excelling Against the Odds*. London: Ofsted.

Ofsted (2009b) *Twenty Outstanding Primary Schools: Excelling Against the Odds*. London: Ofsted.

Ofsted (2013a) *Unseen Children: Access and Achievement 20 Years On*. London: Ofsted.

Ofsted (2013b) *School Report on Rosendale Primary School*. London: Ofsted.

Ofsted (2014a) *The Report of Her Majesty's Chief Inspector of Education, Children's Services and Skills 2013/14*. London: Ofsted.

Ofsted (2014b) *School Report on Sir John Cass's Foundation and Red Coat Church of England Secondary School*. London: Ofsted.

Ofsted (2015) *School Report on Sir John Cass's Foundation and Red Coat Church of England Secondary School*. London: Ofsted.

Oliner, S. (2001) 'Ordinary Heroes', *Yes! Magazine* (5 November). Available at: http://www.yesmagazine.org/issues/can-love-save-the-world/ordinary-heroes.

Oliner, S. (2004) *Do Unto Others: Extraordinary Acts of Ordinary People – How Altruism Inspires True Acts of Courage*. Colorado, OK: Basic Books.

Organisation for Economic Co-operation and Development (OECD) (1999) *Measuring Student Knowledge and Skills: A New Framework for Assessment.* Paris: OECD.

Organisation for Economic Co-operation and Development (OECD) (2010) *The High Cost of Low Educational Performance.* Paris: OECD.

Organisation for Economic Co-operation and Development (OECD) (2012) *Better Skills, Better Jobs, Better Lives: A Strategic Approach to Skills Policies.* Paris: OECD.

Organisation for Economic Co-operation and Development (OECD) (2013a) *Education Indicators in Focus. 2013/01 January.* Paris: OECD.

Organisation for Economic Co-operation and Development (OECD) (2013b) *PISA 2012 Results: Creative Problem Solving.* Vol. V: *Students' Skills in Tackling Real-Life Problems.* Paris: OECD.

Organisation for Economic Co-operation and Development (OECD) (2014) *Skills Beyond School.* Paris: OECD.

Organisation for Economic Co-operation and Development (OECD) (2015) *Education Policy Outlook 2015: Making Reforms Happen.* Paris: OECD.

Oser, F. (1991) 'Professional Morality: A Discourse Approach (The Case of the Teaching Profession)', in W. Kurtiness and J. Gewirtz (eds.), *Handbook of Moral Behavior and Development*, Vol. 2: *Research.* Hillsdale, NJ: Lawrence Erlbaum Associates, pp. 191–228.

Oser, F. and Althof, W. (1993) 'Trust in Advance: On the Professional Morality of Teachers', *Journal of Moral Education* 22: 253–272.

Owen, J. (2016) 'UK Under Fire for Recruiting an "Army of Children"', *The Independent* (24 May).

Oxfam (2006) *Teaching Controversial Issues.* London: Oxfam.

Oxford Cambridge RSA (OCR) (2006) *Skills for Life.* Cambridge: OCR.

Oxford Royale Academy (2014) '8 Trends That Will Matter to Your School-Age Children' (9 August). Available at: http://www.oxford-royale.co.uk/articles/trends-matter-school-age-children.html.

Pagander, L. and Read, J. (2014) 'Is Problem-Based Learning (PBL) an Effective Teaching Method? A Study Based on Existing Research'. Available at: http://www.diva-portal.org/smash/get/diva2:726932/FULLTEXT01.pdf.

Page, D. (2013) 'Managing Serious Teacher Misbehaviour', *School Leadership & Management: Formerly School Organisation* 34(3): 269–283.

Pagliaro, M. (2011) *Exemplary Classroom Questioning: Practices to Promote Thinking and Learning.* Lanham, MD: Rowman & Littlefield.

Palmer, S. (2006) *Toxic Childhood: How The Modern World Is Damaging Our Children and What We Can Do About It.* London: Penguin.

Paton, G. (2009) 'School is Boring and Irrelevant, Say Teenagers', *The Telegraph* (21 January).

Paton, G. (2012) 'Working-Class Pupils Lose Out Because They Are Too Polite', *The Telegraph* (20 August).

Paton, G. (2014a) 'New Plan for Britain's First State-Funded "Virtual School"', *The Telegraph* (28 November).

Paton, G. (2014b) 'Nicky Morgan: Lessons in Character "Just as Important" As Academic Grades', *The Telegraph* (16 December).

Paton, G. (2014c) 'School Leavers "Lack Skills Needed to Get Entry Level Jobs"', *The Telegraph* (24 February).

Peal, R. (2014c) *Progressively Worse: The Burden of Bad Ideas in British.* London: Civitas.

Peng, W. J., McNess, E., Thomas, S., Rong Wu, X., Zhang, C., Li, J. Z. and Tian, H. S. (2014) 'Emerging Perceptions of Teacher Quality and Teacher Development in China', *International Journal of Educational Development* 34: 77–89.

Perkins, D. (1995) *Outsmarting IQ: The Emerging Science of Learnable Intelligence.* New York: Free Press.

Perkins, D. (2014) *Future Wise: Educating Our Children for a Changing World.* San Francisco, CA: Jossey-Bass.

Peters, R. S. (1965) 'Education as Initiation', in R. D. Archambault (ed.), *Philosophical Analysis and Education.* London: Routledge & Kegan Paul, pp. 87–111.

Peters, R. S. (1966) *Ethics and Education.* London: George Allen & Unwin.

Petrie, N. (2011) *Future Trends in Leadership Development* (August). Available at: http://www.ccl.org/leadership/pdf/landing/FutureTrends.pdf.

Pilkington, K. (2014) *The Moaning of Life: The Worldly Wisdom of Karl Pilkington.* Edinburgh: Canongate.

Pinder, R. (1987) *Why Don't Teachers Teach Like They Used To?* London: Hilary Shipman.

Plowden, B. (1967) *Children and Their Primary Schools: A Report of the Central Advisory Council for Education (England)* [Plowden Report]. London: HMSO.

Polanyi, M. (1967) *The Tacit Dimension.* London: Routledge & Kegan Paul.

Pollard, A. (2014) *Reflective Teaching in School*, 4th edn. London: Bloomsbury Academic.

Pollard, A. and Tann, S. (1993) *Reflective Teaching in the Primary School: A Handbook for the Classroom.* London: Cassell.

Pollard, A. and Triggs, P. (1997) *Reflective Teaching in Secondary Schools.* London: Continuum.

Pollard, A. and Triggs, P. (2000) *What Pupils Say: Changing Policy and Practice in Primary Education.* London: Continuum.

Pollock, J. (2012) *Feedback: The Hinge That Joins Teaching and Learning.* Thousand Oaks, CA: Corwin.

Pope, G. (2013) *Questioning Technique Pocketbook*. Alresford: Teachers' Pocketbooks.

Postman, N. (1982) *The Disappearance of Childhood*. New York: Vintage Books.

Pota, V. (2015) 'Over Testing Risks Squeezing Out Creative Skills in Pupils', *The Telegraph* (9 April).

Precey, M. (2015) 'Teacher Stress Levels in England "Soaring", Data Shows', *BBC News* (17 March). Available at: http://www.bbc.co.uk/news/education-31921457.

Prensky, M. (2009) '*H. sapiens* Digital: From Digital Immigrants and Digital Nativest Digital Wisdom', *Innovate* 6(3): article 1.

PricewaterhouseCoopers (2007) *Independent Study Into School Leadership*. London: DfES.

Pring, R. (1976) *Knowledge and Schooling*. Wells: Open Books.

Pring, R. (2005) *Philosophy of Education: An Introduction*. London: Continuum.

Punch, K. and Oancea, A. (2014) *Introduction to Research Methods in Education*, 2nd edn. London: Sage.

Randerson, J. (2008) 'The Path to Happiness: It Is Better to Give Than Receive', *The Guardian* (21 March).

Ratcliffe, R. (2014) 'We Need More Teachers, and We Need Them Now', *The Guardian* (30 June).

Reay, D. (2012) 'Think Piece: What Would A Socially Just Education System Look Like?' London: Centre for Labour and Social Studies. Available at: http://classonline.org.uk/docs/2012_Diane_Reay_-_a_socially_just_education_system.pdf.

Reiss, M. J. (2001) 'How to Ensure That Pupils Don't Lose Interest in Science', *Education Today* 51(2): 34–40.

Resnick, L. (1987) 'Learning In School and Out', *Educational Researcher* 16(9): 13–20.

Reynolds, D. (1992) *School Effectiveness: Research, Policy and Practice*. London: Continuum.

Rheingold, H. (2010) 'Attention, and Other 21st-Century Social Media Literacies', *EDUCAUSE Review* 45(5): 14–16.

Rheingold, H. (2012) *Net Smart: How to Thrive Online*. Cambridge, MA: MIT Press.

Richards, C. (2001) *Changing English Primary Curriculum: Retrospect and Prospect*. Stoke on Trent: Trentham Books.

Richardson, H. (2014) 'Pupils Begin "Tough" New National Curriculum', *BBC News* (1 September). Available at: http://www.bbc.co.uk/news/education-28987787.

Richardson, H. (2015) 'Pupils Have Sats Test Panic Attacks, Says NUT Study', *BBC News* (4 April). Available at: http://www.bbc.co.uk/news/education-32174569.

Riddell, C. (2015) *My Little Book of Big Freedoms: The Human Rights Act in Pictures*. London: Amnesty International.

Ridley, M. (2004) *Nature via Nurture: Genes, Experience and What Makes Us Human*. London: Harper Perennial.

Robertson, A. (2016) 'Muslim Schoolboy, 10, Quizzed By Police After Writing "I Live In a Terrorist House" When He Meant "Terraced"', *Daily Mail* (20 January).

Robinson, C. (2014) *Children, Their Voices and Their Experiences of School: What Does the Evidence Tell Us?* York: Cambridge Primary Review Trust.

Robinson, K. (2015) *Creative Schools: The Grassroots Revolution That's Transforming Education*. London: Random House.

Robinson, M. (2013) *The Trivium in the 21st Century*. Carmarthen: Crown House Publishing.

Robinson, V. M. J. (2007) *School Leadership and Student Outcomes: Identifying What Works and Why*. Winmalee, NSW: Australian Council for Educational Leaders.

Rogoff, B. (1990) *Apprenticeship in Thinking: Cognitive Development in Social Context*. Oxford: Oxford University Press.

Rolfe, G., Freshwater, D. and Jasper, M. (2001) *Critical Reflection for Nursing and the Helping Professions: A User's Guide*. Basingstoke: Palgrave Macmillan.

Rosenshine, B. (2012) 'Principles of Instruction', *American Educator* (spring): 13–39.

Ross, A. (2000) *Curriculum: Construction and Critique*. London: Falmer Press.

Ross, T. (2013) 'Over-60s Are Told: Go Back to University and Retrain', *The Telegraph* (20 February).

Rousseau, J.-J. (1979 [1762]) *Emile: Or, On Education*, tr. A. Bloom. New York: Basic Books.

Rowe, M. B. (1978) *Teaching Science As Continuous Inquiry*. New York: McGraw-Hill.

Rowe, M. B. (1987) 'Slowing Down May Be a Way of Speeding Up' *American Educator* (spring): 38–43.

Rowling, J. K. (2000) *Harry Potter and the Goblet of Fire*. London: Penguin.

Rubin, C. M. (2015) 'The Best Ways a Teacher Can Demonstrate Leadership in the Classroom?', *HuffPost Education* (The Blog) (26 June). Available at: http://www.huffingtonpost.com/c-m-rubin/the-best-ways-a-teacher-can-demonstrate-leadership-in-the-classroom_b_7654578.html.

Ruddock, J. and Flutter, J. (2003) *Consulting Pupils: What's In It for Schools?* London: RoutledgeFalmer.

Rutter, M., Maughan, B., Mortimore, P., Ouston, J. and Smith, A. (1979) *Fifteen Thousand Hours: Secondary Schools and Their Effects on Children*. Cambridge, MA: Harvard University Press.

Sadler, D. R. (1989) 'Formative Assessment and the Design of Instructional Systems', *Instructional Science* 18: 119–144.

Sammons, P., Sylva, K., Melhuish, E., Siraj-Blatchford, I., Taggart, B., Smees, R., Draghici, D. and Toth, K. (2012) *Influences on Students' Dispositions in Key Stage 3: Exploring Enjoyment of School, Popularity, Anxiety, Citizenship Values and Academic Self-Concepts in Year 9*. London: Institute of Education.

Samuel, M. (2006) 'Romeo, Wherefore Art Thou Talking Stupid?', *The Times* (6 June).

Savill, R. (2010) 'Extra Hour in Bed "Boosts Pupils' Exam Results"', *The Telegraph* (21 March 2010).

Savin-Baden, M. (2003) *Facilitating Problem-Based Learning: Illuminating Perspectives*. Buckingham: Open University Press/SRHE.

Schleicher, A. (2014) 'Learning from the World's Educational Leaders: An OECD Perspective on Within-School Variation', *Teaching Leaders Quarterly* (autumn): 1–3.

Schleisser, A. (ed.) (2012) *Preparing Teachers and Developing School Leaders for the 21st Century: Lessons from Around the World*. Paris: OECD.

Schön, D. (1983) *The Reflective Practitioner: How Professionals Think In Action*. New York: Basic Books.

School Curriculum and Assessment Authority (SCAA) (1995) *Spiritual and Moral Development*. Discussion Paper 3. London: SCAA.

Schools Council (1981) *The Practical Curriculum*. Working Paper No. 70. London: Methuen.

Schrum, L. and Levin, B. B. (2009) *Leading 21st Century Schools: Harnessing Technology for Engagement and Achievement*. Thousand Oaks, CA: Corwin.

Schunk, D. H. and Ertmer, P. A. (1999) 'Self-Regulatory Processes During Computer Skill Acquisition: Goal and Self-Evaluative Influences', *Journal of Educational Psychology* 91(2): 251–260.

Schwarz, R. (2013) 'The "Sandwich Approach" Undermines Your Feedback', *Harvard Business Review* (19 April). Available at: https://hbr.org/2013/04/the-sandwich-approach-undermin/.

Scott, K. (2010) 'Primary School Pupils Learn Lessons in Empathy', *The Guardian* (22 November).

Scottish Executive (2007) *A Curriculum for Excellence: Building the Curriculum 2*. Edinburgh: Scottish Executive.

Sebba, J. and Robinson, C. (2010) *Evaluation of UNICEF UK's Rights Respecting Schools Awards*. London: UNICEF.

Seldon, A. (2015) *Beyond Happiness: The Trap of Happiness and How to Find Deeper Meaning and Joy*. London: Yellow Kite.

Sellgren, K. (2014) 'Warning of Worsening in UK Skills Shortage', *BBC News* (30 January). Available at: http://www.bbc.co.uk/news/education-25945413.

Selvarajah, S. (2015) 'Headhunters for Headteachers: Schools Pay Firms up to £50,000 to Find Leaders', *The Guardian* (23 June).

Senge, P. (2006) *The Fifth Discipline: The Art and Practice of the Learning Organization*. New York: Currency Doubleday.

Sergeant, H. (2009) 'Too Many Initiatives, Not Enough Teaching', *The Guardian* (27 November).

Shacklady, G. (2013) 'Dealing with Swearing and Bad Language in Class', *The Guardian* (Teacher Network Teacher's Blog) (22 April). Available at: http://www.theguardian.com/teacher-network/teacher-blog/2013/apr/22/schools-swearing-behaviour-teaching.

Shapira-Lishchinsky, O. (2010) 'Teachers' Critical Incidents: Ethical Dilemmas in Teaching Practice', *Teaching and Teacher Education* XXX: 1–9.

Sharkey, J. (2004) 'Lives Stories Don't Tell: Exploring the Untold in Autobiographies', *Curriculum Enquiry* 34(4): 495–512.

Sharp, C., Eames, A., Sanders, D. and Tomlinson, K. (2005) *Postcards from Research-Engaged Schools*. Slough: NFER.

Shayer, D. (1972) *The Teaching of English in Schools, 1900–1970*. London: Routledge & Kegan Paul.

Shenk, D. (1998) *Data Smog: Surviving the Information Glut*. New York: HarperCollins.

Sherrington, T. (2013) 'Teachers as Researchers: The Ultimate Form of Professional Development?', *The Guardian* (22 February).

Shim, H. S. and Roth, G. (2008) 'Sharing Tacit Knowledge Among Expert Teaching Professors and Mentees: Considerations for Career and Technical Education Teacher Educators', *Journal of Industrial Teacher Education* 44(4–5): 5–26.

Shuayb, M. and O'Donnell, S. (2008) *Aims and Values in Primary Education: England and Other Countries*. Primary Review Research Survey 1/2. Cambridge: University of Cambridge, Faculty of Education.

Shuayb, M., Sharp, C., Judkins, M. and Hetherington, M. (2009) *Using Appreciative Inquiry in Educational Research: Possibilities and Limitations*. Slough: NFER.

Shulman, L. S. (1987) 'Knowledge and Teaching: Foundations of the New Reform', *Harvard Educational Review* 57(1): 1–22.

Sinek, S. (2009) *Start With Why: How Great Leaders Inspire Everyone to Take Action*. London: Penguin.

Sing, A. (2014) 'Most Children "Play Outside for Less Than an Hour a Day"', *The Telegraph* (11 July).

Siraj, I. and Taggart, B. (2014) *Exploring Effective Pedagogy in Primary Schools: Evidence from Research*. London: Pearson.

Siraj-Blatchford, J. (2010) 'Analysis: Computers Benefit Children', *Nursery*

World (5 October). Available at: http://www.nurseryworld.co.uk/nursery-world/news/1095245/analysis-computers-benefit-children.

Skilbeck, M. (1976) 'Basic Questions in Curriculum', in R. Bell, D. Pitt and M. Skilbeck (eds.), *The Scope of Curriculum Study*. Milton Keynes: Open University Press, pp. 45–96.

Skinner, B. F. (1958) 'Teaching Machines', *Science* 128: 969–977.

Skinner, B. F. (1963) *Science and Human Behavior*. New York: Macmillan.

Skinner, D. (2010) *Effective Teaching and Learning in Practice*. London: Continuum.

Slavin, R. E. (1987) *Cooperative Learning: Student Teams*, 2nd edn. Washington DC: National Education Association.

Slavin, R. E. (2011) 'Instruction Based on Cooperative Learning', in R. Mayer (ed.), *Handbook of Research on Learning and Instruction*. London: Taylor & Francis, pp. 344–360.

Smith, A. (2011) *High Performers: The Secret of Successful Schools*. Carmarthen: Crown House Publishing.

Smith, L. (2002) 'Piaget's Model', in U. Goswami (ed.), *Blackwell Handbook of Cognitive Development*. Malden, MA: Blackwood, pp. 515–537.

Smithers, R. (2003) 'Silence of the Little Lambs: Talking Skills in Decline', *The Guardian* (4 March).

Snook, I., Clark, J., O'Neil, A. and Openshaw, R. (2009) 'Invisible Learnings? A Commentary on John Hattie's Book: *Visible Learning: A Synthesis of Over 800 Meta-Analyses Relating to Achievement*', *New Zealand Journal of Educational Studies* 44(1): 93–106.

Snowman, D. (ed.) (2001) *Past Masters: The Best of History Today*. Stroud: Sutton.

Sotto, E. (1994) *When Teaching Becomes Learning: A Theory and Practice of Teaching*. London: Continuum.

Specialist Schools and Academies Trust (2010) *Enterprise Education in Primary Schools*. London: SSAT.

Stamou, E., Edwards, A., Daniels, H. and Ferguson, L. (2014) *Young People At Risk of Drop-Out from Education: Recognising and Responding to Their Needs*. Oxford: University of Oxford.

Standish, P., Blake, N., Smith, R. and Smeyers, P. (2000) *Education in an Age of Nihilism: Education and Moral Standards*. Abingdon: Routledge.

Stenhouse, L. (1975) *An Introduction to Curriculum Research and Development*. London: Pearson Education.

Sternberg, R. (1983) *How Can We Teach Intelligence?* Philadelphia, PA: Research for Better Schools.

Stewart, W. (2012) 'Think You've Implemented Assessment for Learning?', *TES* (13 July).

Stewart, W. (2015) 'Leave Research to the Academics, John Hattie Tells Teachers', *TES* (22 April).

Stringer, E. T. (2013) *Action Research*, 4th edn. Thousand Oaks, CA: Sage.

Stringfield, S., Reynolds, D. and Schaffer, E. (2008) *Improving Secondary Students' Academic Achievement through a Focus on Reform Reliability*. London: CfBT.

Stronge, J. (2010) *Effective Teachers = Student Achievement: What the Research Says*. New York: Routledge.

Sullivan, B., Glenn, M., Roche, M. and McDonagh, C. (2016) *Introduction to Critical Reflection and Action for Teacher Researcher*. London: Routledge.

Sutton Trust (2011) *Improving the Impact of Teachers on Pupil Achievement in the UK: Interim Findings*. London: Sutton Trust.

Swaine, J. (2009) 'Britons "Swear 14 Times Day On Average"', *The Telegraph* (16 January).

Swinford, S. (2014) 'Christians Lie and Wives Must Have Sex or Go to Hell, Trojan Horse Pupils Told', *The Telegraph* (18 July).

Taba, H. (1962) *Curriculum Development: Theory and Practice*. New York: Harcourt, Brace and World.

Tabberer, R. (2013) *A Review of Initial Teacher Training in Wales*. Cardiff: Welsh Government.

Taggart, C. (2011) *I Used to Know That: Stuff You Forgot from School*. London: Michael O'Mara Books.

Tait, P. (2015) 'Causes of Growing Mental Health Problems Sit Largely Within Schools', *The Telegraph* (2 December).

Tame, P. (2015) 'Silver Surfers: A Growing Market Full of Digital Opportunities', *Digital Marketing* (9 April).

Tan, M. (2015) 'Are We Products of Nature or Nurture? Science Answers Age-Old Question', *The Guardian* (19 May).

Taylor, C. (2005) *Excellence in Education: The Making of Great Schools*. London: David Fulton.

Teaching Council (2012) *Code of Professional Conduct for Teachers*. Dublin: Teaching Council.

Telegraph (The) (2014) 'Six New Ways to Teach Children More Effectively', *The Telegraph* (9 October).

Telegraph (The) (2015) 'Headteachers Are Just Big Bullies, Schools Union Says', *The Telegraph* (6 April).

Thaler, R. and Sunstein, C. (2009) *Nudge: Improving Decisions About Health, Wealth and Happiness*. London: Penguin.

Thomas, G. (2013) *Education: A Very Short Introduction*. Oxford: Oxford University Press.

Thorndike, E. L. (1904) *An Introduction to the Theory of Mental and Social Measurements*. New York: Science Press.

Tirri, K. (1999) 'Teachers' Perceptions of Moral Dilemmas at School', *Journal of Moral Education* 28(1): 31–47.

Torp, L. and Sage, S. (2002) *Problems as Possibilities: Problem-Based Learning for K-16 Education*. Alexandria, VA: ASCD.

Tough, P. (2012) *How Children Succeed: Grit, Curiosity and Hidden Power of Character*. London: Arrow.

Trilling, B. and Fadel, C. (2009) *21st Century Skills: Learning for Life in Our Times*. San Francisco, CA: Jossey-Bass.

Tripp, D. (2012) *Critical Incidents in Teaching*. Abingdon: Routledge.

Tulgan, B. (1999) *FAST Feedback*. Amherst, MA: HRD Press.

Tulley, G. (2007) '5 Dangerous Things You Should Let Your Kids Do' [video], *TED* (February). Available at: https://www.ted.com/talks/gever_tulley_on_5_dangerous_things_for_kids?language=en.

Tyler, R. W. (1949) *Basic Principles of Curriculum and Instruction*. Chicago, IL: University of Chicago Press.

UNICEF (2013) *Child Well-Being in Rich Countries: A Comparative Overview*. Innocenti Report Card 11. Florence: Innocenti Research Centre Report.

Urquhart, C. (2012) 'Teenagers Value the Simple Things in Life', *The Observer* (6 October).

Vaughan, R. (2015) 'Wilshaw: Teacher Recruitment is the Biggest Challenge Facing England's Schools', *TES* (16 September).

Vega, V. (2012) 'Project-Based Learning Research Review', *Edutopia* (3 December). Available at: http://www.edutopia.org/pbl-research-learning-outcomes.

Vincent, K., Cremin, H. and Thomas, G. (2005) *Teachers and Assistants Working Together*. Buckingham: Open University Press.

Walsh, J. A. and Satters, B. D. (2011) *Thinking Through Quality Questioning: Deepening Student Engagement*. London: Sage.

Warneken, F. and Tomasello, M. (2006) 'Altruistic Helping in Human Infants and Young Chimpanzees', *Science* 311: 1301–1303.

Warneken, F. and Tomasello, M. (2007) 'Helping and Cooperation at 14 Months of Age', *Infancy* 11: 271–294.

Warneken, F. and Tomasello, M. (2009) 'The Roots of Human Altruism', *British Journal of Psychology* 100: 455–471.

Warneken, F. and Tomasello, M. (2013) 'Parental Presence and Encouragement Do Not Influence Helping in Young Children', *Infancy* 18: 345–368.

Waters, M. (2013) *Thinking Allowed on Schooling*. Carmarthen: Crown House Publishing.

Watkins, C. (2003) *Learning: A Sense-Maker's Guide*. London: Association of Teachers and Lecturers.

Watkins, C. (2009) 'Easier Said Than Done: Collaborative Learning', *Teaching Times* 1(1): 22–25. Available at: https://www.ioe.ac.uk/about/documents/Watkins_09_collaborative.pdf.

Weale, S. (2015a) 'Fifth of Secondary School Pupils "Wake Almost Every Night to Use Social Media"', *The Guardian* (15 September).

Weale, S. (2015b) 'Labour's Tristram Hunt Calls on Parents to Play More with Their Young Children', *The Guardian* (1 May).

Webb, R. and Vulliamy, G. (2002) 'The Social Work Dimension of the Primary Teacher's Role', *Research Papers in Education* 17(2): 165–184.

Webster, R., Russell, A. and Blatchford, P. (2013) *Teaching Assistants: A Guide to Good Practice.* Oxford: Oxford University Press.

Weinstein, C. E., Husman, J. and Dierking, D. R. (2000) 'Self-Regulation Interventions with a Focus on Learning Strategies', in M. Boekarts, P. Pintrich and M. Zeidner (eds.), *Handbook of Self-Regulation.* San Diego, CA: Academic Press, pp. 727–747.

Wellcome Trust (2010) '*Marks Tell You How You've Done … Comments Tell You Why*': Attitudes of Children and Parents to Key Stage 2 Science Testing and Assessment.* London: Wellcome Trust.

Wells, K. (2009) *Childhood in a Global Perspective.* Cambridge: Cambridge University Press.

Welsh Government (2015) *Reflective Practice.* Cardiff: Welsh Government.

West, L. (2004) 'The Trouble with Lifelong Learning', in D. Hayes (ed.), *The Routledge Guide to Key Debates in Education,* London: Routledge, pp. 138–143.

West-Burnham, J. (2003) 'Leading to Learn', in J. B. Davies and J. West-Burnham (eds.), *Handbook of Educational Leadership and Management.* London: Pearson, pp. 51–59.

White, J. (2012) *The Aims of Education Restated.* Abingdon: Routledge.

Whitehead, T. (2009) 'One in Four of the Population Will Be Over 65 By 2033', *The Telegraph* (8 December).

Whitty, G. and Wisby, E. (2007) *Real Decision Making? School Councils in Action.* London: DCSF.

Wiggins, G. and McTighe, J. (2005) *Understanding by Design.* Alexandria, VA: ASCD.

Wildman, R. and Niles, J. (1987) 'Reflective Teachers: Tensions Between Abstractions and Realities', *Journal of Teacher Education* 3: 25–31.

Wiliam, D. (2015) *The Journey to Excellence: Personalised Learning.* Available at: http://www.journeytoexcellence.org.uk/videos/expertspeakers/personalisedlearningdylanwiliam.asp.

Williamson, B. and Paynton, S. (2009) *Curriculum and Teaching Innovation: Transforming Classroom Practice and Personalisation.* Bristol: Futurelab.

Willingham, D. (2010) *Why Don't Students Like School? A Cognitive Scientist Answers Questions About How the Mind Works and What It Means for the Classroom.* San Francisco, CA: Jossey-Bass.

Willis, J. (2007) 'The Neuroscience of Joyful Education', *Educational Leadership* (summer). Available at: http://www.ascd.org/publications/educational-leadership/summer07/vol64/num09/The-Neuroscience-of-Joyful-Education.aspx.

Winch, C. and Gingell, J. (1999) *Key Concepts in the Philosophy of Education.* London: Routledge.

Wolf, A. (2002) *Does Education Matter? Myths About Education and Economic Growth.* London: Penguin.

Wood, K. (2011) *Education: The Basics.* Abingdon: Routledge.

Woolcock, N. (2015) 'Steel Town Schools Show Their Mettle', *The Times* (10 October).

World Health Organization (WHO) (1999) *Partners in Life Skills Education.* Geneva: WHO.

Wragg, E. C. (1991) *Assessment and Learning in the Primary School.* London: Routledge.

Wragg, E. C. (2001) *Assessment and Learning in the Secondary School.* London: Routledge.

Wragg, E. C. and Brown, G. (2001) *Questioning in the Secondary School.* London: Routledge.

Wright, O. (2015) 'Ministers Turning to Behavioural Psychology to Tackle Policy Problems', *The Independent* (22 July).

Young, M. (2007) *Bringing Knowledge Back In: From Social Constructivism to Social Realism in the Sociology of Education.* Abingdon: Routledge.

Zaccaro, S. J., Kemp, C. and Bader, P. (2004) 'Leader Traits and Attributes', in J. Antonakis, A. T. Cianciolo and R. J. Sternberg (eds.), *The Nature of Leadership.* Thousand Oaks, CA: SAGE, pp. 101–124.

Zhao, Y. (2014) *Who's Afraid of the Big Bad Dragon?* San Francisco, CA: Jossey-Bass.

Index